Best Practice in Social Work

Best Practice in
Social Work

Critical Perspectives

edited by
KAREN JONES,
BARRY COOPER
and
HARRY FERGUSON

First published in 2008 by
PALGRAVE MACMILLAN
Houndmills, Basingstoke, Hampshire RG21 6XS and
175 Fifth Avenue, New York, N.Y. 10010
Companies and representatives throughout the world.

PALGRAVE MACMILLAN is the global academic imprint of the Palgrave
Macmillan division of St. Martin's Press, LLC and of Palgrave Macmillan Ltd.
Macmillan® is a registered trademark in the United States, United Kingdom
and other countries. Palgrave is a registered trademark in the European
Union and other countries.

ISBN-13: 978–1–4039–8501–9 paperback
ISBN-10: 1–4039–8501–4 paperback

This book is printed on paper suitable for recycling and made from fully
managed and sustained forest sources. Logging, pulping and manufacturing
processes are expected to conform to the environmental regulations of
the country of origin.

A catalogue record for this book is available from the British Library.

A catalog record for this book is available from the Library of Congress.

Catalog Card Number: 2007048543

10   9   8   7   6   5   4   3   2
17 16 15 14 13 12 11 10 09 08

Printed in China

For Andy Malinowski 1949–2004

Contents

Acknowledgements

The aim of this book is to profile social work at its best and producing it has been a very satisfying experience as we savoured the cumulative impact of bringing together so much of what is best about social work practice. As all the academic and practice contributors came from the same region, we were able to hold regular meetings where we discussed the meaning of critical thought and best practice, both in general and as it is applied to each chapter. We want to thank the contributors for their hard work, creativity and commitment to the project, and not just for their own chapters but their contribution to enhancing the quality of the book as a whole. We are grateful to our academic colleagues for their commitment to trying to use critical social theory in ways that attempt to expand understandings of best social work practice. A focus on practice, on what social workers actually do, is at the heart of the book and we owe a great debt to the practitioners who permitted their practice examples to be used and we thank them for sharing their experiences. We are also grateful to the senior managers in the organisations where the practice went on for so enthusiastically supporting the material being used in the book. Our editor at Palgrave, Catherine Gray, provided tremendous encouragement and intellectual support, for which we are very grateful. For their invaluable love and support we want to thank: Hannah Greenslade, Emily Greenslade and Oliver Bennett; Maggie Pickering; Clare Mackinnon and Ellen Ferguson. Ellen's vision helped greatly with the cover.

The book is dedicated to the memory of our late colleague Andy Malinowski, whose tragically premature death prevented him from completing his chapter, but whose enthusiastic support for the project meant so much and was typical of him.

NOTE: All references to and identifying information about service users and other professionals in the book have been changed to protect their anonymity.

Karen Jones
Barry Cooper
Harry Ferguson

Bristol, July 2007

Notes on contributors

Jonathan Coles qualified as a special educational needs teacher in 1979 and works as a part-time lecturer at the University of the West of England. Much of his work has been with young people and adults who have been labelled as having learning difficulties and/or emotional and behavioural difficulties, in both education and social care settings. He has worked in Higher Education on a part-time basis since 1989, combining this employment with freelance consultancy, education and training. He has a particular commitment to self-advocacy and service user involvement in the development of services and professional practice.

Peter Connors is Learning and Development Manager for Aspects and Milestones Trust. He has been a senior operational manager and has led the commissioning of a number of community services for people with learning disability. His previous experience includes management within the NHS and running a housing organisation providing services for people with learning disabilities. He has a Management MA together with a Diploma in Management Studies, a Health Service Management qualification and is an experienced NVQ Assessor and Verifier. He set up Aspects and Milestones' own City and Guilds accredited NVQ Assessment Centre in 2001 and also runs Q Training NVQ Assessment Centre.

Barry Cooper is Lecturer in Social Work at The Open University, having been a visiting lecturer at University of the West of England. He has previously worked as a child care and mental health social worker since 1980 and as a social services training officer for practice teaching and post-qualification award programmes in Bristol. His doctoral research studies at Bristol University focused upon constructivist assessment perspectives within social work practice and education, and he has published a number of journal articles exploring these themes.

Jane Dalrymple is a Senior Lecturer at the University of the West of England. She has practised as a social worker in the child care field and for five years was the Director of a national advocacy service. She is the author of a number of publications about advocacy for children and young people.

Anne Farmer is a manager with Bristol Children and Young People's Department. She qualified as a social worker in 1980 and has been practising within children's services since. She has specialised in child protection work whilst retaining a strong interest in the learning and development of both student and qualified social workers. She has for many years been a tutor and visiting lecturer at University of the West of England and currently chairs the Assessment Panel moderating the work students complete on their practice placements.

Harry Ferguson is Professor in Social Work at University of the West of England. He previously held the Chair in Social Policy and Social Work at University College, Dublin, and also worked at University College Cork and Trinity College, Dublin. He is a qualified social worker and holds a PhD from the University of Cambridge. Harry has researched and published widely in the areas of child abuse, protection, domestic violence, fatherhood, masculinities and welfare, and the sociology of social work. His books include *Protecting Children in Time: Child Abuse, Child Protection and the Consequences of Modernity* (Palgrave, 2004).

Alison Gardener has been working as a social worker in the south West of England since 2001, specialising in work with older and disabled people as part of an Adult Care Team. She has a particular interest in linking the theory and practice of social work.

Des Gorman is a social worker with Bristol City Council. He has worked in social services in Bristol for 17 years, mainly with older people and in a number of practice and managerial roles in home care, residential and intermediate care and most recently as SW and acting team manager in intermediate care.

Hilary Horan works for Barnardos as the Childrens Services Manager for the regional Family Group Conference and Advocacy Service. She has been involved in setting up and managing seven FGC services and managed the first FGC service in the United Kingdom to routinely offer independent advocates to children. Hilary previously worked in various Local Authority Social Services Departments and worked for five years as an Independent Chair of Child Protection Conferences and five years as a Guardian ad Litem. She has three fine sons and an enchanting grandson!

Karen Jones is a Senior Lecturer in social work at the University of the West of England. Her practice background is in adult social work, particularly the areas of learning difficulties and health-related practice.

Karen currently leads the post-qualifying award in adult social work and has a research interest in this area and in social work education more generally. Her current research is looking at ways of understanding and theorising the nature of contemporary adult social work practice.

Celia Keeping is a social worker in a Community Mental Health Team in North Somerset where she worked as an Approved Social Worker for almost ten years. She is a member of a psychotherapy team which offers psychoanalytical psychotherapy within the NHS. Celia is also a Senior Lecturer in the Faculty of Health and Social Care at University of the West of England where she teaches social work students, nurses and public sector managers. She is interested in the application of psychoanalytic theory to partnership working, professional identity and research methodology.

Sarah Leigh is a Senior Lecturer in Social Work at the University of the West of England. Her background in practice is in childcare and more recently in child protection and working with looked-after children. Her research and teaching interests are in the arena of service users' views on child protection social work within the UK New Labour government's modernisation agenda and good practice in the field of long-term complex child care work, including inter-professional and multi-agency working. She is currently researching with social workers who work with asylum seekers and refugees. Sarah has returned to child care practice twice over her time at University of the West of England to refresh her knowledge and skills. She increasingly teaches in a multi-professional context at University of the West of England including teachers, nurses, physiotherapist, midwives and the police.

Elspeth Loades is a Planning and Development Manager with Bristol City Council, Children and Young People's Services. She has several years of experience as a social worker practitioner, team manager and strategic planner.

John O'Gara is an Approved Mental Health Social Worker for South Gloucestershire Council, working as a member of an emergency duty social work team covering the authorities which used to be Avon. He has been involved in supervising and assessing pre-and post-qualifying social workers, including candidates for the post-qualifying, the Practice Teaching Award and trainee ASWs. He is an Associate Lecturer on mental health for the Open University and a Visiting Lecturer in social work at University of the West of England.

Imogen Powell is an Approved Mental Health Social Worker in mental health in an Assertive Outreach Team. She has worked in the learning difficulties field and in the voluntary sector. At the time of her practice covered in this book she worked for Bristol City Council in a Mental Health team for older adults where she worked for 9 years. In 2005 she trained and began to work as an Approved Social Worker.

Bruce Senior is Head of School for Health, Community and Policy Studies in the Faculty of Health and Social Care at University of the West of England. From his first social work experiences in London in the 1970's he has been interested in the political, social and emotional aspects of organisational life. Currently, he pursues this interest in both the higher education and social care settings and, in particular, the question of how organisations impact on teams and individuals and how they in turn can influence organisational behaviour.

Kate Spreadbury is Safeguarding Adults Coordinator in Bristol City Council. Her past work experiences include lecturing and tutoring on a Diploma in Social Work course, practice teaching and training social workers and social care staff. Her operational work has mainly been as a social worker and team manager in mental health teams. She also specialised in working with people who had been sexually abused as children or were currently in abusive situations.

Pat Taylor is a Senior Lecturer in Health and Social Care in the Faculty of Health and Social Care at the University of the West of England. She has worked in community development and the voluntary sector and has extensive experience of working with community based and service-user-led groups and in helping them establish their role in partnership working. She has worked within the NHS and social care to promote public and service user\carer involvement and to develop its potential to influence mainstream practice. She continues this interest in her current research. She is currently leading the patient service user and carer initiative in the new social work degree and within the faculty as a whole and retains strong links with practice in the field to enable her to fulfil this role.

Judith Thomas is an experienced social worker who is now a Principal Lecturer at the University of the West of England where she has been the programme leader for the Practice Teaching Award and the BSc(Hons) Social Work. Judith's research interests include reflective practice, professional and interprofessional education. She is editor (with Barrrett and Sellman) of *Interprofessional Working in Health and Social Care* (Palgrave, 2006).

Introducing critical best practice in social work

KAREN JONES, BARRY COOPER AND HARRY FERGUSON

The aim of this book is to present examples of best practice in social work from a range of critical perspectives. There is a remarkable paucity of writing in social work which focuses in a systematic way on accounts of best practice and an almost complete absence of such work in the literature on 'critical practice'. The best practice approach presented here is 'critical' in two senses. First, it is an urgently needed response to the deep negativity surrounding the profession. This often leads to the 'best' in social work remaining hidden from view. Second, it is an approach that proposes the adoption of a 'critical' sociological stance through which the best social work practices need to be understood and analysed.

Our starting point is that social work operates largely within a climate of negativity whereby few have a good word to say publicly about it. It is characterised by a 'deficit' culture which positions social work as fair game for persistent criticism, not only from politicians, the media and inquiries into apparent 'failures' to protect children and adults but also from some social work organisations themselves and from some academics and social work literature. In fact, so poor has been the public image of social work in the United Kingdom that since 2001 the government has run advertising campaigns on television and in the print media to try to improve public perceptions of the profession and attract more recruits to fill vacancies caused by the recruitment and retention problems which many employers have been experiencing.

There has long been a tradition of positive writing which values the social work profession, its practice wisdom and skills (Howe, 1993; Hanvey and Philpot, 1994; Coulshed, 1998; Stepney and Ford, 2000; Doel and Shardlow, 2005; Payne, 2005; Trevithick, 2005). Some recent social work literature explores 'good practice' in particular service areas (Pritchard, 2001; Tibbs, 2001; Frank, 2002). This is supplemented by a growing number of guides to 'what works' in practice (MacDonald and Winkley, 1999; Buchanan and Rictchie, 2004) and a welcome focus on the 'learning organisation' (Gould and Baldwin, 2004). Vitally important work has been produced on the notion of 'critical reflection' and 'reflective practice' which illuminates the ways in which practitioners think, talk about and generally make sense of and 'construct' social work in everyday practice (Gould and Taylor, 1996; Taylor and White, 2000; Fook, 2002). Parton and O'Byrne's (2000) concept of 'constructive social work' has the dual intention of illuminating how practitioners go about their work and how they can do it positively. All the chapters in this book are influenced in various ways by these important strands of work. Yet there remains a large gap in knowledge and the need for a dedicated body of work where the notion of 'best practice' is theorised and the actual work done showcased as a basis for learning and development in policy and practice.

Meanwhile, the 'radical' or 'critical' tradition in social work has produced vital knowledge about the impact of power and social structures on service users, and its impact has been such that the notion of 'anti-oppressive practice' and promoting equality is now central to social work education (Dalrymple and Burke, 2007; Thompson, 2006). Yet, as Harry Ferguson shows in Chapter 1 of the book, attempts to develop realistic accounts of the ways in which critical practice can be done have only begun (Brechin, 2000; Adams et al., 2002, 2005; Fook, 2002; Healy, 2005). Meanwhile, there is an almost total absence of dedicated accounts of such work done well. The bringing together of critical analysis and best practice results in what we call a 'critical best practice perspective' (Ferguson, 2003). The book aims to correct for the remarkable fact that it is very difficult to find in the literature of social work examples of critical best practice that can help to inform the learning of students and all those concerned with social work.

We argue in this book that it is time to replace the deficit model of social work. Instead of a focus on what does not get done (well), we propose an approach which draws out the strengths and profiles the best practice that routinely goes on. The aim is to create a perspective whereby learning can occur through best practice set out as a model for developing systems, knowledge and practice capabilities. Claims for 'best practice', we suggest, should be analysed from the perspectives of the individual practitioners, service users and managers involved and critically informed by social theories. Thus, critical best practice refers to social work which is skilfully supportive, therapeutic and challenging of power structures, yet authoritative and which can be shown to deserve to be called the 'best' because it contains aspects of all of these.

THE DISTINCTIVE CONTRIBUTION OF CRITICAL BEST PRACTICE PERSPECTIVES

Our argument is that the concept of critical best practice perspectives elaborated through the book has a number of distinctive features. Its core distinguishing feature is that every chapter of the book offers detailed description and analysis of actual social work practice drawn from real events and cases. This, as we pointed out above, is quite unique in books about social work. What tends to be offered in 'critical' texts is prescriptions about what social workers should not do – in terms of avoiding being oppressive – but with little indication as to how social workers can practice in progressive, skilful ways, which values their expertise and good authority, while being as respectful of and fair to service users as possible.

A second distinguishing characteristic of the book leads directly on from the first, in how a detailed focus on practice makes visible the deep complexity of social work practices. This exposes the deep limitations of the notion of 'anti-oppressive practice' (AOP) which is so dominant in social work. The principle of at all times needing to avoid being disrespectful, harmful and inappropriately controlling towards service users and unfairly discriminating against them must always hold. However, the intimate accounts of practice in this book suggest that what is needed instead is a much stronger focus on ethical dilemmas (Beckett and Maynard, 2005; Banks, 2006; Webb, 2006). AOP tends to reduce practice to a series of choices which imply identifiably good and bad options and courses of action. But in the real world of practice, matters are rarely so straightforward. Often, for instance, children need to be taken into care even when this is the last thing their parent's want. Individuals have to be detained in mental health institutions against their will because they are viewed as a high risk to themselves or others. The chapters in this book have in common the fact that there were no straightforward actions which could protect or promote the welfare of one person or group without possibly causing distress or even deeply hurting and restricting their's and other's rights and freedom. To refer to such actions in the language of 'oppression' itself risks being oppressive to those involved, as it fails to recognise the interminable nature of the ethical dilemmas involved. The choice, as this book shows, is not how only to do good, but how to do least harm while practising skilfully, fairly and using good authority.

Third, the book grapples with the neglected issue of defining and showing what is meant by 'best practice'. A new public discourse has begun in the United Kingdom about 'excellence' in social work, as exemplified by the creation in 2001 of the Social Care Institute for Excellence (SCIE), which is developing a 'best practice' knowledge base, standards and guidance for social care and social work (see, www.scie.org). The notions of 'excellence' and 'best practice' require refinement and debate, and we seek in this book to contribute to the clarification of these important concepts. We are proposing and developing a radical and realistic redefinition of the 'best'. This means that the best practice examples used throughout the book are good illustrations of what it is possible to achieve. They are not perfect – nothing is. Nor do they mean that there were no constraints on what the practitioners could do. From a strengths perspective (Saleebey, 2006), they highlight what the authors believe was the best that was achieved at that time, in that situation and by that combination of people, processes and circumstances.

Fourth, at the centre of best practice perspectives is the practitioner's voice, together with that of the service user and any other stakeholders who contribute to and co-construct the practice. We emphasise the practitioner perspective because it has tended to be marginalised and there is much that needs to be learned from them about how social workers actually practice and how this is done in critically best practice ways. Social work intervention has to be created through negotiation and agreement/disagreement by the people involved, and all the uniqueness, difference and diversities of individual perspectives needs to be brought out. Part of the urgency for such a perspective arises in the context of recent demands in the United Kingdom and internationally for 'evidence-based social care'. While the need for 'evidence for practice' in social work has been promoted for some time (Shaw, 1999), government policy now asserts that decisions in professions like social work should be based less on 'opinions' and more on data about 'what works' (Department of Health, 1998). The meaning of 'evidence-based practice' for social work is a contested notion however (compare Webb, 2001 and Sheldon, 2001), and one of our aims in this book is to contribute to a conception of 'evidence' which includes notions of 'best practice' as they are developed by the various contributors.

We hope the book provides clear and original insights into the range of knowledge, skills, organisational conditions and personal resources that are required to be an effective social worker. Achieving critical best practice is an extraordinary accomplishment, involving the effective interweaving of the bureaucratic, ethical, emotional, communicative and spiritual dimensions of social work. Best practice in social work can and does make a profound difference to vulnerable people's lives, which is the most important reason why we need to learn from it and develop it.

OUTLINE OF THE BEST PRACTICE COVERED IN THE BOOK

Through the 15 chapters that follow, the book seeks to apply a critical, theoretical analysis to descriptions of social work practice. The intention is for these illustrations and perspectives to provide a picture of what happens in real social work encounters with service users, other professional colleagues and managers, in order to expand understandings of the skills, strengths and dynamics of these practices and relationships. The book covers a range of service user groups, and forms of practice in different contexts, but cannot claim to have covered all the possible areas, as no single text ever could. What we have been able to include is a good balance of chapters that address children's and adult's services, as well as different types of service provision and practice experiences. These include casework, day care and family support, statutory work in mental health, adult protection and child protection, initial 'duty' interviews, assessments, advocacy, long-term therapeutic social work, supervision and peer support, inter-professional 'partnership' working and organisational management.

In trying to integrate theory and practice we sought contributors from academic colleagues at the University of the West of England and social workers and managers in practice who were known to us through placements, post-qualifying courses, as ex-students and so on. Four chapters are single-authored by academics, drawing on research studies and recordings which include the voices of practitioners and service users; two are single-authored by practitioners who use theory to analyse their own practice and one is single-authored by an academic who also spends part of her time in practice, while eight chapters are jointly written by practitioners and academics. Given our geographical proximity, the group met frequently in the writing of the book in the hope of achieving as much coherence of approach and thematic unity as possible across the chapters.

We hope that individually and collectively the chapters provide insights into particular issues and approaches, while adding up to something significant in the overall character of critical best practice that they offer. Not every chapter can deal with every aspect of critical best practice in its entirety and the depth that is possible, and some chapters illuminate particular aspects more than the others. For this reason the book is broken into three Parts which deal with distinct aspects of critical best practice. Part I has five chapters which outline and discuss various theoretical issues and the concept of critical best practice perspectives, while focusing on distinct practice issues. In Chapter 1 Harry Ferguson traces the development of critical ideas in social work thinking and practice and outlines the key themes of a critical best practice perspective. The second half of the chapter applies the theory to practice by illustrating a social worker's nuanced and careful approach to a situation of domestic abuse and suspected physical abuse of children which is shown to involve the careful balancing of competing perspectives and contradictory issues of care and control. The fact that the family were from a minority ethnic group, the travelling community, increased the challenge to achieve best practice that was critical by being ethically sensitive, skilful and authoritative.

In Chapter 2, Alison Gardener provides a critical reappraisal of the concept of 'anti-oppressive practice'. She argues that while it still has some value, the notion of AOP is insufficient to meet the challenges of accounting for the complex ethical dilemmas and nuances of how power must be exercised that social workers routinely confront in their practice. Through an analysis of her own work with three younger disabled adults, Alison demonstrates the importance of balancing complex and competing perspectives in order to practice in ways which are ethically grounded and value based. Her chapter, like the book as a whole, seeks to develop a language and theoretical understanding to make better sense of this complexity by grounding it in intimate accounts of best practice.

In Chapter 3, Karen Jones with social worker Imogen Powell also use theory from critical post-modernism to explore best practice with 'Amelia', an older woman with dementia. They draw out Imogen's skilled engagement with the service user and show how fine practice judgements can incorporate both a realistic assessment of risk and a genuine responsiveness to the client's own sense of meaning and place. Centrally, this involved detailed negotiations about the meaning of home and putting in place services which could enable Amelia to safely live there.

In Chapter 4, Celia Keeping argues that an understanding of the emotional content and dynamics of relationships in social work is central to achieving best practice. She writes about what began as an emergency mental health assessment of 'Jane', a young woman experiencing acute psychological distress, and how it developed into a five-year relationship. Celia draws on theories which sensitise us to the importance of issues of class, gender and ethnicity in understanding people's problems and working with them. Her particular focus though is on theories from psychoanalysis and how they help to demonstrate the importance of emotional engagement in building a secure, trusting and empathetic relationship with Jane over a five-year period.

Part I of the book concludes with Chapter 5, where Barry Cooper introduces arguments from constructivist theoretical perspectives. These are used to illustrate the creative thinking, quick judgements and skilled negotiations that characterise critical best practice in engagements between social workers and service users. The analysis is based on an interview between Sally, an experienced children and families' social worker and 'Adam', a father, who is being interviewed as part of the early stages of a multi-agency investigation into allegations made by his teenage daughter. The chapter demonstrates the importance of language and communication and illustrates how robust working relationships can be skilfully created with service users, despite apparent conflict, within the duties and obligations of a statutory child protection intervention.

Having laid the conceptual as well as at least some of the practical foundations, the book moves into Part II to consider in further depth critical best practice interventions and interactions. Chapters 6–12 are based on a critical analysis of social work activity from a variety of practice and theoretical perspectives. The rationale for the order they come is the lifespan, beginning with work with children and the first stage of intervention into cases and moving into subsequent chapters to cover work with adults and older people. Chapter 6 acts as a 'bridge' between Parts I and II and the principles and interventions of critical best practice. In developing a different stage of the interview used in his previous chapter, Barry Cooper focuses on how the negotiations that are at the heart of social work interventions are permeated by struggles for power and meaning. The chapter explores the powerful dynamics that can arise from processes of social judgements that underpin the social work assessment and some of the skilful ways in which service users can be kept included in statutory child protection investigations. It shows the ways in which assessment in social work has been officially redefined to mean what is covered in 'assessment frameworks', formats and procedures and goes beyond these and illuminates the routine ways in which social workers are skilfully assessing people all the time in their work.

In Chapter 7, Sarah Leigh and Anne Farmer write about their discussions with a group of children and families social workers around what constitutes critical best practice. They take a complex child protection case, identified by the group, as the subject of their detailed critical best practice analysis. This shows how the social worker carefully assessed and managed the issue of substantiated physical abuse of 14-weeks-old 'Jamie' by his middle-class father, Andrew. The practice involved highly skilled supportive work with Sandra, the highly stressed mother, developing her capacities to be a safe, reflective parent, while patiently and skilfully working with Andrew and other agencies who provided counselling and other services. The effect was that the father, having gained significant insight into his own history of abuse in childhood and much greater ability to know and manage his emotions and behaviour, eventually returned to live in the family home, while Sandra gained similar kinds of self-understanding and improvements in parenting capacity. The children came to be viewed as safe, and their names were removed from the child protection register.

In Chapter 8, Harry Ferguson also considers critical best practice in child care, with respect to family support and child protection. He draws on the theoretical perspective of 'individualization' and the 'democratisation of the family', taken from the work of Anthony Giddens. His analysis draws on interviews with a number of professionals and members of the 'Smith' family, including ten-year-old 'Joanne' who was experiencing substantial emotional abuse and neglect. Here a social worker and a family support worker together enabled a mother and a child, and albeit to a lesser extent, a father, to engage in 'life-planning' and gain an important degree of mastery over their lives and develop safer, more loving and supportive relationships. Jane Dalrymple and Hilary Horan write in Chapter 9 about the child's voice as central to critical best practice with children and young people. They tell the story of 'Matty' who was at high risk of entering care due to neglect and how his advocate, Joe, worked with and alongside him, together with a social worker and other professionals. The chapter demonstrates how the child's voice can be allowed to be heard within the complex dynamics of decision-making in child welfare and the positive and empowering outcomes which can follow from genuine participation.

In Chapter 10, Kate Spreadbury, an adult protection co-ordinator, writes with Karen Jones about the ethical complexity inherent in situations of adult abuse. Kate reflects critically on her own practice and on that of a social work colleague in enabling a couple at the centre of adult protection concerns to voice their own interpretation of their relationship, in ways which challenged and ultimately deepened the understanding of professionals involved, enabling them to take actions and risks which were clearly focused on the needs and desires of the victim, while remaining ethically sound. Chapter 11 also focuses on ways of amplifying the voices of disempowered service users as a cornerstone of critical best practice. Peter Connors is a learning and development manager in a large care-provider organisation for people with learning difficulties. He writes with Jonathan Coles about their joint involvement in a video project to facilitate a group of service users to voice and visualise their life experiences and choices. This is critical best practice both in the deeply respectful, humanistic and rights based nature of the process of engagement with service users, and in the learning resources this work has provided to contribute to the education and training of social care professionals. Chapter 12 is written by Jon O'Gara, a mental health practitioner, who tells the story of his brief, statutory intervention in the life of 'Justine', a young mother who was threatening to throw herself and her baby from the balcony of her tower-block home. He explores the ethical tensions and dilemmas inherent to using statutory powers in emergency mental health practice and the skills and judgement involved in the process of ascribing meaning and intention to people experiencing mental distress, while at the same time trying to respect their rights and protect them and others they place at risk.

Part III of the book covers a range of critical best practice issues from the perspective of different practice settings and cultures. While never losing sight of actual service delivery, these three chapters concern the context of practice in and across organisations. Social work is increasingly constituted by a requirement to work collaboratively with other agencies, and Pat Taylor and Karen Jones write with social worker Des Gorman in Chapter 13 about partnership working as best practice within a multi-professional team. Des's work with 'Mr Green', an older man who is struggling to cope in his sheltered flat, is shown to be critically best because of how its fluid and critical approach to the boundaries between social workers and service users and between social workers and other professionals resulted in a genuine partnership in practice.

In Chapter 14, Judith Thomas and Kate Spreadbury draw on their experience as social work educators, trainers and supervisors in writing about the importance of promoting critical best practice through supervision, learning and development. Their analysis highlights the value of creating spaces where practitioners can safely reflect, challenge and be challenged. Through case studies of social worker's experiences they demonstrate that such opportunities are present within partnership models of supervision, but may also arise through more and less formal opportunities for sharing and development. They outline an important model for agencies and individual and organisational learning through the development of 'communities of practice'.

In Chapter 15, Bruce Senior writes with Elspeth Loades, an experienced social work manager, about the ways in which social work practitioners affect and are affected by their organisations. They show how the organisational context is typically either ignored in the social work literature or treated as a problem or constraint to good practice. Drawing on evidence from their conversations with Alison Gardener (who writes about her practice in Chapter 2) and with a number of other social workers, they provide a multi-dimensional picture of the centrality of skilled organisational work to achieving best practice in how a reflective approach to bureaucratic rules and relationships with managers enables social workers to do what they do well. Their chapter reveals the creative and confident practice which can be achieved by critical practitioners who are both self-aware and organisationally aware. The book concludes with a chapter by us as editors which reflects upon the key messages of the book and the meanings and future of critical best practice analysis.

REFERENCES

Adams, R., Dominelli, L. and Payne, M. (eds) (2002) *Critical Practice in Social Work* (Basingstoke: Palgrave).

Adams, R., Dominelli, L. and Payne, M. (eds) (2005) *Social Work Futures: Crossing Boundaries, Transforming Practice* (Basingstoke: Palgrave).

Banks, S. (2006) *Ethics and Values in Social Work* (Basingstoke: Palgrave, 3rd edition).

Beckett, C. and Maynard, A. (2005), *Values & Ethics in Social Work: An Introduction* (London: Sage).

Brechin, A. 'Introducing Critical Practice' in Brechin, A., Brown, H. and Eby, M. A. (eds) (2000) *Critical Practice in Health and Social Care* (London: Sage/Open University).

Buchanan, A. and Rictchie, C. (2004) *What Works for Troubled Children?* (Ilford: Barnardo's).

Coulshed, V. and Orme, J. (1998) *Social Work Practice: An Introduction* (Basingstoke: Macmillan).

Dalrymple, J. and Burke, B. (2007) *Anti-Oppressive Practice Social Care and the Law*, (Maidenhead: Open University Press, 2nd edition)

Department of Health (1998), *Modernising Social Services* (London: The Stationery Office).

Doel, M. and Shardlow, S. (2005) *Modern Social Work Practice: Teaching and Learning in Practice Settings* (Aldershot: Ashgate)

Ferguson, H. (2003) 'Outline of Critical Best Practice Perspective on Social Work and Social Care' *British Journal of Social Work*, 33: 1005–1024.

Fook, J. (2002) *Social Work: Critical Theory and Practice* (London: Sage).

Frank, J. (2002) *Making it Work: Good Practice with Young Carers and Their Families* (London: Children's Society, Princess Royal Trust for Carers).

Gould, N. and Taylor, I. (eds) (1996), *Reflective Learning for Social Work* (Aldershot: Arena).

Gould, N. and Baldwin, M. (eds) (2004) *Social Work, Critical Reflection and the Learning Organisation* (Aldershot: Ashgate).

Hanvey, C. and Philpot, T. (eds) (1994) *Practising Social Work* (London: Routledge).

Healy, K. (2005) *Social Work Theories in Context* (Basingstoke: Palgrave).

Howe, D. (1993) *An Introduction to Social Work Theory* (Aldershot: Arena).

MacDonald, G. and Winkley, A. (1999) *What Works in Child Protection?* (Ilford: Barnardo's).

Parton, N. and O'Byrne, P. (2000) *Constructive Social Work* (London: Macmillan).

Payne, M. (2005) *Modern Social Work Theory* (Basingstoke: Palgrave, 3rd edition).

Pritchard, J. (ed.) (2001) *Good Practice with Vulnerable Adults* (London: Jessica Kingsley Publishers).

Saleebey, D. (ed.) (2006) *The Strengths Perspective in Social Work Practice* (New York: Longman)

Shaw, I. 'Evidence for practice' in Shaw, I. and Lishman, J. (eds) (1999) *Evaluation and Social Work Practice* (London: Sage).

Sheldon, B. (2001) 'The Validity of Evidence Based Practice in Social Work: A Reply to Stephen Webb' *British Journal of Social Work*, **31**: 801–809.

Stepney, P. and Ford, D. (2000) *Social Work Models, Methods and Theories: A Framework for Practice* (Lyme Regis: Russell House).

Taylor, C. and White, S. (2000) *Practicing Reflexivity in Health and Social Care* (Maidenhead: Open University Press).

Thompson, N. (2006) *Anti-discriminatory Practice* (Basingstoke: Palgrave).

Tibbs, M. (2001) *Social Work and Dementia: Good Practice and Care Management* (London: Jessica Kingsley).

Trevithick, P. (2005) *Social Work Skills: A Practice Handbook* (Maidenhead: Open University Press).

Webb, S. A. (2001) 'Some Considerations on the Validity of Evidence Based Practice in Social Work' *British Journal of Social Work*, **31**: 57–59.

Webb, S. A. (2006) *Social Work in a Risk Society* (Basingstoke: Palgrave).

Part I

Critical Best Practice:
Critical Perspectives

1 The theory and practice of critical best practice in social work

HARRY FERGUSON

The aim of this chapter is to introduce the notion of a critical best practice perspective on social work which is at the core of this book. It is the first of five chapters in Part I of the book which outline and discuss the concept of critical best practice perspectives and various theoretical issues, while focusing on practice. As was pointed out in the editors' introduction, social work has become dominated by a 'deficit approach' where the focus is on what does not get done (well), and on how social work supposedly 'fails'. So great have these problems become in the United Kingdom that following a recent very high profile inquiry into the death from abuse of 8–year-old Victoria Climbie, the profession was pronounced by the *Times* newspaper (January 29, 2003) to be 'in terminal decline'. The central aim of a critical best practice (CBP) perspective is to promote positive learning about social work by setting out examples of best practice; that is, outlining and analysing instances where it is argued that what social workers did was done well, with all the benefits that can accrue from this for service users.

The 'critical' element here arises from how social theory is used to critically analyse and develop understandings of such best practice. Indeed, a key reason why such practice can be regarded as 'best' is because it contains a 'critical' component where social workers have used their powers and capacities to critically reflect in a way that is both skilful and deeply respectful to service users, being mindful of their often marginalised social position and vulnerability, while at the same time using good judgement and authority. This approach constitutes a strategic attempt to develop a more positive perspective on researching, learning about and, most importantly, doing social work, from critical perspectives. Deficit culture has left us without a knowledge base of best critical practice and devoid of a tradition of celebration, pride or sense of achievement on which to build or fall back on and has helped to create a context where governments can feel able to ride roughshod over social work. Social work needs to showcase what it routinely does well by developing knowledge of best practice on which to base learning and positive growth by making this visible both within the profession and to the public. This is the essential aim of a CBP perspective. The first part of the chapter outlines the development of critical perspectives in social work and the theoretical basis of CBP perspectives. The chapter then develops the discussion through an analysis of CBP in an actual case.

IN SEARCH OF 'BEST PRACTICE'

What does it mean to speak of and search out 'best practice'? There is and never can be a fixed definition of best practice in social work. It is a product of its time and place. Social work has existed as a profession since the end of the nineteenth century, and while the language of 'best practice' is quite new, every era since has had its own standards of what it consisted of (Means and Smith, 1998; Ferguson, 2004). In effect, best practice is a social construction. This means that even within particular times and places what constitutes best practice is contested and open to debate. Moreover, the entire idea could be contested on the basis that if one believes that society is riddled with conflicts and inequalities how is it ever possible or legitimate to say that anything can be 'best' or worth celebrating? This raises the key question of 'best' according to whom and what criteria? A classic example of how the answers to such questions change over time is that for many today the inclusion of the service user's perspective is seen as vital, which is quite different to 30 years ago when it was the policy maker, social worker and the academic as 'experts' who had the monopoly on defining what was best.

Another sign of our times is the significant development of the 'evidence-based practice' movement. In the United Kingdom, government policy now asserts that decisions in professions like social work should be based less on 'opinions' and much more on data about 'what works', on 'evidence' (Department of Health, 1998). Here the 'evidence' for what is 'best' is that which can be *proved* scientifically to be so. The key approach to achieving this is the 'experimental' research design known as the randomised control trial. Control groups which do not receive the intervention are included to permit a more robust evaluation of the precise impact of the intervention in question (Macdonald, 2001). Its focus tends to be on the use of bigger samples randomised into experimental and control groups and the outcomes of particular interventions in terms of statistical averages, probabilities and calculations based on numerical data (MacDonald and Sheldon, 1992).

Such approaches can have something valuable to offer, especially if combined with other, qualitative, research methods (Strange et al., 2001). But unlike health care where they are extensively used and it is far easier to measure the impact of a treatment on patient's well-being, experimental designs have serious limitations in social work. They tend to be monopolised by researchers as experts to the exclusion of the voice of service users (Margison, 2001). A major problem is that the scientific notion of 'evidence' contains a very limited view of what practice actually is and how it is created (Shaw, 1999; Webb, 2001). Best practice is not the same as 'what works' in that its conception of practice is about more than outcome. It is about social action, process and the nuances of how practice is done. It includes critical attention to those processes which may not be amenable to or even seen as relevant to measurement but which are the essence of what social work is. For instance, a user who is involuntary and not cooperating with the service can be constructively engaged in a best practice way, even though positive performance indicators about them as (good enough) parents/carers/patients/citizens and the outcome of intervention (as good enough) may be absent. While the very designation 'best' implies that often the intervention has worked, many lessons about best practice can be drawn from what in a strict scientific sense of outcomes *has not* worked.

The case study I provide below exemplifies this in how a huge amount of social work and other professional practice goes into situations where outcomes are messy, unclear, even poor, yet the practice was skilfully done and in a manner which upholds social work's democratic value base. A crucial aim of a CBP perspective is to capture the very 'work' that *is* social work, the actions taken, what gets said and done and with what consequences, which constitute particular kinds of practice. In the chapters that follow, countless such examples of how such good work gets done are given, ranging from the use of gestures, types of questions, the management of emotion, the constructive use of statutory powers, to changing professional attitudes and dominant beliefs about situations, management and organisations, providing advocacy, practical and material support, and changing users beliefs and behaviours.

Producing such knowledge means adopting theories and methods that give primacy to trying to understand people's experience and the meanings it has for them. Compared to the deductive reasoning which underpins positivist experimental research approaches, this is a more inductive process of knowledge building. Theory and understandings of practice are developed out of the everyday experience of professionals and service users and people's capacities for 'critical reflection' (Fook, 2002). This type of approach is reflected throughout this book in the gathering and analysis of people's 'narratives' to make sense not merely of practice, but *best* practice. Crucially, what constitutes achievable standards of 'best' is determined not from a single source, such as agency rules and policy, but from a range of sources, including service users, managers, front-line professionals. How the practice was (co-) constructed and given meaning by these different actors can then be explored. A key challenge of CBP analysis is to build from these diverse narratives a unifying representation of (best) practice. Practice may mean different things to different people, but it is possible to identify and make claims about what constitutes 'best'. However, the search for best practice is not about some unqualified celebration of 'good works', but a standard for evaluation of 'best' which is rigorously, sociologically critical. Crucially, the focus is not on idealised images of best practice, but attainable ones within the possibilities of current working realities. This means a commitment to profiling the best practice that can be found to be going on and critical analysis of such practice.

IN SEARCH OF THE 'CRITICAL'

All of this raises the key question of what is meant by 'critical'? What then is and should be the relationship between theory, 'criticality' and social work? At first sight, the notion of CBP seems like a contradiction in terms. For how can one be critical of something that is best? 'Critical' here is meant in the sociological sense of critique as opposed to being negative. This does not mean always trying to be 'nice' and constructive. Asking awkward questions and being a nuisance in questioning the way society is structured, the nature of power and so on, is a vital part of what intellectual debate involves (Fuller, 2005). 'Critics', as Ian Shaw (2005: 1244) observes of social work, 'are not universally liked'. Here 'critical theorising' is seen as involving a commitment to using such critique to not merely understand the world but to try to change it, for the betterment of service user's lives.

The radical or 'critical' imagination in social work began to engage in such critical theorising with the birth of the 'radical social work' movement in the early 1970s. It emerged in response to a profession then dominated by social casework with its alleged tendency, under the influence of theories such as psychoanalysis, to reduce all problems to the individual failings of clients. Social work courses were dominated by psychological theories, with minimal use of ideas drawn from areas such as sociology or politics. At the same time social work was professionalising and its training became embedded in the increasingly popular critical social sciences in the expanding university sector, which critiqued power relations in society and the place of service users, professionals and the state within it. Social work, or at least the traditional ways of doing it through social casework, was now scorned by radicals as a method to control the poor and the oppressed and began to be seen by radicals as part of the problem rather than a possible solution to social ills. In a classic political cartoon of the time two 'slum kids' hold a conversation: 'We've got rats', says one; 'Shit man', says the other, 'we've got social workers' (Pearson, 1975: 133). Drawing on the work of Karl Marx, the message was that state social work 'cooled out' the anger of working class people blocking the revolutionary potential of political change. The radical social work movement helped engineer an inversion of values. Now social workers were characterised as 'social policemen'; it was they, not their 'problem families' who could not be trusted.

Bailey and Brake's pioneering text *Radical Social Work* defined it as being about 'understanding the position of the oppressed in the context of the social and economic structure they live in' (Bailey and Brake, 1975: 9). At first, radical social work was concerned solely with social class, and drew heavily from the theories of Karl Marx. Corrigan and Leonard's (1978), *Social Work Practice Under Capitalism: A Marxist Approach* exemplified this singular focus on state social work as a means to demonising and controlling the poor to benefit the 'ruling classes' and the reproduction of capitalism (on this perspective in social work today, see Ferguson and Lavelette, 2004, 2006). Responses at that time typically involved expressions of a new identity politics which were premised on ways for social workers to show solidarity with excluded minorities and clients. In 1978, while on my first ever social work placement, the first senior social worker from social services I ever met just happened to be a proudly out gay man. Among the team of social workers he supervised was a man who insisted on wearing woolly jumpers and jeans full of holes and whose hair and beard were long and often dirty. At first I mistook him for a homeless client and wondered how he had managed to get inside the office! This is precisely as he wanted it. Radicals consciously dressed down to show support with and try not to alienate agency clients, leaving no doubt as to whose side they were on (Wilson, 1985).

The actual number of radical social workers always appeared to be quite low (at least if applying the woolly jumper test). Yet a process had been established through which the value base of social work firmly embraced the view that diversity and difference were to be *affirmed* not feared or excluded (Thompson, 1993; Dalrymple and Burke, 1995). In the 1980s, with the influence of feminism and the women's movement, gender, sexism and sexuality reached the radical agenda, while racism (Dominelli, 1988), disability rights (Oliver, 1990) and gay and lesbian rights would soon follow (Brown, 1997; Hicks, 2000). Thus by the 1990s, the focus of radicalism in social work had broadened as it absorbed the influence of new developments in social theory and new social movements. This kind of critical awareness of tackling discrimination has been crucial in enabling social work to try to respond respectfully to the diverse needs of all social groups. Notions of anti-discriminatory practice, anti-oppressive practice and empowerment became part of the mainstream of theory and practice. The upshot has been a loosening of the traditional classifications and boundaries between 'us' (professionals) and 'them' (clients/service users), of 'the boundaries set up to distinguish what is external to and what is internal to a collectivity' (Lash and Urry, 1987: 297). The ethical imperative became one of needing to include clients within the social work collectivity, an outcome of which is that in the 2000s the language has become one of 'service users' who it is expected will routinely be worked with in dignified and empowering ways.

However, huge problems continue to surround the way in which critical social work theory has too often remained at the level of negative critique, idealistically prescribing what should *not* be done, while the actual practicalities of what *can* and often *should* be done, and *how* is ignored or left at the level of aspiration. Thus it has largely avoided any encounter with best practice, leaving out how critical practice can be done well. This has also contributed to the deficit culture in which the dominant view is that there is always something inherently wrong with social work, that practice is never (quite) good enough. Sometimes it is not. But, we contend in this book, it sometimes is, and we need to learn from such instances of best critical practice. In a similar vein, Shaw (2005) draws attention to how 'critical' in social work too often means 'censoriousness', where a legitimate agenda to pursue social justice and social transformation is adopted without reflexive careful judgement. Shaw regards the introduction of the practitioner voice in the research process as a key way to achieve such judgement, wisdom and grounded knowledge of critical practice.

There are however some signs that a more grounded and practically useful radicalism is emerging in the notion of 'critical social work' or 'critical practice' that has begun to take coherent shape since the late 1990s (Adams et al., 1998, 2002, 2005; Fook, 1999, 2002; Healy, 2000, 2005). Also significant are the notions of 'reflective practice' and the 'reflective practitioner' and the ways in which practitioners creatively and skilfully 'construct' their work (Parton and O'Byrne, 2000; Taylor and White, 2000; Houston et al., 2001; Scourfield, 2003). To different degrees these writings reflect an awareness of the need to transcend the often idealistic theoretical prescriptions of critical theorising to include greater clarity with regard to what needs to be skilfully done in practice as well as thought and aspired to. Brechin (2000: 35) for instance, usefully suggests that 'critical practice' refers to a capacity to integrate at least four levels of knowledge and action: a critically reflective use of self and sound skills base; working with a value base that respects others as equals; adopting an open approach to practice; and understanding individuals (including oneself) in relation to a socio-political and ideological context within which meanings are socially constructed.

Yet this shift in theory and critical practice is incomplete. Much more remains to be done to recognise the complexity of social work and people's lives. The radical/critical tradition in social work has tended to set up crude oppositions between 'bad system'/'good service user'; 'powerful oppressive system'/ 'powerless victimized client'; 'oppressive managerial system'/ 'powerless victimized social worker'. While this is changing, it still goes on. The focus needs to be on what both the 'system' and service users contribute to the meanings and outcomes of interventions (Williams and Popay, 1999). A more fluid understanding of power, human agency and creativity are required in practice (Healy, 1999, 2005). The influence of what is called 'post-modernism' is important here. Post-modernism suggests that it is no longer valid to speak and write as if there is a single unitary way of describing and analysing social phenomena. Thus, for instance, it is problematic to claim to explain social work through a perspective based only on social class and Marxist theory – or any other single theoretical perspective. There are many perspectives and voices and it is now recognised that they all need to be heard if the complex nature of 'truth' is to be established (Pease and Fook, 1999). This is especially true in social work where traditionally the voices of 'experts' have dominated and other perspectives have historically been marginalised or silenced. The quite recent emergence of the recognition of the service user's voice in social work is a classic example of a previously silenced group beginning to be heard. All discourses and practices are seen to be run through with power, and post-modernism is sceptical of simplistic ideas of progress and constantly asks questions such as, who says what the nature of people's problems are or that interventions are 'helpful'? Access to knowledge about social work is no longer available just through what experts say. The way is opened for detailed analyses of the possibly diverse meanings best social work practice has for practitioners, service users and carers alike. Knowledge is seen as being 'situated' in particular relationships, language, circumstances, conditions that require detailed inquiry, rather than simply being 'out there' to be discovered. The chapters in this book draw in various ways on such 'critical' and 'constructive' theoretical frameworks.

As Hoggett (2001) points out, critical theorising needs also to include attention to the psyche and do justice to the complexity of what it is to be human. This means grasping our irrationalities, the impact of the unconscious and our capacity for sabotaging and destroying ourselves and others, as much as good intentions, resilience and creativity (see also Holway, 2001; Froggett, 2002; Cooper and Lousada, 2005). This opens the way to a theory of practice which incorporates an understanding of relationships and people's emotions, inner-lives and how they interact with external influences and processes (Trevithick, 2003; and Celia Keeping, this volume). Being open to such human complexity is necessary to enable us to go beyond the purity and simplicity that has dogged so much radical theorising in social work, to recognise that best practice analysed in such a critical way is not always about doing the right thing all of the time. Some of the best practice profiled in this book deserves that label because it involved workers using critical reflection and changing direction having realised that they had made a mistake. There is then, a commitment here to rendering visible the struggle involved in being 'critical', the human challenge of practicing empathy and values such as tolerance while so often dealing with the pain, cruelty and suffering that comes from its opposite, with all the feelings of inner-conflict this can provoke.

Similar issues arise in the need for much greater recognition of the complexity involved in using power in social work. A significant proportion of statutory service users are 'involuntary clients' – as many as a third of all cases in some studies (Ferguson, 2005) – yet the bulk of social work theory, and certainly critical theorising, persists in ignoring or denying this and implying that all 'service users' want to be helped and can have their needs met if only the services would cease oppressively controlling them. But some people are dangerous, destructive, irresponsible and a risk to others or themselves, and sometimes it is necessary to limit their freedoms and try to get them to change. Very often the best practice issue is not *if* such constraint is valid, but *how* it is done in a respectful, critically reflective way which provides as much scope as possible for the service users to plan their own life. This is invariably a contradictory undertaking. When statutory powers are used to detain adults under mental health legislation or to remove children from home, rarely can there be a straightforward 'good' outcome. Such work can involve even adding to the suffering of some (relatives, parents etc.) in pursuit of promoting the safety and well-being of another (who may not even want or appreciate it). Power in and of itself is not oppressive. It can be in how it is exercised, but equally it is a positive and necessary resource, depending entirely on how it is used. A concept of 'good authority' has to be central to critical practice in social work. Several of the chapters in this book grapple with the tensions and the ethical dilemmas that invariably surround child and adult protection.

The notion of criticality and best practice being developed here is based on a crucial assumption: that social work is a creative enterprise and that how practitioners, teams and organisations go about doing it is influenced by their capacities to reflect and act; their 'agency'. This is often referred to in social work as 'critical reflection' or 'reflexivity' (see De'Cruz et al., 2007). However, best practice is categorically not something that floats free of the organisational and social context in which it goes on. It derives its legitimacy from the State and its laws and is at all times embedded in 'structures', 'systems'. Over the past two decades social work has undoubtedly become a much more state regulated, managed and controlled enterprise. There are more procedures and guidelines to follow, performance targets are set and social work is routinely managed, audited and inspected to see if it is reaching them. However, many commentators assume or read into this the erosion of virtually all autonomy for practitioners. Whereas once the lament of radicals was a fear of social workers being 'social policemen', now it is a fear of being policed and held prisoner by an all-encompassing managerial system, dispensing scarce services (not welfare, or care, or therapy) to pre-ordained categories of people at risk (Webb, 2006). There is some evidence that in the United Kingdom bureaucracy has penetrated quite deep into the psyches of some practitioners. For instance, Cooper and Lousada (2005) argue that the minds of practitioners and indeed managers have become 'colonised' by procedure and organisational rules and refer to a social worker who had no conception of doing anything other than what was directed in the ever expanding rule-book. A key task for critical theorising of social work under such highly managerial conditions is to find ways to inspire people and equip them with the knowledge and skills to recognise their own capacity for action and how they can and do make a difference. All of the chapters in this book attempt to do this.

Best practice goes on even in systems that are judged to be over-managed, 'bad', oppressive and producing poor outcomes. But even this statement is problematic as we need to transcend the very thinking which treats 'the system' in this way as if it had an existence independent of the human beings who work in it. CBP refers to the ways in which professionals work creatively with and within structures to carve out actions which make a (positive) difference to service user's lives. This does not mean simply accepting 'structures' for what they are but having an understanding of them as providing rules and resources that are given meaning through human action (Giddens, 1984). These rules and resources (such as the law, agency procedures, welfare services, tacit knowledge) are not in any simple sense constraining but can *enable* (best) practice in how they are mobilised by the radical imaginations and creative actions of lay and professional actors, who together co-construct what practice is. As Bruce Senior and Elspeth Loades' chapter in this book shows, agency rules and management can be supportive to workers who have more discretion about how to do their work than is often recognised.

A CBP perspective then can be defined as solution-focused in that it attempts to be strategic in terms of identifying ways of working that offer positive resources to professionals in guiding their work, but in a manner which takes full account of issues of power, inequalities and constraint, as well as creativity in how skilful social intervention makes a difference. Many of the chapters in this book show that the workers involved were keenly aware of how 'structural' factors created limitations which both impacted on the lives of service users and threatened efforts to alleviate those problems. Yet despite and because of these apparent barriers, good practice was achieved. A central aim of a CBP perspective is to produce knowledge which demonstrates good work which is skilfully supportive, therapeutic and challenging of power structures, yet authoritative, and which can be shown to deserve to be called best because of how it contains aspects of all of these.

A CRITICAL BEST PRACTICE PERSPECTIVE IN ACTION

Having stated that a focus on actual practice is central to a CBP perspective, I now want to turn to such analysis. This principle has to be compromised here in that a shorter amount of space than is desirable can be devoted to it given the necessity to discuss the meanings and parameters of a CBP perspective. I will use extracts from a single case to illustrate examples of CBP analysis. This case covers a 15-month period of work in a high-risk child protection case which involved physical abuse and domestic violence in relation to a Traveller family of eight children, aged between 15 and 2 years at the time of the referral. The case is taken from a large study of child care and protection in three social work teams in the Republic of Ireland (Ferguson and O'Reilly, 2001). All significant actors involved in the case were interviewed, ten in total: the area social worker, public health nurse, family support worker, counsellor, school principal and police; the mother and father were interviewed (separately), as were two of the children, aged 10 and 9 (together). The case file was also read.

There had been long-standing social work involvement which included five other children with disabilities who were looked after by the state for non-child protection reasons. The case was open for child protection concerns at the time of new referral in the study, which came from a school principal whose home the mother had arrived at one night stating that she was in fear of her husband who was threatening to 'burn all the family in the caravan'. The principal wrote to the social work department:

> They were very distressed. The mother was crying, trembling and very frightened. She said the father has hit and beaten her and was very violent ... . Daughter also referred to her black eye incident and said that her father kicked her to the face and gave it to her and that she didn't get it from a bicycle fall as previously stated.

The alleged black eye to the child had been investigated by social workers and the police six months earlier and the young person, then aged 10, said she had not been abused. In relation to the new referral, the mother, here called 'Mrs Gates', withdrew the allegations of violence by her husband and denied that he hit her or the children, while the father denied ever hitting his children. Yet, according to the social worker, 'the children said it did happen, even though it was denied when I spoke to them'. The case was re-referred twice within a year by the school who were concerned about hygiene and care of a six-year child. Five child protection case conferences were held within the study period and nine child protection 'updates' were submitted by the social worker to the official child protection monitoring system. The children were also the subject of a statutory Supervision Order. Mr Gates was also known to have abused his wife, who explained in the research how following one incident alone her husband's violence caused her to have 48 stitches to her face. 'I was bleeding all night. The face is the worst one everyone can see it ... I got a big stove on top of me. He threw a fireplace on top of me, four or five months after I was pregnant'. The father also acted in a violent and threatening manner towards professionals. He 'lunged toward' the public health nurse on one occasion when she called to the caravan. According to the police, 'there is no reasoning with him; he is a very violent individual'.

THE ACTUAL SOCIAL *WORK* INVOLVED IN (BEST) PRACTICE

Huge professional efforts just about managed to secure the children's safety. I suspect that had a research methodology been included which used statistical methods to measure child development and well-being and parenting capacities, the 'evidence' would have shown little improvement. Yet, there are many instances here of best practice, in the spirit in which that term is being used here, in terms of *actions*: of what was done and how. This is an example of the great deal of social work that goes into situations where positive outcomes in the sense of improving parenting can even seem poor because the very nature of the work involves huge struggle around preventing further harm. Managing to prevent further harm and the children having to be removed is in itself a key best practice outcome. In that sense it did broadly succeed, especially in how a client who was involuntary and determined not to cooperate with the service was constructively engaged in a best practice way.

A crucial best practice issue concerns the strategies adopted by professionals to ensure their own personal safety and thus maximise their capacity to gain access to vulnerable adults and children. Unless professionals feel safe and secure, child safety cannot be secured (Ferguson, 2005). The larger research study from which this case is taken showed that men/fathers are not worked with to anything like the same degree as women/mothers (Ferguson and O'Reilly, 2001). Other research also suggests referrals involving violent men are 'filtered out of the system by social workers fairly readily' (Buckley, 2003). In this case, workers courageously did work with the father which meant having to adopt strategies that ensured both their own personal safety and access to the mother and children. For the (male) school Principal, 'If I was making a visit to the caravan, I'd always have a man come with me'. The family support worker employed the tactic when visiting the caravan of, 'If he is really angry I will physically remove myself towards the door and I will say, "will we have a fag lad?" and my lighter is in the car. I won't go back where I was sitting; I will stand at the door or sit nearer the door'. For the (female) social worker, 'On two occasions I was accompanied by two male social workers. He can be quite verbally aggressive, quite threatening [saying], "Have you ever been hit?", you know things like that'. In being accompanied on the visits and getting good supervision and peer support at the office, the worker received the kind of emotional support that is crucial to enabling her to 'contain' her anxiety in the midst of complex psychodynamic processes and stay focused on the safety needs of the children and woman. This also begins to illustrate how professionals engage with, develop and try to sustain relationships with service users and resistant clients.

THE CREATIVE USE OF STATUTORY POWERS AND THEIR CONTRADICTORY EFFECTS

This was best practice not simply because the violent father was worked with but because of *how* this was done. It went well beyond simply 'challenging' a man about his behaviour, which can increase levels of danger for workers and women and children (Milner, 2004). The father was mandated by the Court via the Supervision Order to attend a counsellor who was employed by the social services department. According to the father, this was also part of a probation order which arose because, 'I lost my temper, over a [police man]'. This is commendable because research and practice wisdom suggests that for this kind of work to have any chance of succeeding it needs to be part of a sanction which institutionalises the man's accountability to the State for his violence. And if he does not then engage with the programme he can be sanctioned. Group programmes show the best outcomes (Shepard and Pence, 1999), but because none were available in the locality, creative individual work had to suffice. Although happening too late for this case, the available resources changed when a senior practitioner in the region helped to start a group work programme for violent men, thus showing how such creative efforts can influence 'structures' and generate more widely the conditions for best practice.

The aim of the counsellor's work with the father was 'to look at what is causing, what is underlying the violence and what has built up to the violence and what is happening for the individual ... [I] try to understand what is happening for him and then try to reflect that back to him, so that he is more aware when he is more likely to be violent, so that he can counteract his build up process.' The (male) counsellor emphasised that abused women's rights to personal safety should be paramount. Yet his perspective – rightly in my view – was that couple counselling could not be considered safe practice in this case because the perpetrator had not accepted full responsibility for his abuse. While the woman might be safe from abuse while actually in the counselling session, she is at risk of further abuse when she leaves it. In effect, the woman is placed in a 'double bind' where to talk of the abuse could put her in very grave danger (Adams, 1988: 187; Stark and Flitcraft, 1996). Similarly, a focus on anger management without an even more strategic attempt to challenge the offender's belief system and issues of power and control can actually increase the danger to the victim (Dobash and Dobash, 1992: 245; Mullender 1996: 225; Hearn, 1999). Gondolf (1993: 247) argues that couple counselling is best introduced only after the perpetrator has successfully completed an intervention programme for violent men and after six to twelve months of known non-violent behaviour. What was also nicely avoided in this practice was a limiting of the abuser's responsibility for the violence through a process of 'mitigation' (Milner, 1996), which minimises it by blaming things like alcohol. While it is legitimate to regard alcohol as lowering inhibitions, the underlying cause has to be seen as the man's abuse of power and need to control (Morran and Wilson, 1999).

On no less than nine occasions during the study period the social worker referred further incidents of concern to the Child Protection Notification Committee. The father was suspected of continuing to hit the children – and his wife. The case file notes that visible marks were evident on one child that could have been consistent with ring marks. In response, the social worker confronted the father about the abuse, which he denied, and increased the number of visits to the caravan. Even this had contradictory consequences, when, in balancing the care and control aspects of the work towards greater control, the family regarded this as coercive and retaliated by pulling back from intervention, thus heightening the risk to the children. They moved away from the area because, as the father explained, 'She [the social worker] was telling me she'd put the kids in care ... . I didn't really like it. I moved away. I thought I was going to get rid of them [social workers], but they still kept coming round off me.' Pressure from the professional system caused 'closure' in the family system (Reder et al., 1983). When the family did not comply with the Supervision Order by permitting access to the home, the social worker adopted a more controlling stance and brought in male colleagues to support her in confronting the father. What defused this tension was the father's assurance that he would cooperate and go to counselling, and that social workers could see the children when they wanted to. One year on, the father was becoming resigned to social work intervention. '[Social workers] will probably see me for another three or four years, but I don't mind that's their job like.'

Over time the social worker felt the father was gaining control over his violent behaviour. For instance, he chose to follow due process of law as opposed to fighting with a man who destroyed his caravan. 'He actually responded by not going down and killing [the man], which he probably would have done previously. He seems to be dealing with his anger a bit better outside of the home.' The challenge was to get him to extend this to his behaviour inside the home.

EMPATHY, SKILL AND CRITICAL JUDGEMENT IN PRACTICE

The practitioners faced the considerable challenge of not only protecting the children and mother from the father, but also ensuring that the mother's actions (or perhaps lack of them in not leaving) did not endanger the children. A considerable body of feminist research has shown that the effect of mothers being scrutinised in their parental role – especially while fathers are not – carries the risk in domestic violence cases of the abused woman not getting support and protection and being held responsible for both it and protecting the children (Featherstone, 2004). Much hung on whether or not Mrs Gates was willing to make a statement against her husband and stand by it. When this did not happen some professionals became disillusioned. For the police officer:

> The mother has done it [made a formal complaint] on one or two occasions ... you go and investigate in relation to going to Court, which invariably you would, because of his history and past convictions and in the meantime they have made up. These two seem to stick together like glue ... [and it] leads to total apathy with the members of the [police], particularly so with this couple.

The family support worker asked rhetorically, 'What can you do? She has been offered a caravan someplace else, a Barring Order [which would exclude the man from the home], and she won't take any of it on board.' The provision of support for the mother was made all the more difficult because the father was always present when professionals called to see her. The public health nurse 'got very little opportunity to talk to her, because as I say, I seldom got them separate'. The family support worker eventually pulled out because the father was so 'controlling' she couldn't support the mother. The first case conference recommended that a court order barring the man from the home be sought. The social worker implemented the decision by giving Mrs Gates the choice but completely understood why she did not want to pursue it at this time.

> Basically I didn't think it was appropriate at the time. [The mother] isn't *strong* enough yet to do it, she'd have to be strong to cope with the children, to cope with the demands of getting a place to live, she'd have to be strong to do all that after the Order and I don't think the mother is at present. She says that a Barring Order will not protect her from [the father] and when she does leave, she always comes back.

This nuanced, deeply empathetic social work practice went beyond an emotional reaction and approach which sought to blame or 'rescue' the mother or children. Social services had powers under the Domestic Violence Act (1996) to pursue civil Protection and Barring Orders on behalf of women who are not in a position to procure an order on their own behalf. But these were very rarely taken due to the State's reluctance to take statutory responsibility for the protection of adults. The decision not to take out a Barring Order was viewed in relation to the perceived repercussions that such an Order might have on the mother and the fact that there were not adequate safeguards available to ensure her protection. The time following an abused woman taking action to protect herself is known to be highly dangerous, as perpetrators often resort to extreme violence and even murder in seeking to reassert control and dominance (Dobash and Dobash, 1992). Neither the mother nor some of the professionals had trust that an adequate protective response by the police would follow breaches of the Barring Order. Thus the risk assessment concluded that, within the current legal system, its interpretation by agencies and the available resources, the risk of removing the mother from the home or insisting that she leave for the sake of the children was greater than leaving them there. The professionals worked as effectively as they could in using the rules and resources at their disposal to enable them to practice as creatively as possible, in a woman and child-centred way (see also, Wise, 1995).

CULTURALLY SENSITIVE AUTHORITATIVE PRACTICE

Traveller people are among the most oppressed ethnic minority groups in the western world and have long held that status in Ireland, experiencing high infant-mortality rates, much shorter life-expectancy than the settled community and persistent, extreme racism (O'Connell, 2002). The workers faced a very difficult challenge of taking account of issues of class and ethnicity and respecting the family's culture while needing to be authoritative in seeking to protect the children. In many respects how they handled it approximated to best practice. For example, many of the recommendations from the case conferences were focused on trying to ascertain a suitable caravan halting site for the family to live on. Implicit in this was the belief that the risk would be reduced if and when the family had more space and amenities. The public health nurse believed that, 'If they had a halting site it would take all the pressure and stress off the family'.

More adequate housing was a legitimate focus for intervention, not least because the parents themselves wanted it, rather than it being imposed by professionals on the basis of their cultural assumptions. According to the social worker, parenting issues were hard to address because of the family's lack of resources. 'How can you clean the kids when you don't have anywhere to wash them ... and parenting at that level was difficult [to address] until they are based in a place where they do have facilities.' In this regard, even though the authorities failed to deliver on a halting site, this Traveller family did get some material and considerable moral support to help them cope with their social exclusion and lack of resources. This is reflected also in the attempts that were made to support the abused woman and children in that Mrs Gates was offered a caravan of her own away from her husband, and support in getting a Barring Order against her husband.

This was an example of CBP to the extent that the professionals took account of the impact of extreme social disadvantage on the family while avoiding the danger that too concerted a focus on secondary problems such as alcohol use and housing could have been at the expense of making the father accountable for his violence, diluting attention away from the child abuse and domestic violence. Similarly, as a victim/survivor of serious violence, the choices Mrs Gates made to stay were looked upon sympathetically in a way that took account of just how difficult it is for abused women to leave, and the added difficulties Traveller women can face. Yet the woman's responsibility to her children and the impact of her decision-making on them still had to be dealt with authoritatively. The counsellor's view was that: 'It's not just with [the father] that work needs to be done. [Mrs Gates] has an acceptance for violence as well, which is not acceptable.' However, Mrs Gates did not keep her appointment to meet with a psychologist and consistently resisted, and even sabotaged, attempts to help her.

Statutory protection in the form of Care Orders was also not regarded as a solution, as account was taken by social workers of the eight children's cultural background: 'I just don't feel it's the right step for them. And we're talking about a whole new culture of people and houses. The son, if in care, would run away. There's no way you could ever move him'. Another key factor influencing the decision not to go for Care Orders was the five children who were already accommodated due to non-child protection concerns (learning difficulties), and knowledge of those Traveller children's difficulties in care and the parent's suffering in relation to them. Implied here was a recognition that if accommodated in care the children would require a trans-racial placement due to the absence of carers from their own community, which damages the identities of children from minority groups (Small, 1986). In short, especially because of the family's cultural background, the professionals had little confidence in the ability of the looked-after children system to do much better than the parents.

Once again, this kind of professional judgement was made possible through relationship-based CBP. Crucially, part of the social worker's approach to safeguarding the children was getting to know them through doing direct work with them. As the 10-year-old girl put it in the research interview, 'We go in [to see the social worker] and out every couple of months. We used to go in every couple of weeks. She'd say, "How are you today and how's mammy and daddy?"... I think its alright [talking to the social worker], you go away for a while and come back'. Yet, the elder boy did not like being asked questions about his home life. 'I hate it, disgusting. They hold you up for too long, too much stupid questions that's what I hate ... I don't like going in on my own because you won't be able to answer all. You need your sister to answer some, you have to be safe like'. This is the young male service user who was viewed as not confinable if received into care and his resistant attitude helps us to see why. On the other hand, the children were unanimous about what they wanted the social worker to do for them. 'Talk to daddy and mammy like they do when people fight they help them. That's what they do with daddy and mammy.'

The workers faced the challenge of taking culture into account without engaging in 'cultural relativism', the view that no culture has a right to judge another's lifestyle and child-rearing practices and tolerating abusive practices on the assumption they are 'normal' within particular cultures (Dingwall et al., 1995). What was achieved here was credible authoritative ethnically sensitive practice (Connelly et al., 2005) in that it took the alleged child and woman abuse deeply seriously while trying to find solutions which took full account of the family's culture and what it was possible to achieve in promoting the children's well-being.

CONCLUDING REMARKS

In making the case for CBP, the point is not that the practice was perfect – whatever that might look like – or beyond question. The case in focus was chosen precisely because it illustrates well the complexity involved in defining, doing and analysing best practice. Questioning it is in fact the whole point, as by seeing it laid out we are able to engage with it and clarify our own definitions of best practice in terms of how we would respond. This returns us to the vital question concerning the kinds of critical theorising that should be incorporated into nourishing new forms of 'radical imagination' and best practice in social work. I have suggested that we need forms of theorising which must be able to work effectively at a number of inter-related levels, incorporating the personal, the organisational and the social/political. This means addressing head-on the intimacies of people's lives and how social work practices 'wrap' themselves around people's vulnerabilities, strengths, dangerousness, suffering and resilience. It concerns the politics of the personal as experienced through lived experience and practice, what I have elsewhere called 'life politics' (Ferguson, 2001, 2004). This involves accounting for power and the structural factors that contribute to people's problems by addressing them through analysis of how they materialise in people's inner and outer lives in actual practice.

A CBP perspective has a similar orientation to and shares the concerns of what evaluation researchers call 'appreciative inquiry', where the production of knowledge for the constructive development of policy and practice is based on agency staff and service users being asked about what works well, what is of value? It identifies 'what is best and most successful as a means for moving forward' (Preskill and Coghlan, 2003: 1). A CBP perspective is solution-focused in that it goes beyond deficit approaches to provide examples of ways of working which are viewed as working, focusing on the who, what, when and where of effective responses instead of the who, what, when and where of problems (De Jong and Miller, 1995). In many respects it involves applying a strengths-based perspective (Saleebey, 2006) to social work itself where its successes are affirmed. Once these strengths are brought to awareness and thereby made available for public consumption both inside and outside the profession, social work can mobilise them to create solutions tailor-made for the lives of service users and to promote the healthy development of the profession itself. The core objective is to identify the best work that is going on, so that what is done well will be acknowledged, celebrated, learned from and done more often. The cumulative effect of more and more CBP being performed could then be the transformation of the system in its own image.

REFERENCES

Adams, D. (1988), 'Treatment models of men who batter: A pro-feminist analysis', in K. Yllo., K. Bograd and M. Bograd (eds), *Feminist Perspectives on Wife Abuse* (Newbury Park: Sage).

Adams, R., Dominelli, L. and Payne, M. (1998), *Social Work: Themes, Issues and Critical Debates* (Basingstoke: Macmillan).

Adams, R., Dominelli, L. and Payne, M. (eds) (2002), *Critical Practice in Social Work* (Basingstoke: Palgrave).

Adams, R., Dominelli, L. and Payne, M. (eds) (2005), *Social Work Futures: Crossing Boundaries, Transforming Practice* (Basingstoke: Palgrave).

Bailey, R. and Brake, M. (1975), *Radical Social Work* (London: Edward Arnold).

Brechin, A. (2000), 'Introducing critical practice', in A. Brechin., H. Brown and M. Eby, (eds), *Critical Practice in Health and Social Care* (London: Sage).

Brown, H. C. (1997), *Social Work and Sexuality: Working with Lesbians and Gay Men* (Basingstoke: MacMillan, 1998)

Buckley, H. (2003), *Child Protection: Beyond the Rhetoric* (London: Jessica Kingsley).

Connolly, M., Crichton-Hill, Y. and Ward, T. (2005), *Culture and Child Protection: Reflexive Responses* (London: Jessica Kingsley).

Cooper, A. and Lousada, J. (2005), *Borderline Welfare: Feeling and Fear of Feeling in Modern Welfare* (London: Karnac).

Corrigan, P. and Leonard, P. (1978), *Social Work Practice Under Capitalism: A Marxist Approach* (London: Macmillan)

Dalrymple, J. and Burke, B. (1995), *Anti-Oppressive Practice, Social Care and the Law* (Buckingham: Open University Press).

De'Cruz, H., Gillingham, P. and Melendez, S. (2007), 'Reflexivity, its Meanings and Relevance for Social Work: A Critical Review of the Literature', *British Journal of Social Work*, Vol. 37, 73–90.

De Jong, P. and Miller, S. (1995), 'How to interview for client strengths', *Social Work*, Vol. 40, pp. 729–736.

Department of Health (1998), *Modernising Social Services* (London: The Stationery Office).

Dingwall, R., Eekelaar, J. and Murray, T. (1995), *The Protection of Children* (Aldershot: Avebury, 2nd ed.).

Dobash, R. and Dobash, P. (1992), *Women, violence and social change* (London: Routledge).

Dominelli, L. (1988), *Anti-racist social work: A Challenge for White Practitioners and Educators* (Basingstoke: Macmillan).

Featherstone, B. (2004), *Family Life and Family Support* (Basingstoke: Palgrave).

Ferguson, H. (2001), 'Social Work, Individualisation and Life Politics', *British Journal of Social Work*, Vol. 31, 41–55.

Ferguson, H. (2004), *Protecting Children in Time: Child Abuse, Child Protection and the Consequences of Modernity* (Basingstoke: Palgrave).

Ferguson, H. (2005), 'Working with Violence, the Emotions and the Psycho-social Dynamics of Child Protection: Reflections on the Victoria Climbié Case, *Social Work Education*, Vol. 24, No. 7, pp. 781–795

Ferguson, H. and O'Reilly, M. (2001), *Keeping Children Safe: Child abuse, Child Protection and the Promotion of Welfare* (Dublin: A&A Farmar).

Ferguson, I. and Lavalette, M. (2004), 'Beyond Power Discourse: Alienation and Social Work', *British Journal of Social Work*, Vol. 34, pp. 297–312

Ferguson, I. and Lavalette, M. (2006), 'Globalization and Global Justice: Towards a Social Work of Resistance', *International Social Work*, Vol. 49, pp. 309–318

Fook, J. (1999), 'Critical reflectivity in education and practice', in B. Pease and J. Fook (eds), *Transforming Social Work Practice: Postmodern critical perspectives* (London: Routledge).

Fook, J. (2002), *Social Work: Critical Theory and Practice* (London: Sage).

Froggett, L. (2002), *Love Hate and Welfare*, (Bristol: Policy Press).

Fuller, S. (2005), *The Intellectual* (London: Icon Books).

Giddens, A. (1984), *The Constitution of Society* (Cambridge: Polity).

Gondolf, E. W. (1993), 'Male Batterers', in R. Hampton (ed.), *Family Violence: Prevention and Treatment* (pp. 230–257) (Newbury Park, CA: Sage).

Healy, K. (1999), 'Power and Activist Social Work', in B. Pease and J. Fook (eds), *Transforming Social Work Practice: Postmodern Critical Perspectives* (London: Routledge).

Healy, K. (2000), *Social Work Practices: Contemporary Perspectives on Change* (London: Sage).

Healy, K. (2005), *Social Work Theories in Context: Creating Frameworks for Practice* (Basingstoke: Palgrave Macmillan).

Hearn, J. (1999), *The Violences of Men* (London: Sage).

Hicks, S. (2000), 'Sexuality' in M. Davies (ed.), *The Blackwell Encyclopaedia of Social Work* (Oxford: Blackwell).

Hoggett, P. (2001), 'Agency, Rationality and Social Policy', *Journal of Social Policy*, Vol. 30, No. 1, pp. 37–56.

Holway, W. (2001), 'The Psycho-social Subject in 'Evidence-based Practice', *Journal of Social Work Practice*, Vol. 15, No. 1, 9–22.

Houston, S., Magill, T., MaCollum, M. and Spratt, T. (2001), 'Developing Creative Solutions to the Problems of Children and their Families: Communicative Reason and the use of Forum Theatre', *Child and Family Social Work*, 6(4) 285–294.

Lash, S. and Urry, J. (1987), *The End of Organised Capitalism* (Cambridge: Polity).

Leonard, P. (1997), *Postmodern Welfare: Reconstructing an Emancipatory Project* (London: Sage).

Macdonald, G. (2001), *Effective Interventions for Child Abuse and Neglect* (London: Wiley).

Macdonald, G. and Sheldon, B. (1992), 'Contemporary Studies of the Effectiveness of Social Work', *British Journal of Social Work*, Vol. 22, pp. 615–643.

Margison, F. (2001), 'Practice-based Evidence in Psychotherapy', in C. Mace, S. Moorey, and B. Roberts (eds), *Evidence in Psychological Theories* (London: Brunner-Routledge).

Means, R. and Smith, R. (1998), *From Poor Law to community Care: The Development of Welfare Services for Elderly People 1939–1971* (Bristol: Policy Press).

Milner, J. (1996), 'Men's Resistance to Social Workers', in B. Fawcett, B. Featherstone, J. Hearn and C. Toft (eds), *Violence and Gender Relations, Theories and Interventions* (London: Sage).

Milner, J. (2004), 'From "Disappearing" to "Demonized": The Effects on Men and Women of Professional Interventions Based on Challenging Men Who are Violent', *Critical Social Policy*, Vol. 24, pp. 79–101.

Morran, D. and Wilson, M. (1999), 'Working with Men who are Violent to Partners – Striving for Good Practice', in H. Kemshall and J. Pritchard (ed.), *Good Practice in Working with Violence* (Jessica Kingsley Publishers: Philadelphia).

Mullender, A. (1996), *Rethinking Domestic Violence: The Social Work and Probation Response* (London: Routledge).

O'Connell, J. (2002), 'Travellers in Ireland: an examination of discrimination and racism', in R. Lentin and R. McVeigh (eds), *Racism and Anti-Racism in Ireland* (Dublin: Beyond the Pale Publication).

Oliver, M. (1990), *Understanding Disability: From Theory to Practice* (Basingstoke: Macmillan).

Parton, N. and O'Byrne, P. (2000), *Constructive Social Work* (Basingstoke: Palgrave).

Pearson, G. (1975), *The Deviant Imagination* (London: Macmillan).

Pease, B. and Fook, J. (eds) (1999), *Transforming Social Work Practice: Postmodern Critical Perspectives* (London: Routledge).

Preskill, H. and Coghlan, A. T. (2003), *Using Appreciative Inquiry in Evaluation* (San Francisco: Jossey-Bass).

Reder, P., Duncan, S. and Gray, M. (1983), *Beyond Blame: Child Abuse Tragedies Revisited* (London: Routledge).

Saleebey, D. (ed.) (2006), *The Strengths Perspective in Social Work Practice* (New York: Longman).

Shaw, I. (1999), 'Evidence for practice', in I. Shaw and J. Lishman (eds), *Evaluation and Social Work Practice* (London: Sage).

Shaw, I. (2005), 'Practitioner Research: Evidence or Critique?' *British Journal of Social Work*, Vol. 35, No. 8, pp. 1231–1248.

Sheldon and Macdonald (1999), *Research and Practice in Social Care: Mind the Gap* (Exeter: Centre for Evidence-Based Practice).

Shepard, M. and Pence, E. (1999), *Coordinating Community Responses to Domestic Violence: Lessons from Duluth and Beyond* (London: Sage).

Small, J. (1986), 'Trans-racial placements: conflicts and contradictions', in Ahmed, S., Cheetham, J and Small, J. *Social Work with Black Children and their Families* (London: Batsford/BAFF).

Stark, E and Flitcraft, A (1996), *Women at Risk: Domestic Violence and Women's Health* (London: Sage Publications).

Strange, V., Forrest, S., Oakley, A. and the Ripple Study Team (2001), 'A listening trial: 'qualitative' methods within experimental research', in S. Oliver and G. Peersman (eds), *Using Research for Effective Health Promotion* (Buckingham: Open University Press).

Taylor, C. and White, S. (2000), *Practising Reflexivity in Health and Welfare: Making Knowledge* (Buckingham: Open University Press) .

Thompson, N. (1993), *Anti-Discriminatory Practice* (London: Macmillan).

Trevithick, P. (2003), Effective Relationship-based Practice: A theoretical Exploration, *Journal of Social Work Practice*, Vol. 17, No. 2, 163–176.

Webb, S. (2001), 'Some Considerations on the Validity of Evidence-based Practice in Social Work', *British Journal of Social Work*, Vol. 31, 57–79.

Webb, S. (2006), *Social Work in a Risk Society* (Basingstoke: Palgrave).

Williams, F. and Popay, J. (1999), 'Balancing polarities: developing a new framework for welfare research' in Williams, F., Popay, J. and Oakley, A., (eds), *Welfare Research: A Critical Review* (London: UCL Press).

Wilson, E. (1985), *Adorned in Dreams: Fashion and Modernity* (London: Virago).

Wise, S. (1995), 'Feminist ethics in practice', in R. Hugman and D. Smith (eds), *Ethical Issues in Social Work* (Routledge, London).

2 Beyond anti-oppressive practice in social work: best practice and the ethical use of power in adult care

ALISON GARDENER

INTRODUCTION

When I was studying for my Social Work Diploma in 2000, it was a requirement that every piece of work I wrote demonstrated my commitment to anti-oppressive practice (AOP). I was encouraged to analyse the cultural and structural oppression embedded in society and to demonstrate how, as a social worker, I was both working within those oppressive structures and actively seeking to challenge them. That AOP was social work's defining theoretical basis was something I felt that I could not safely question – or not if I wanted to qualify. So, when I wrote about my practice, I would try to fashion what I was doing into an anti-oppressive mould. I often felt caught in something of a double bind. On the one hand, I was committed to challenging oppression and, on the other, I had no choice but to oppress. At a basic level, how could I balance the conflicting rights of a disabled person and their carer? If I supported one, was it not inevitable that I would oppress the other? Or, if I believed I had a legal and ethical duty to seek to have restrictions placed on a woman with dementia, how could I escape the fact that my intervention was highly oppressive?

As a result, the analysis of my practice would be largely negative, focusing on what I had *not* done well or what had *not* been possible.

All names and some circumstances have been changed to ensure the anonymity of the service users.

When it came to my post-qualifying social work course, I decided to turn this experience on its head and to use my own practice to interrogate the anti-oppressive model. I wanted to find a way of thinking about and theorising what I did which was both critical *and* positive. This chapter is based on the result. I intend first to look briefly at the key ideas behind AOP and outline some of the reasons why I find them a problematic theoretical basis for social work. Then, by analysing elements of my own practice with three different service users, I want to examine in more detail some of the very real difficulties with the ways in which AOP is often conceived. At the same time, I aim to use the notion of critical best practice (CBP) outlined in Chapter 1 to re-interpret or re-imagine that same practice through a more complex and positive critical lens.

The focus here is on my own perception of my work as it was not possible to elicit the views of the service users themselves directly for the purpose of this chapter. I am mindful throughout that I am conveying my own interpretation of events and include the perspective of service users and carers only to the extent of repeating aspects of what they told me as the work was in progress.

ANTI-OPPRESSIVE PRACTICE

AOP has been defined in different ways and different terminology is sometimes used, but at its core is the idea that individuals and groups are disadvantaged by the way in which society is structured. Thompson's 'PCS' model (Thompson, 1997) illustrates how discrimination operates at a personal, cultural and structural level, analysing how individuals and groups are stereotyped, infantalised, pathologised, excluded or rendered invisible. People may be directly discriminated against, but less overtly and more problematically, the very cultural norms, values, language and structures of a society will discriminate against the less powerful groups within it. Whilst a shared culture can create a positive sense of belonging and stability, individuals and minority groups within it may so internalise the existing order of things that they can conceive of no alternative, in effect colluding with their own oppression. The power of some groups over others is, therefore, evident not only in words and actions but also in what is *not* thought about or said or done: 'the most effective and insidious use of power is to prevent ... conflict from arising in the first place' (Lukes, 2005: 27).

Within this context, social work is seen as an overtly political activity, and the primary role of the social worker is not to help people cope with their circumstances, but to challenge the cultural assumptions and oppressive social structures that have been instrumental in creating those circumstances: 'The driving force of AOP is the act of challenging inequalities' (Burke and Harrison, 2002: 230).

In many ways, it is difficult to disagree with this. Ever since the radical social work of the 1970s, social work has clung on to its commitment to social justice, even in the face of mounting bureaucracy and managerialism. Whilst the General Social Care Council's Code of Practice (GSCC, 2002) makes no reference to inequality beyond that of respecting individual rights, the British Association of Social Work continues to insist that social justice remains one of its core values (BASW, 2002). Working with adults in a statutory setting, I am constantly confronted by the ways in which many older and disabled people are disadvantaged. The department for which I work, states that its aim is to 'empower' the community and to ensure that its service users have 'the same rights of citizenship' as everyone else. But, how can this mean anything to the older person who cannot move to the residential home of their choice because it is more expensive than the local authority rate – which is set so low that it will not buy *any* local private residential home place? Questioning and criticising the structures in which we work continues to be a requirement of best critical social work practice.

And yet, there still seems to me to be a considerable gulf between what I am actually *doing* and much of the theoretical underpinning of AOP. Statutory social workers are working within legal and policy restraints and, generally, with individuals rather than groups or communities, so our sphere of influence is necessarily limited. Collectively, it is social movements such as the disabled people's movement rather than the social work profession which have been effective in campaigning for political and social change (Wilson and Beresford, 2000). But, paradoxically, Wilson and Beresford (2000: 554) also dismiss AOP as social work's 'sacred cow' on the basis that social workers represent *so much* power. From a service user perspective, they argue that it is intellectually dishonest for social work to claim that AOP is its key theory when one of its main functions is that of social control.

Perhaps a standpoint that views social work's role principally in structural terms answers our own need for a sense of mission and purpose more than it provides a coherent theoretical basis for what we do. The danger is that, if we are taught that AOP is the foundation of good social work, we will continually feel demoralised, because if social work is defined in those terms we can never do a good job. We may share the values of AOP, but we are unable to fulfil its demands, working within and representing structures that we can do very little to change. Yet, real and meaningful social and personal change does occur for individuals, families, groups and communities as a result of social work intervention, and we need to find a language and develop theories which can account for how this happens. Despite encouraging a strengths-based approach when working with service users, social work very often takes a deficit-based stance in thinking about itself, focusing predominantly on what it fails to do (Ferguson, 2003b). No doubt there are failures, but perhaps this is partly because what it seems to be setting out to achieve is not achievable – at least, not within the context of statutory social work. Our aim then, is to outline what is possible and best in critical practice.

COLIN AND MARY

Colin had been indicating for some time that he was thinking of moving out of his home. His relationship with his partner, Mary, had not been entirely easy before his motorbike accident, and he felt it had broken down further since then. Colin was in his early 60s and the accident six years ago had left him with a cognitive impairment, unable to speak or read more than a very few words and affected by periods of depression. He had a daughter in her late teens and his relationship with her was particularly difficult.

Colin asked me to support him in discussing this with Mary. At the meeting, she said that she would not stand in Colin's way, but she feared that a move would increase his sense of isolation and could be counter-productive. She became very agitated and angry with Colin as she thought about the practical and financial implications for herself and their daughter. Colin himself appeared increasingly distressed and tearful and eventually indicated that he had changed his mind and no longer wished to move.

When communicating with Colin, I frequently had to ask him closed questions. Although he had no difficulty in understanding, the only verbal way he had of responding was by saying 'yes', 'no' or 'don't know'. There was therefore always a danger that I defined the terms of the conversation. In other meetings, I encouraged Colin to indicate what he wanted to say through gesture and drawing, but in the context of an emotional discussion, this did not seem possible. I had underestimated the difficulty of including him, and was constantly drawn into conversation with Mary, so that I felt that he was literally being silenced. Colin had requested that only I came to the meeting, but I regretted that he did not have his own advocate. As a result, I decided that I needed to speak to Colin again on his own and suggested to both him and Mary that I would meet up with them a few days later.

At our second meeting, Colin appeared much calmer. I felt that he might have changed his mind simply because the meeting had got too difficult. So I stated very clearly that he had the right to move, if this was what he wanted and that I, and others who worked with him, would promote his right to choose, whatever practical and emotional problems might arise. However, Colin remained clear that he was, at present, wanting to stay at home.

Anti-oppressive discourse suggests that people belong to mutually exclusive groups, some powerful and some powerless, who are in conflict: 'Power is seen as concerned with personal and social relationships where one person or group consistently prevents others, who are seen as powerless, from achieving their needs or aspirations' (Payne, 1997: 258, citing Dalrymple and Burke, 1995). From a Disability rights perspective, it has been argued that the relationship of a disabled person to a carer is, almost by definition, one of subordination (Priestley, 1999), which would make Colin the 'oppressed' party with Mary in control. Working anti-oppressively, I might then have concluded that my role was to support Colin 'against' his wife, aiming at 'a constant lowering of the power imbalance through a continual process of identifying the sources of power differentials and eliminating as many of these obstacles as possible' (Dominelli, 2002: 8).

However, defining people's relationships in terms of rights and power is clearly simplistic. First, within the framework of Community Care legislation in the United Kingdom, social workers are expected to work in partnership with both service users *and* carers, and there is an increasing emphasis on the rights of carers to assessment and support in their role (The Carers (Recognition and Services) Act 1995; The Carers and Disabled Children Act 2000; The Carers (Equal Opportunities) Act 2004). But even if this were not the case, how could I decide whether Colin or Mary had more power? Whose rights should take precedence? Colin was, as a disabled man, excluded from many aspects of society, particularly by his communication difficulties. His income from benefits was very low and he had given Mary Power of Attorney, so that she had control of his finances. From a feminist perspective, Mary was living in a culture in which there is still an assumption that women should be able and willing to care for all of their family, however demanding the circumstances, even when they are holding down a full-time job and managing a household (Orme, 2001). Mary, as well as Colin, had had to cope with the consequences of his accident and all the attendant difficulties and trauma. When Colin was particularly frustrated and angry, the atmosphere at home could be extremely stressful and Mary worried about the effect this had on their daughter: 'Hemmed in by conflicting obligations ... and contradictory social injunctions ... women often find themselves to be in a situation from which there is *no exit*; someone is always being let down' (Hoggett, 2001, citing Mendus, 1993).

Cognitive impairments following a head injury have been called an 'invisible injury' (Japp, 2005: 21), one that is not understood or supported in the way that a more 'visible' impairment would be. Both Colin and Mary were discriminated against by the absence of appropriate, long-term services for head injury survivors, which makes them more dependent on their families (House of Commons Health Committee, 2001). Feminist and Disability rights analyses contribute much to our understanding of human situations and dividing people into 'powerful' or 'powerless' groups is a potent political tool. However, by defining individuals in political terms ('service user' or 'carer'), we run the risk of failing to relate to them as people (Pease and Fook, 1999). The dichotomous and rights-based stance of anti-oppressive discourse struggles to account for the complex dynamics of real human feelings and relationships. Colin may have felt unable to act because of Mary's opposition, but it also seemed that he himself was in conflict; he wanted both to leave Mary *and* to repair and renew his relationship with her.

A social work practice which is both 'best' and 'critical' is rooted firmly in this all too human complexity. My role was not to take sides or make judgements about what the outcome should be (it was, after all, their life and not mine) but to adopt a 'not-knowing' approach (Brechin, 2000: 32), accepting the uncertainty of the situation, rather than seeing it as a problem to be solved. My practice was not 'best' because it was perfect or because there was nothing I would have done differently (in retrospect, I wish I had found an advocate for Colin at that first meeting). But, I could *do* my best to support both Colin and Mary whilst they came to their own decisions, allowing myself to be guided both by what they themselves were saying and by my critical understanding of the structures and power dynamics in which our lives are lived.

Over the following months, my focus was to explore with Colin ways in which he could improve the quality of his life by building up a network outside the home. I introduced him to a group of other people who had had head injuries and arranged for a support worker to assist him on a regular basis. As their relationship grew, this person frequently acted as Colin's advocate. At the same time, I continued to try to support Mary. She refused a Carer's Assessment, saying that she herself did not need any support and rejected the idea of relationship counselling. But, after a while, she contacted me in order to talk about the stress she was under and to request additional respite. As a result, I introduced Colin to a community in a neighbouring region, which offered accommodation to people in need of support in exchange for practical help. This gave Mary a break and also helped to build up Colin's confidence and independence. He had not travelled on his own since his accident but was assisted in doing this and getting there on his own, using communication cards and the train company's service for disabled passengers. He also opened his own bank account to manage his direct payment over which he, rather than Mary, had control. Some time after my own involvement ended, but with ongoing support from his support worker and new social worker, Colin did decide to move out.

This typifies CBP in how it embraced the complexity of working against the discrimination that both the service user and carer experienced, and was deeply practical in acting to help get useful things for the service user and carer done, while also skilfully engaging with trying to help individual's identify and meet their needs and manage the emotional dynamics of their relationships. The relationships I developed with Colin and Mary themselves acted as a 'container' within which at least some of their individual sufferings could be worked through and their self-esteem, well-being and life plans could be developed (for further discussion of this concept of emotional 'containment', see Chapter 4).

SANDRA

Sandra received a direct payment from the state to employ a number of personal assistants due to her physical disabilities. There were however, ongoing problems. She found it difficult to retain staff and the majority of care agencies would no longer work with her, saying that she shouted at their care workers and made unreasonable demands. There had been many attempts by the support service to assist, but the difficulties had continued. The situation came to a head when a funding body decided that Sandra was no longer eligible and stopped their payments. At the same time, a number of her personal assistants resigned, a succession of live-in care workers walked out and several nursing homes withdrew from emergency placement arrangements, saying that they could not work with her.

There is a tendency within anti-discriminatory practice perspectives to 'blame the system' and underemphasise the part played by service users themselves who, like all of us, will sometimes act in ways that are self-defeating, contradictory and destructive (Hoggett, 2001; Ferguson, 2003a). My image of myself as a social worker is based on the principle that I am there, first and foremost, to act on behalf of the service users with whom I am working. I want to see myself as their advocate, working within an often complicated and apparently heartless welfare system and trying to use my knowledge of policy and my powers of persuasion to obtain the assistance that they need. Working with Sandra, it was not difficult to see the situation from her point of view. In arranging her own care, she had the responsibility of running a medium-sized business and, at a time of low unemployment, it was difficult to recruit personal assistants on the low rates of pay provided by social services. Giving Sandra the assistance she needed during the day and night involved hard work and long hours for a single live-in care worker and it was not surprising that it had been difficult and stressful. The emergency placements that had broken down were in relatively inexpensive care homes, without specialist facilities or high staffing levels, and they were in no position to give Sandra the level of assistance she had had at home.

At the same time, I could not ignore the impact of Sandra's own behaviour. If she treated other people so badly, it was not surprising that they refused to work for her. Her live-in care workers were mostly Black women from the African continent, working for low pay with minimal job security. They reported that their treatment by Sandra – who was white British – was not only unreasonable, but racist. From an organisational perspective, Sandra was given a direct payment on the understanding that she could manage her own care arrangements, with assistance and training from a support service. But, when her arrangements broke down, responsibility reverted to social services and the consequent crisis management was immensely time-consuming and expensive. Finding emergency placements was difficult enough, and specialist beds were even harder to come by at short notice. If, in the future, no service providers would work with Sandra, how could social services fulfil its legal obligation to meet her needs?

I went to see Sandra in order to discuss what was happening and to challenge her racist attitudes, but I found the meeting very uncomfortable. Whilst I was clear that her treatment of her care workers was discriminatory and jeopardised her direct payment, she was equally clear that the difficulties lay not with her but with the care workers and the inadequacy of the service provision. As I was speaking, I could hear myself prevaricating and being insufficiently explicit about the difficulties, and the risk that social services would withdraw her direct payment. I reminded Sandra of her legal responsibilities as an employer under the Race Relations Act 1976, but the discussion felt formal and defensive. Our respective positions were stated, but I am not sure that anything significantly changed.

In describing a disability equality workshop with non-disabled people, Casling (1993: 204) suggests that there is a discrepancy between the professed attitudes of non-disabled towards disabled people, 'promoted on the premise of sympathy and care', and the feelings that non-disabled people actually experience of anxiety, guilt and anger. Sandra was severely impaired and could move only her head. When I talked to her, I was intensely aware of myself as a non-disabled person and had a sense that it was wholly inappropriate for me to be making judgements and decisions in relation to her life. How could I really understand what it was like to be physically dependent on other people for every movement and action? Wouldn't I get frustrated and angry? Or would I simply have given up in a way that Sandra had not? I also knew that I had no solution to offer; withdrawing the direct payment would only lead to a stand-off between social services offering a placement to fulfil its legal obligations, and Sandra refusing to accept it.

AOP operates within a modernist theoretical framework that seeks to explain society in terms of conflict between those with and without power. Society and its problems are defined in terms of having single origins (what are called 'meta narratives'). Marxist theory, for instance, regards the key explanation for social life as being social class differences and the relationship between those who own the means to produce wealth (capitalists) and those who sell their labour power (workers). Marxist theory (as was shown in Chapter 1) has had an important influence on radical perspectives in social work (Corrigan and Leonard, 1978). However, real social work at its best has to consider different and competing perspectives (multiple rather than 'meta' narratives). Thus radical thinking in social work has taken the important theoretical direction which Fook (2002) calls 'critical practice'. Informed by post-modernism it is useful for making sense of the diverse 'voices' and meanings that surround social work interventions. We are frequently working in situations of ethical complexity and having to think critically about individual rights, political perspectives, personal and societal values and the legal, policy and financial restrictions within which we are working. CBP sits more comfortably within a post-modern paradigm, in which reality is not seen as objectively 'out there', but as made up of many subjective experiences and perspectives. In Sandra's case, social service's perspective was largely that she was 'not managing' and 'disruptive'; the care agencies' perspective was that Sandra was an unreasonable and racist employer. Sandra's perspective was that she was trying to organise the assistance she needed within an under-funded, inadequate and bureaucratic system. My own perspective was that there was truth in all of these, but none of them told the whole story.

But there are difficulties with this. One of the main criticisms of post-modern thought is the danger that it leads to what the philosopher John Caputo has described as an 'anything goes relativism [in which] nothing is true, everything is possible, one belief or perspective is as good as another' (Caputo, 2001: 60). In relation to social work, the fear is that these relativistic tendencies undermine its commitment to social justice (Ife, 1999; Noble, 2004). A purely post-modern social worker (if such a thing could exist!) might look at Sandra's situation and acknowledge the different perspectives as equally valid. But how would that help them to act? If all perspectives are as good as each other, ethical debate is no longer relevant. And, if you believe that profound injustices and discrimination *do* exist – that people are systematically discriminated against in the way society is organised – this relativism will do nothing to challenge the *status quo*. Post-modern social work, with no values, no politics and no ethics, would not be social work at all.

Perhaps, however, a post-modern approach to social work offers no moral framework because this is not what it is about; it is not so much an analysis of how the world should be as an exploration of how we understand it (Fook, 2002). It is not asking us to abandon our values, because they are not what it is talking about. Looking at it like this, we can accept that there are different and competing versions of reality without rejecting wholesale what has gone before: 'The "post-" [in "post-modern"] should not be understood to mean "over and done with" but rather *after having passed through* modernity' (Caputo, op cit).

As has already been said in Chapter 1, best practice is not just about positive outcomes, and much good social work happens in situations where outcomes are unclear or further harm prevented. I could not solve the problems surrounding Sandra's care. The system is under-resourced and inflexible but, even if it had not been, Sandra might not have been able to retain the staff that she needed; her own attitudes and behaviour played a major part. However, this does not mean that my practice was bad or ineffectual. Practically, I was able to clarify for Sandra the complicated rules surrounding her funding and provide information on relevant appeal and complaints procedures. I wrote to one of the funding bodies to express my view that their guidelines were discriminatory, which persuaded them to make an exception in Sandra's case. My stance throughout was to treat Sandra as an equal, sharing my knowledge and working on the basis that she was an expert in relation to her own care. And, crucially, while challenging her racism, I made sure that Sandra's own perspective was heard and I highlighted some of the structural issues which impacted on her care arrangements, so that she herself was not viewed simply as problematic.

SIMON

Simon was given early retirement in his 50s, and his employers con-tacted social services because they were worried that he would be iso-lated and unable to manage without the support that they had been giving him. Simon had a congenital impairment and used a power-assisted wheelchair to get around. His house was dirty and in some dis-repair, and it looked as though he himself rarely washed or changed his clothes. There was rotting food in the fridge and freezer and evidence that he had spent most of his substantial savings on things that he could and would never use, which accumulated in boxes in his bunga-low. Simon's former colleagues said that he had got into financial diffi-culties, his personal care had deteriorated and that they were very unsure of what he was eating. However, Simon himself seemed unper-turbed. He laughed a lot and said that things were 'perfectly fine', that he cooked and ate well, was enjoying his retirement and would occupy himself with making models and collecting postcards.

The AOP perspective, quite rightly, places a strong emphasis on accept-ing difference: 'Practising equality requires the practitioner to value 'difference' in lifestyles and identities instead of settling for a clone of oneself as expressed by demanding a uniform conformity in others' (Dominelli, 2002: 9). Alongside this, there is a deep and healthy dis-trust of any concept of 'normality', with an understanding that any apparent consensus about what is or is not 'normal' is likely to be only a consensus of the powerful majority. The tendency is always to see someone's 'difference' as positive and the state's push towards conformity as negative, so that socially constructed concepts such as 'self-neglect' are viewed with suspicion. There is certainly truth in this: we do need to consider critically how norms of socially acceptable hygiene are established and whose problem it is if they are not met (Lauder et al., 2002). But at the same time this does not mean that self-neglect does not exist or that it is unethical for the state to try to prevent people from harming themselves.

As I worked with Simon, I became increasingly uncertain about his ability to manage or to understand the consequences of his actions, especially in relation to his finances. I felt that I needed another opinion and, with Simon's permission, I requested a mental health assessment. To my great frustration, the GP would not see him unless he went to the surgery, which Simon refused to do. When I then referred him directly to the Community Mental Health Team, they concluded that he was not eligible for a specialist assessment. In social work practice, we frequently have to perform a difficult balancing act between our statutory responsibilities and individual freedoms. Much of the language of UK government policy is couched in terms of 'risk management', so much so that in the current government's *Fair Access to Care* criteria, eligibility for services is defined in terms of the risks to a service user if assistance is not provided (DOH, 2003b). But equally pervasive is the rhetoric of choice and independence. Legally, all adults who have the mental capacity to make decisions about their lives also have the right to put themselves at risk, provided those risks are themselves not against the law. The recent White Paper, *Independence, Wellbeing and Choice* (DOH, 2005: 10) states that 'people should be able to live with their own risk' and the Department of Health's Guidance on working with Vulnerable Adults, *No Secrets* (DOH, 2000), is clear that provided an adult is able to understand their situation and make decisions the state cannot intervene to protect them if this is against their wishes.

Without any clear guidance relating to Simon's mental capacity to manage his money or make decisions about his care, I was left in a quandary. I had no power to intervene against his will, but remained worried about the harm he could come to. I could have argued that living the way he did was his choice and that if I intervened to allay my own anxieties I would also deny him his right to take risks. On the other hand, *not* intervening is often the easier option and there is a danger that we use the principle of an individual's right to choose simply as an excuse to do nothing (Pritchard, 2001). Mindful of both these pitfalls, I tried to steer a middle course between being over-protective (to allay my fears) and leaving Simon entirely to his own devices. My starting point was to see to what extent I could work with him and persuade him to make some changes. Over the following months, there were some small improvements; he accepted assistance with clearing some of the rubbish, regular cleaning and agreed to mobile meals, whilst continuing to decline any help with his personal care. I suggested that he should consider giving someone Power of Attorney, but Simon did not want to do this. Eventually, working with a friend of his, we came to a partially successful voluntary agreement in which he allowed her to oversee his financial affairs. Whilst I was frequently trying to be as persuasive as possible, I was also explicit about Simon's rights. When his friend would sometimes, in understandable exasperation, tell him that he would 'have to go into a home', I tried to ensure that both he and she understood that, if his house was re-possessed, we would work with him to find alternative, independent accommodation, if that was what he wanted. 'Persuasion' here is shorthand for the use of a range of interviewing and counselling skills, including carefully framed questions, active listening and reframing of the service user's perspectives (Trevithick, 2003), which are central to CBP.

However, persuasion is sometimes not enough. There is no escaping the fact that part of a social worker's function is control; we have both the power and a duty to intervene against the will of a service user to protect them, or someone else, from harm. Within the terms of AOP, it is difficult to see these powers as anything but problematic, something that we have to do, but which does not 'fit' the theory. But whilst our powers and responsibilities need to be handled with a critical awareness, it is not helpful only to see them in problematic terms. Power can easily be abused, but exercising power is not intrinsically oppressive. We can still fulfil our duties and use our powers well and with respect.

Simon drove a car, and it became increasingly clear that he was unsafe. His GP had been informed, but had not contacted the Licensing Authority. I was not only concerned about the risks both to Simon and to others but also knew that he relied heavily on his car, and losing it would dramatically reduce his independence and increase his isolation. I was loath to contact the Licensing Authority without a second opinion and advice on any possible adjustments that could be made to the car. So I suggested that I should organise a driving assessment, to which Simon agreed. The assessors were also concerned and advised that Simon would need a full off-road test, only available some distance away, which he declined. By this time, he had had two further minor accidents and it had become evident that he was still driving without tax and insurance, despite a number of attempts to help him sort them out. I discussed the situation in supervision and decided that, with the information I had, I had no option but to write to the Licensing Authority, and I informed Simon that I would be doing this. His license was revoked, but he went on driving. Again, I advised him that it was my duty to inform the police, which I subsequently did. My actions were wholly against Simon's wishes, but I felt, on balance, that I was doing the 'right' thing. I could not do what Simon wanted (which was for me to ignore the situation), but I could be open and honest with him about what I was doing. I tried to minimise the negative consequences of my actions, organising transport and a support worker to assist him with going shopping and seeing other people during the week.

In the end, my intervention was not enough to prevent a crisis. Simon's diet made him very ill, his debts mounted and his mortgage company moved towards repossessing his house. After a spell in hospital, he confounded all my expectations by deciding that he wanted to sell up and move into a care home, where he enjoyed feeling well, eating good food and having company. The outcome was 'good' in that Simon was safe and insisted that he was happy. At the same time, I found it strangely sad that this cheerful and unconventional man, who had been so frustrating to work with, had taken so easily to institutional life.

CONCLUSION

The picture that has emerged in the analysis of my work with Colin, Mary, Sandra and Simon is, above all, a complex one. I have suggested that the paradigm of AOP, which views the world in conflictual and dichotomous terms (the powerful *versus* the powerless, the state *versus* the individual, the anti-oppressive social worker *versus* the managerial system) and sees individuals as belonging to one or the other of these discrete groups is deeply flawed. My argument has been that, whilst AOP contains some crucial insights, they are not on their own an adequate basis for theorising what we actually *do* when we 'do' social work. It cannot do justice to how we have to work with real people and real relationships, with all the diversity and complexity that that implies.

It was suggested in the introduction to this book that social work theory needs to 'rediscover its soul'. If that discovery is going to be made anywhere, it will be in the way social workers relate to the service users with whom they work. Radical traditions, with their focus on structural change, have under-emphasised the individual nature of what we do, as if the small canvas on which we work is somehow contrary to a wider political engagement. Within the rights-based ethic, 'care' itself has been equated with 'oppression' (Meagher & Parton, 2004) and words like 'compassion' have become deeply suspect: 'Even … [the word] "empathy" – once a mainstay of welfare discourse – resonates like a faintly embarrassing echo of a more therapeutically assertive age' (Froggett, 2002: 112).

Meanwhile, what service users themselves are calling for is

> courtesy and respect, being treated as equals and as individuals, and as people who make their own decisions … people who are experienced and well informed, able to explain things clearly and without condescension and who "really listen"… people who are able to act effectively and make practical things happen. (Harding and Beresford, 1996 cited in Croft & Beresford, 2002: 390)

I have argued, however, that a desire to treat service users as equals should not lead to an idealisation of practice and a refusal to face up to the use of power and authority that is often called for. A social work practice which is both 'best' and 'critical' is, first and foremost, informed by a belief that how we are and what we do in relation to another person matters profoundly. At the same time, when we root our practice in individual lives, we do not and cannot preclude politics; 'treating others as equals' is, itself, a political as well as a personal stance: 'the work of politics doesn't get done without a recognition that my good or dignity has no substance, no life, without someone else's good or dignity being involved … . It is an acknowledgement that someone else's welfare is actually *constitutive* of my own' (Williams, 2000: 77). To take that acknowledgement seriously is, by definition, to concern ourselves with social justice.

From this individual and political foundation, we can perhaps understand social work as a kind of negotiation. Working with service users and taking what they are telling us as our starting point, we act as intermediaries between them and the structures of welfare. Sometimes all that is needed is information or very practical assistance, but often we have to weigh up and analyse different and conflicting perspectives, whilst we work towards as good an outcome as is possible for the service user. Crucially, as part of that analysis, we also bring to our work a critical awareness of power relations and of how they are embedded in the way in which we understand and structure our world (Brechin, 2000). Analysing our work as social workers is a difficult business in which we have to face up to the contradictory and messy nature of what we do. But perhaps it needs to be difficult; after all, we are often making decisions that profoundly affect people's lives. It is only by wrestling with the complexity, questioning both ourselves and the structures in which we are working, that we can begin to work effectively in ways that are critically best, that is client-centred, ethical and creative.

REFERENCES

Brechin, A. (2000) 'Introducing Critical Practice' in A. Brechin., H. Brown and M. A. Eby (eds) *Critical Practice in Health and Social Care* (London: Sage).

British Association of Social Work (2002) *Ethics* [online]. Available from: http://www.basw.co.uk/articles.php?articleId=2&page=3[Accessed 8 August 2005].

Burke, B. and Harrison, P. (2002) 'Anti-Oppressive Practice' in R. Adams., L. Dominelli and M. Payne (eds) *Social Work: Themes, Issues and Critical Debates* (2nd ed.) (Basingstoke: Macmillan).

Caputo, J. (2001) *On Religion* (London: Routledge).

Casling, D. (1993) 'Cobblers and Songbirds: The Language and Imagery of Disability', *Disability, Handicap and Society*, **8** (2).

Corrigan, P. and Leonard, P. (1978), *Social Work Practice Under Capitalism: A Marxist Approach* (London: Macmillan).

Croft, S. and Beresford, P. (2002) 'Service Users' Perspectives' in Davies, M. (ed.) *The Blackwell Companion to Social Work* (Oxford: Blackwell).

Department of Health (2000) *No Secrets: Guidance on Developing and Implementing Multi-agency Policies and Procedures to Protect Vulnerable Adults from Abuse* (London: HMSO).

Department of Health (2003b) *Fair Access to Care Services: Guidance on Eligibility Criteria for Adult Social Care*. Available from: http://www.dh.gov.uk/assetRoot/04/01/96/41/04019641.pdf [Accessed 25 July 2005].

Department of Health (2005) *Independence, Well-being and Choice: Our Vision for the Future of Social Care for Adults in England* (London: HMSO).

Dominelli, L. (2002) 'Anti-oppressive Practice in Context' in R. Adams, L. Dominelli and M. Payne *Social Work: Themes, Issues and Critical Debates* (2nd ed.) (Basingstoke: Macmillan).

Ferguson, H. (2003a) 'Welfare, Social Exclusion and Reflexivity: The Case of Child and Woman Protection', *Journal of Social Policy*, **32** (2), 199–216.

Ferguson, H. (2003b) 'Outline of a Critical Best Practice Perspective on Social Work and Social Care', *British Journal of Social Work*, 33, 1105–1024.

Fook, J. (2002) *Social Work: Critical Theory and Practice* (London: Sage).

Froggett, L. (2002) *Love, Hate and Welfare: Psychosocial Approaches to Policy and Practice* (Bristol: Policy Press).

General Social Care Council (2002) *Codes of Practice for Social Care Workers and Employers* (London: GSCC).

Hoggett, P. (2001) 'Agency, Rationality and Social Policy', *Journal of Social Policy* **30** (1), 37–56.

House of Commons Health Committee (2001) *Head Injury: Rehabilitation. Third Report* (London: House of Commons)

Ife, J. (1999) 'Postmodernism, Critical Theory and Social Work' in Pease, B. and Fook, J. (eds) *Transforming Social Work Practice* (London: Routledge).

Japp, J. (2005) *Brain Injury and Returning to Employment: A Guide for Practitioners* (London: Jessica Kingsley).

Lauder, W., Anderson, I. and Barclay, A. (2002) 'Sociological and Psychological Theories of Self-neglect', *Journal of Advanced Nursing,* **40** (3), 331–338.

Lukes, S. (2005) *Power A Radical View* (2nd ed.) (Basingstoke: Palgrave/Macmillan).

Meagher, G. and Parton, N. (2004) 'Modernising Social Work and the Ethics of Care', *Social Work and Society,* **2** (1), 10–27.

Noble, C. (2004) 'Post-modern Thinking. Where is it taking Social Work?' *Journal of Social Work,* **4** (3), 289–300.

Orme, J. (2001) *Gender and Community Care: Social Work and Social Care Perspectives* (Basingstoke: Palgrave)

Payne, M. (1997) *Modern Social Work Theory* (Basingstoke: Macmillan).

Pease, B. and Fook, J. (1999) 'Post-modern Critical Theory and Emancipatory Social Work Practice' in Pease, B. and Fook, J. (eds) *Transforming Social Work Practice* (London: Routledge).

Priestley, M. (1999) *Disability Politics in Community Care* (London: Jessica Kingsley).

Pritchard, J. (2001) 'Neglect: Not Grasping the Nettle and Hiding Behind Choice' in Pritchard, J. (ed.) *Good Practice with Vulnerable Adults* (London: Jessica Kingsley).

Thompson, N. (1997) *Anti-discriminatory Practice* (2nd ed.) (Basingstoke: BASW/Macmillan).

Trevithick, P. (2003) *Social Work Skills* (Buckingham: Open University Press).

Williams, R. (2000) *Lost Icons: Reflections on Cultural Bereavement* (Edinburgh: T&T Clark).

Wilson, A. and Beresford, B. (2000) 'Anti-oppressive Practice: Emancipation or Appropriation' *British Journal of Social Work,* **30**, 553–573.

3 Situating person and place: best practice in dementia care

KAREN JONES WITH IMOGEN POWELL

This chapter is the result of a collaboration between Karen, a social work tutor and academic and Imogen, an experienced social work practitioner in a local authority mental health team for older adults. The first-person voice within the writing is Karen's, while the practice described is Imogen's.

The emphasis within Critical Best Practice (CBP) on openness and learning from real, situated practice has demanded different skills and presented new challenges in comparison with much of the academic writing I have done in the past. What follows then, is my attempt to understand and analyse good practice with adults with dementia through the illumination of a genuine practice situation. The application of ideas which I have found significant and helpful as a practitioner and as an academic are offered as a critical response to the particular social work situation described here. At the same time, the chapter offers an introduction to some of the key theoretical themes which occur elsewhere in the book.

CRITICAL PRACTICE

The term 'critical' is a contested idea and Chapter 1 of this book provides a detailed introduction to some of the shades of meaning and debate surrounding the notion of critical practice within the past and present activity of social work. Central to this chapter is the fact that 'critical' in this context does not imply a negative or destructive impulse, but rather something closer to Ann Brechin's definition of 'open minded, reflective appraisal that takes account of different perspectives, experiences and assumptions' (Brechin, 2000: 26).

My own interpretation of critical practice is influenced by those writers who have attempted to draw on post-modern ideas to critique, enhance and develop the critical tradition within social work (e.g., Rojek et al., 1988; Parton, 1994; Leonard, 1997; Pease and Fook, 1999; Healy, 2000; Powell, 2000). These theoretical perspectives are used not only to analyse the practice described here, but they also reflect a critical thread which runs through several chapters in the book.

The contribution of post-modern critical theory to an understanding of contemporary social work, and to the development of specific practice approaches is broad, contested and subject to on-going debate. Some writers embrace the post-modern label more wholeheartedly than others; it is nevertheless possible to identify a recent trend in critical thinking for social work, which favours contextual understandings of practice situations over prescriptive evidence-based approaches and single methodologies. The argument here is not that the knowledge and research base of professional expertise is unimportant, but rather that the context within which knowledge and skills are exercised is unique to specific situations and individuals.

The post-modern emphasis within social work tends to be on empathic engagement with people's stories as a path to negotiated change rather than on the imposition of expert solutions. These ideas have been used to develop critical approaches which question taken for granted assumptions, particularly those embedded in language and which embrace complexity, uncertainty and ambiguity rather than attempting to eliminate it.

CRITICAL *BEST* PRACTICE

CBP seeks to showcase what social work routinely does well (Ferguson, 2003). In many respects the case described below *is* routine and unremarkable. It is the stuff of day to day practice for Imogen and other members of the integrated health and social work mental health team in which she works, but it is also the story of an individual's experience of dementia and of a unique practice intervention.

My aim is not to raise all the practice issues involved in this case or even to tell the whole story of Imogen's involvement. It is rather to highlight practice which was *best* in a particular context, thereby enabling learning, reflection and the drawing out of key critical themes for the positive development of this area of work.

AMELIA

Amelia, who was in her early eighties, lived alone in a council house, which had also been her parents' home until their deaths. She had never married and as far as her friends and family were aware, had not had any long-term intimate relationships. At the point at which Imogen became involved, Amelia had been diagnosed with probable Alzheimer's type dementia. She was referred to the mental health team by staff at the day hospital, which she had been attending for some time. The referral described Amelia's growing confusion, and increasingly erratic attendance at the day hospital; it suggested that she now needed to be assessed for residential care. Amelia's nearest relative was her cousin Bob, who was in his early sixties and lived in the same area of town. He had never been particularly close to his cousin, but for several years had visited once a fortnight to do her shopping. At the point of referral, Amelia had begun to make bizarre and anxious telephone calls to Bob, often at strange times of the day or night; as a consequence, he was becoming increasingly drawn into the role of carer.

ENGAGING AND ASSESSING

The initial referral said that Amelia had a history of not opening the door to staff from health or social care services, so Imogen met with her on two occasions at the day hospital, in order to begin to build a trusting relationship. Once a relationship had started to be established, Imogen arranged to meet with Amelia in her own home. Here too Imogen took time and care not to *impose* a process on Amelia. In reflecting on the case, Imogen spoke of how she enabled Amelia to *tell her own story* rather than trying to introduce *the assessment agenda* immediately:

> I came to understand Amelia in her social context through discussing her personal history with her. She was keen to talk about her past — about her time in the RAF and how she then came home to live with her parents and became part of the local community. It enabled me to understand her strong attachment to her home and her reluctance to engage with people in authority whom she perceived as a threat to her security. As her short-term memory began to fail, Amelia drew comfort from long-term memories of her home and her life with and without her parents.

Understanding the importance of home and all that it represented, was central to the way in which Imogen built and maintained a relationship with Amelia. This kind of individually responsive approach is not always easy to maintain within the proceduralised framework of community care assessment. Standard tools for assessing the needs of older people typically address housing *issues* such as tenure, access and maintenance. While these areas are rightly becoming more central within social policy for older people in the United Kingdom (Heywood et al., 2002), a focus on the functionality of housing can ignore psychosocial aspects of the meaning of home for older people.

A similar pattern is found in housing research, which has often focussed on the external manifestations of housing issues such as health (Sterling, 1997; Wilkinson, 1999), homelessness (Crane, 1999) or home ownership (Saunders, 1990). Research which does look more closely at the psychosocial dimension of older people's experience of home generally paints a positive picture of its significance. (e.g., Harrison and Means, 1990; Langan et al., 1996). However, there are still gaps in our understanding of this aspect of older people's experience. Heywood et al., (2002) conclude that there is a need to draw on approaches from the field of Ageing Studies in order to develop a better understanding of the meaning of home for older people. Their suggestion that such an approach might attend closely to individual biographies and personal interpretations of past experiences is reflected in the way in which Imogen intuitively sought to understand Amelia's past experiences and current needs.

The context of Imogen's involvement was a multi-professional assessment under community care legislation. This chapter could have taken Imogen's skilled approach to working with other professionals and agencies, as its focus. The way in which she worked flexibly with the notion of assessment and went beyond simple proceduralism, had much in common with the practice of partnership working described in Chapter 13. The particular aspect of skilled practice which I want to illuminate here however, is the individualised attention through which the social worker ensured that Amelia's personality and sense of self remained at the heart of the assessment.

By avoiding jargon and prioritising empathetic engagement over an agenda led by the expectations of her agency or other service constraints, Imogen enabled Amelia to communicate what was most important to her. By accepting the importance of Amelia's home and neighbourhood, Imogen was able to gradually negotiate community-based support options, which would enable Amelia to remain in her own home as she strongly wished to do. These included local day care, home care and the support of a volunteer from an organisation for older people. In many respects, this is not an unusual social work activity; the aim of community care policy in the United Kingdom is to enable people to remain in their own homes for as long as possible after all. What is particularly impressive is the level of understanding which Imogen developed from really attending to an individual's story. Amelia was much less suspicious of support options which emerged from her own story, within a carefully developed relationship of trust, than she was of previous attempts by health professionals to impose care solutions.

The engagement with individual biography which Imogen demonstrated so clearly, is often cited as an important element of critical practice. Adams (2002) for example, argues that critical practitioners situate people's histories, with an awareness of context which brings together past and present, while Parton and O'Byrne (2000) draw on post-modern ideas to develop the notion of *constructive* practice. They argue for the importance of language in developing understanding as a collaborative process when they make the deceptively simple point that: 'Telling one's story and having it heard respectfully is a very necessary ingredient for change to begin to occur' (Parton and O'Byrne, (2000, 5).

RESPONDING TO DEMENTIA

There has been a profound shift in the way in which dementia is understood during the past twenty years. Consequently, while the medical model still dominates many areas of treatment, dementia is no longer described only in terms of brain functioning. New understandings of the social, psychological consequences of the condition have lead to greater emphasis on the personal experiences of people with dementia, and the wider social context within which their experience is situated.

For social workers and others whose role lies at the interface between the personal and the social, working with those affected by dementia is challenging on a number of levels. The experience of dementia is often characterised by uncertainty, change and fear, both for those who have the disease and for people close to them. Social work with people with dementia and their carers is, therefore, likely to involve complex and conflicting needs, shifting relations of power and powerlessness and a high degree of risk. As a relatively common disease of later life with the potential to affect any of us, dementia may also evoke powerful feelings of fear and threat for individual workers (Cheston and Bender, 1999). Social work with people with dementia is complicated, difficult and personally demanding.

CRITICAL PRACTICE AND DEMENTIA CARE

The emphasis on individual experience and identity, which is central to post-modern critical and constructive approaches in social work, is increasingly acknowledged as fundamental to good dementia care. The recognition that purely medical approaches are likely to create disempowerment, and to threaten individual identity have resulted in a growing emphasis on the personal and social experiences of dementia (e.g., Sabat and Harré, 1992; Cheston and Bender, 1997; Kitwood, 1997, 1999; Proctor, 2001). As Cheston and Bender point out, people with dementia: 'Are social beings ...all of us live and are cared for within a social world of relationships and communication. It is through these relationships that we establish a sense of who we are – our identity or as Tom Kitwood referred to it, our personhood' (1999: 80–81).

Kitwood's influential work promotes the notion of *personhood* as central to empowering and respectful approaches to dementia care. The experience and recognition of personhood, he suggests, depends on positive social responses which value individual identity:

> To have an identity is to know who one is; it involves maintaining a sense of continuity with the past and some kind of consistency across the course of present life. Identity involves having a 'narrative' – a story to tell about oneself and one's life. (Kitwood, 1997a: 20)

This is precisely the approach taken by Imogen in her work with Amelia. Rather than characterising Amelia in terms of her medical diagnosis, Imogen engaged with her as an individual with a vivid and interesting life history.

QUESTIONING THE TAKEN FOR GRANTED

Amelia was initially referred to the Mental Health Team for 'residential care' because she was 'not coping' at home. Any referral which prejudges the outcome of an assessment clearly contradicts the spirit and guidance of the National Health Service and Community Care Act 1990 and Imogen, at an early stage in her work with Amelia, rightly challenged the referring agency about their assumption. The world of health and social care, like other large occupational groups, has developed its own jargon and ways of using language. While this linguistic shorthand may be inevitable, there is a danger that the language of referral and assessment can contain subtle judgements, which endow people with taken for granted needs or characteristics. These judgements may be inadvertent, but words and phrases like 'non compliant', 'not coping' and 'at risk', which embody a range of assumptions may helpfully be deconstructed by the skilled practitioner in favour of other, more helpful narratives of individual experience.

This is not to say that judgements about risk and individual struggle are not central to the assessment of people with dementia, rather that the sort of reflexive, empathic engagement which Imogen demonstrated, enabled her to make *better* judgements than she might otherwise have done. As Imogen said:

> There is often an assumption from family and others that the best place for people (with dementia) is the place where there is supposedly least risk and most support, especially when people live on their own. The idea of being 'cared for' has warm associations and it is the right thing for lots of people, but Amelia hated it. She was terribly independent. It was easy to understand by listening to her story that her well-being depended much more on having her independence and autonomy respected than on removing every element of risk from her life.

ANTI-OPPRESSIVE PRACTICE AND BEYOND

The radical strand within social work has raised awareness amongst social workers of the impact of structural oppression on the lives of those with whom they work. This has led to the promotion of an explicitly *anti-oppressive* approach to social work practice (Mullaly, 1997). Our aim in this book is to resist easy or simplistic notions of anti-oppressive practice. We are rather seeking to promote learning from practice which acknowledges the complexity of power relations and demonstrates the positive impact which an awareness of power can bring (Chapter 2 opens up these debates in more detail). Imogen's practice was therefore anti-oppressive in the best sense. Her work with Amelia challenged ageist assumptions about the needs of older people and sought to counter oppression by respecting Amelia's individuality and promoting her right to be listened to and to make choices.

Post-modern thinking has contributed to debates about the nature of anti-oppressive practice by emphasising the importance of *negotiation* between social workers and service users in order to reach a shared perception of the individual's unique situation (Howe, 1994; Parton, 1994). The personal narratives which are drawn out through this process are important both in themselves and for the part they play in telling a collective story of disempowerment. Imogen's attention to Amelia's personal story enabled her to negotiate care options which respected Amelia's desire to remain in her own home for as long as possible. Through this very individually focussed intervention, Imogen was also challenging the taken for granted notion that residential care is an inevitable early outcome for people living alone with dementia. She later reflected on this in terms of her personal and professional development as an anti-oppressive practitioner:

> As a specialist practitioner it's easy to think you know what's best for people, but everyone's different – Amelia was completely her own person, even when she was very confused. In this area of work, understanding oppression is about knowing how people are subject to all kind of dehumanising assumptions just because they belong to this category of 'people with dementia'. That's really important, but what Amelia also reminded me, was that the group is made up of as many individual stories as there are people with dementia and that the way oppression works is through personal experience.

Questioning the taken for granted, whether in a written referral or a conversation, involves unpicking the way in which language constructs ideas, and supposedly neutral accounts can hide subject positions. Staff at the Day Hospital constructed Amelia's *home* as a 'risk' and a 'problem'. Through her conversations with Amelia, Imogen allowed a different, more authentic reality to emerge, within which home was a source of safety and security at the centre of an increasingly risky and threatening outside world. By valuing Amelia's own *narrative identity* (Fook, 2002: 78) Imogen was able to work with her to find ways of reducing the very real risks and problems she was facing.

BUREAUCRACY, MANAGERIALISM AND CREATIVITY

The responsive, individualised approach taken by Imogen in her work with Amelia represents a challenge to the increasingly technical/ managerial focus of social work practice, which has been identified by many commentators in recent years (e.g., Howe, 1992, 1996; Parton and O'Byrne, 2000; Jones, 2001). Workers juggling resource constraints and prescriptive assessment frameworks may be tempted to see older people with dementia as problems to be managed rather than as individuals located within their own changing situations. The assessment of risk in relation to people with dementia, is a particularly challenging and sometimes frightening activity. The abundance of forms and assessment tools which now exist, may offer practitioners the illusion of fixed and certain solutions, but in the end bureaucratisation is no substitute for the preparedness to engage with complexity which critical practice demands. Robert Adams sums this up clearly:

> The critical practitioner acknowledges the inherently problematic situation and takes its essence into account rather than pretending it can be simplified and the problem ignored. Thus, critical practice is likely to embody the conflict that the dilemma holds rather than ducking or working around it. This is extremely testing for the practitioner, who has to establish a direction for the practice, rather than yielding to the temptation to impose a simplistic, often inappropriate solution. (Adams, 2002: 93)

Imogen resisted the sort of technical/ managerial approach which encourages a view of assessment as a one-off event and need as fixed at a single point in time. She was aware that Amelia's needs were bound to change and approached their relationship, not as an exercise in gathering *objective* data, but rather as a process of creative communication, with outcomes which would be renegotiated within a complex and changing context. In this respect, Imogen demonstrated the ability to make fine professional judgements which facilitated the reduction of risk while accommodating uncertainty, and the inevitability of future change. For a further analysis of creative best practice within a context of uncertainty and change, the reader is again referred to Chapter 13, where the work of Des, another social worker in an older person's team, is described.

BALANCING THE NEEDS OF SERVICE USERS AND CARERS

The interests of people with dementia and their caregivers do not always coincide. The process of providing support to Amelia to remain in her own home brought Imogen into some conflict with Amelia's cousin Bob. Bob took his responsibilities as Amelia's nearest relative seriously, but in many respects he was a reluctant carer who had hoped that a social work referral would lead quickly to Amelia being placed in residential care.

There is no doubt that an early placement *would* have improved the quality of Bob's life; he had never been close to his cousin and understandably his priorities lay with his own adult children and grandchildren. Imogen was, therefore, faced with two contradictory sets of needs, in the context of which she sought to negotiate the best possible ways forward:

> Their needs were never reconcilable and it was really important not to deny that, but I was able to share the risk and the responsibility and in many ways that helped Bob more than anything. We gradually introduced more and more practical support at home, but very much at Amelia's own pace. I think Bob moved from thinking that things could only get worse, to seeing that Amelia could make some decisions with the right support and that as a result things could be better for both of them.

Imogen's skill here was to avoid the sort of binary oppositional thinking which would have cast Bob as an oppressor because he felt that residential care was the best solution for Amelia and for himself. Imogen was able to understand Bob within the framework of his own life and to engage with the anxiety, frustration and shame, which were all part of *his* narrative of his cousin's decline.

In spite of this sensitivity, there were occasions during the course of Imogen's work with Amelia when the precarious balance between the needs of carer and service user was temporarily lost. As Amelia's confusion increased, she became more dishevelled and paid less attention to her personal hygiene; this caused Bob considerable stress and anxiety. For a while Imogen found herself engaging more fully with Bob's pained reaction to Amelia's decline than with Amelia's own experience. It was largely as a response to Bob's distress that Imogen arranged a meeting between herself, Bob and Amelia's Day Centre key worker to address the issue of Amelia's personal hygiene. During the meeting a plan was devised for Amelia to be bathed at the day centre, in spite of her previously expressed opposition to this idea. The plan was wholly unsuccessful; not only did it meet with resistance, anger and distress from Amelia but it also temporarily damaged the web of support which Imogen had carefully negotiated with her. Imogen's later reflection on this experience demonstrates the importance within CBP of reflection and learning from mistakes as well as from that which can most easily be understood as *best*.

> Somehow in the process the balance had been lost. Bob had become central and Amelia became the problem to be solved. I had lost focus on providing person centred care and the strategy we had devised so carefully failed because Amelia had not been involved in the planning. This was a learning experience for all of us.

Imogen talked openly to Bob about this experience. The discussion which followed had the positive effect of enabling Bob to see the importance of Amelia's involvement in planning her own care and opened the way for more honest, less conflictual conversations between Imogen and Bob.

WORKING WITH RISK AND CHANGE

Amelia continued to refuse help with bathing at the day centre, but gradually came to accept short periods of respite care at times when she was particularly confused and afraid. Amelia viewed these short stays as 'holidays' during which she would accept help and her health would improve. Once she began to feel better, Amelia would insist on returning home. Although in many respects this was a more intrusive service than the plan to provide a bath at the day centre, the fact that Amelia was able to control it herself and make sense of it as a 'holiday' meant that it was far more successful.

In spite of this success, Amelia was gradually becoming more and more confused. The frequency with which she needed and wanted emergency respite care became greater. She started to get lost in her own neighbourhood and began to experience increasingly distressing hallucinations. Imogen was negotiating an increasingly fine balance between Amelia's right to make her own decisions and the considerable risks her client was facing. Meanwhile, Bob's growing stress and anxiety in the face of increasing demands from his cousin represented a further layer of complexity and need. This changing and uncertain situation meant that Imogen was now continually re-appraising her decisions and actions in relation to Amelia.

An awareness of current law and policy guidance became increasingly important as the option of using mental health legislation to force Amelia to move to a residential home for her own safety became progressively more likely. Imogen regarded the use of statutory powers to remove Amelia from her home as a last resort. However, her critical understanding of the empowering possibilities as well as the protective and controlling functions of legislation enabled her to maintain a person-centred focus, even when considering compulsory measures:

> I was very reluctant to initiate actions which would lead to Amelia having to leave her home. It was the very thing that she had so consistently not wanted. But actually the situation was changing – her freedom and autonomy were becoming compromised by the fact that she was at home alone and frightened. I had to consider whether the least restrictive action to

force her to live somewhere else, would now offer greater freedom than remaining at home.

The fine judgements which Imogen was making about levels of risk were also informed by empirical research evidence. When Amelia began to talk about having been mugged in her own home by two men for example, Imogen turned to research relating to the incidence of hallucinations and feelings of paranoia amongst people with dementia (Burns., Jacoby and Levy, 1990; Cheston and Bender, 1999). It is a mark of Imogen's skill and confidence as a practitioner that she was able to use the research evidence that hallucinations are indeed a common feature of dementia to inform rather than to prescribe her practice. She demonstrated an awareness of this important knowledge base while also maintaining her critically reflective, person-centred approach and continuing to attend to Amelia's own narrative:

> I kept an open mind about whether she had been mugged – it was possible after all, but that story came at a time when she had begun to talk about strange men in the house and the evidence was that these were hallucinations rather than physical experiences. At the same time there were more and more rooms she wouldn't go into – her environment was shrinking around her and she had basically retreated to one small room. What was coming out in everything she said was that home was no longer a safe place to be. When she started giving such a strong message about not feeling safe, I was able to begin to negotiate with her about alternative accommodation.

The fact that Imogen had engaged in such a full and empathetic way with Amelia during their past conversations, enabled her to recognise the significance of this change in the meaning of 'home'. Imogen understood that home no longer represented the source of safety and security for Amelia that it had once done. Almost two years had passed since the initial referral when Imogen raised the possibility of residential care again. This time, Amelia's response was very different; she agreed to go with Bob to visit a number of local residential homes with a view to a permanent move.

Bob and Amelia visited a number of residential homes together. Amelia's response to this process was often ambiguous; there was no doubt that her *capacity* to make an informed decision about her future was now seriously compromised. However, while waiting for a vacancy in her chosen residential home, Amelia began to telephone Bob frequently to ask him when he was going to take her to her 'other home'. For Imogen this seemed to be a further confirmation that the house in which Amelia had lived all her life no longer held the meaning for her that it had once done and that she was seeking safety and security elsewhere:

> It was still a very difficult thing for [Amelia] to move away from her home. On one level it was not at all what she wanted, but in the end it did seem that what she was saying most clearly was that she needed to be somewhere, where she felt safe .... . She's doing really well now. I see her sometimes in the home. She doesn't know who I am, but she knows that she knows me. She thinks I was in the war with her, but that's ok – I know about her war so I can talk to her about it.

CONCLUSION

It is important to acknowledge here that social work with people with dementia can result in less positive and satisfying outcomes than the story you have just read. Amelia's situation could easily have evolved differently. Under slightly different circumstances or within a more prolonged timescale, Imogen would have used mental health legislation to require Amelia to move to a safer environment. While this would have caused distress to all involved, the balance of risk to Amelia could well have made it the best practice decision under the circumstances. In other cases the particular needs of a person with dementia, living alone, might have led to a far more intrusive approach at an earlier stage. The unpredictability of these outcomes underlines the fact that not only are there no blueprints for practice but there are also perhaps fewer recurring patterns than we sometimes like to think.

Imogen's practice with Amelia was particularly good because it was situated within the context of Amelia's life and experience. Imogen drew on social work theory, knowledge of the law and relevant research to inform her decisions, but what was central to best practice in this case was Imogen's empathetic engagement with Amelia's own narrative and the humane, caring response which this engendered. An integral part of this process was an ability to reflect on her practice, which enabled Imogen to use insights from past experience, while at the same time developing new practice wisdom. Jan Fook summarises this important social work skill in her account of the reflective practitioner as someone who can:

> situate themselves in the context of the situation and can factor this understanding in to the ways in which they practice. This ongoing process of reflection allows for the practitioners to develop their theory directly

from their own experience. It allows them to practice in a way which is "situated" in the specific context. (Fook, 2002: 40)

To undertake practice in a way which is genuinely situated, practitioners must engage with all those involved and maintain an openness to individulals' own interpretations. Imogen recognised that good practice is 'co-constructed by all the actors involved' (Ferguson, 2003). Rather than allowing her professional expertise to become the dominant narrative, she used Bob and Amelia's distinctive and changing accounts of their experiences to develop her own practice actions. In this respect, Imogen's practice was explicitly critical. Not only did she disrupt the dominant discourse of older people's dependency, by refusing to take it for granted, but she also sought out Amelia's voice and placed it at the centre of the assessment.

Engaging with people's individual narratives is the opposite of the sort of technical/ managerial approach which we are seeking to counter in this book. Imogen's work with Amelia involved some very precise practice judgements and an ongoing analysis of risk. This skilled response was not grounded in the formulaic, procedural approach, which sometimes characterises assessment of high-risk situations, but in empathetic, reflexive engagement. Imogen continually resisted the *othering* of service users, which can occur when social workers are not imaginatively connected with the difficulties faced by those with whom they are working. This is nowhere more important or more challenging than in social work with people with dementia, who are certainly one of the most disempowered and marginalised groups in society. As Tom Kitwood (1997a) argues, the ability to use 'our own poetic imagination' is central to engagement with the experiences of people with dementia.

The kind of situated practice which this book is seeking to promote and which responds imaginatively to individual narratives, is likely to be highly demanding and professionally challenging. This is social work which resists the notion of assessment as a one-off event and engages imaginatively with complexity and change. It demands of practitioners the confidence not to be reduced to *in*action by the recognition of uncertainty and contradiction, but to *act* compassionately on the basis of situated critical analysis.

REFERENCES

Adams, R. (2002) 'Developing Critical Practice in Social Work' in Adams, R., Dominelli, L. and Payne, M. (eds) (2002) *Critical Practice in Social Work* (Basingstoke: Palgrave).

Brechin, A. 'Introducing Critical Practice' in Brechin, A., Brown, H. and Eby, M. A. (eds) (2000) *Critical Practice in Health and Social Care* (London: Sage/ Open University).

Burns, A., Jacoby, R. and Levy, R. (1990) 'Psychiatric Phenomena in Alzheimer's Disease II: Disorders of Perception', *British Journal of Psychiatry*, **157**: 81–86.

Cheston, R. and Bender, M. (1997) 'Inhabitants of a Lost Kingdom: A Model of the Subjective Experiences of Dementia', *Ageing and Society*, **17**: 513–532.

Cheston, R. & Bender, M. (1999) 'Brains, Minds and Selves: Changing Conceptions of the Losses Involved in Dementia', *British Journal of Medical Psychology*, **72**: 203–216.

Crane, M. (1999) *Understanding Older Homeless People* (Buckingham: Open University Press).

Ferguson, H. (2003) 'Outline of Critical Best Practice Perspective on Social Work and Social Care', *British Journal of Social Work*, **33**: 1005–1024.

Fook, J. (1999) 'Critical Reflection in Education and Practice' in Pease, B. and Fook, J. (eds) *Transforming Social Work Practice* (London: Routledge).

Fook, J. (2002) *Social Work: Critical Theory and Practice* (London: Sage).

Harrison, L. and Means, R. (1990) *Housing: The Essential Element Within Community Care* (Oxford: Anchor Housing Trust).

Healy, K. (2000) *Social Work Practices: Contemporary Perspectives on Change* (London: Sage).

Heywood, F., Oldman, C. and Means, R. (2002) *Housing and Home in Later Life* (Buckingham: Open University Press).

Howe, D. (1992) 'Child Abuse and the Bureaucratisation of Social Work', *The Sociological Review*, **40** (3): 491–508.

Howe, D. (1994) 'Modernity, Postmodernity and Social Work', *British Journal of Social Work*, **24**: 513–532.

Howe, D. (1996) 'Surface and Depth in Social Work Practice' in Parton, N. (ed.) *Social Theory, Social Change and Social Work* (London: Routledge).

Jones, C. (2001) 'Voices From the Front Line: State Social Workers and New Labour', *British Journal of Social Work*, **31**: 547–562.

Kitwood, T. (1997) *Dementia Reconsidered: The Person Comes First* (Buckingham: Open University Press).

Kitwood, T. (1997a) 'The Experience of Dementia', *Ageing and Mental Health*. **1**(1): 13–22.

Langan, J., Means, R. and Rolf, S. (1996) *Maintaining Home and Independence in Later Life: Older People Speaking* (Oxford, Anchor Trust).

Leonard, P. (1997) *Postmodern Welfare: Constructing an Emancipatory Project* (London: Sage).

Mullaly, B. (1997) *Structural Social Work: Ideology, Theory and Practice* (Oxford: Oxford University Press).

Parton, N. (1994) 'Problemantics of Government: (Post) Modernity and Social Work', *British Journal of Social Work*, **24:** 9–32

Parton, N. (ed.) (1996) *Social Theory, Social Change and Social Work* (London: Routledge).

Parton, N. and O'Byrne, P. (2000) *Constructive Social Work* (Basingstoke: Macmillan).

Pease, B. and Fook, J. (1999) *Transforming Social Work Practice: Postmodern Critical Perspectives* (London: Routledge).

Powell, M. (2000) 'New Labour and the Third Way in the British Welfare State: A New and Distinctive Approach?', *Critical Social Policy*, **20**(1).

Proctor, G. (2001) 'Listening to Older Women with Dementia: Relationships, Voices and Power', *Disability and Society*, **16**(3): 361–376.

Rojek, C., Peacock, C. and Collins, S. (1988) *Social Work and Received Ideas* (London: Routledge).

Sabat, S. R. and Harré. R. (1992) 'The Construction and Deconstruction of Self in Alzheimer's Disease', *Ageing and Society*, **12**: 443–446.

Saunders, P. (1990) *A Nation of Home Owners* (London: Unwin and Hyman).

Sterling, T. (1997) 'Housing and Health – Making the Links Count', *Housing Review*, **46**(3): 56

Wilkinson, D. (1999) *Poor Housing and Ill Health: A Summary of Research Evidence* (Edinburgh: The Scottish Office, Central Research Unit).

4 Emotional engagement in social work: best practice and relationships in mental health work

CELIA KEEPING

INTRODUCTION

Jane is a woman in her late thirties who has suffered from mental and physical health problems for many years. My involvement with Jane, as a mental health social worker based in a Community Mental Health Team has lasted for approximately five years. This chapter is an overview of my work with Jane and uses a transcript of a recent meeting to illustrate certain key points. The chapter also reflects my particular interest in psychoanalytic theory. Having begun my career working with children and families and moved on to adult mental health, I have long been convinced of the link between early childhood experiences and disturbances in adult life. Further training in the application of psychoanalytic ideas has reinforced my belief that early patterns laid down in response to childhood events continue to have a powerful and often unconscious impact on later relationships and on one's sense of self. This psychodynamic perspective is intended to compliment some of the more structural critiques outlined in this book and aims to forefront the emotional work that is part of all critical best practice (CBP). The critical framework used to analyse practice in this chapter also integrates psychoanalytical ideas with critical social theory and so recognises the importance of contextualising individual *experience* within the structures of statutory social work and the mental health system. Furthermore, the practice described here, has at its heart, the kind of close, empathetic attention to Jane's experiences – to her *story* that we have placed at the centre of our definition of CBP.

This chapter focuses on the importance of *emotional engagement* within the social work encounter. Whether the core task is statutory assessment, practical assistance or therapeutic support, attention to the quality and nature of the emotional relationship between social worker and service user is intrinsic to best practice. As I hope this chapter will illustrate, conscious and thoughtful emotional engagement on the part of the practitioner with the inner world of the service user is vital to the development of a meaningful, insightful and powerful relationship.

I have consulted Jane about using her material in this way and she has given her agreement. Nevertheless, many of the material facts of Jane's situation have been altered in order to protect her identity.

THE CHALLENGE OF EMOTIONAL ENGAGEMENT: BEING AND DOING

Maintaining a position of emotional engagement as a social worker is not an easy task and can be particularly difficult and demanding if this aspect of the work is constrained or undervalued by the worker's employing agency. Moves towards the bureaucratisation of social work in recent years (Newman & Clarke, 1994; Taylor & White, 2000) can mean that we risk losing sight of the emotional interchange which inevitably occurs between service user and social worker and which is such an important tool for practice. Some writers have argued that emotion itself is in danger of becoming absorbed and quantified within the bureaucratic processes of care management. Hochschild (1983) uses the helpful term 'emotional labour' to describe the often unacknowledged part of paid work which involves the labouring 'of the heart' rather than the mind or the body. She suggests that emotions can be exploited and commodified by organisations, leading to a shift from an individual to a corporate notion of institutionally approved emotion with rules about parameters and expectations of emotional involvement. Helen Gorman sees a danger of this in the shift from social work to care management in the United Kingdom and suggests that:

> the significance of the emotional labour within caring work may have become lost within the administrative and managerial process that dominates it. The maintenance of self-esteem within the job role without becoming cynical about the job itself can be a challenge. (Gorman, 2000: 154)

Where emotional labour is not valued or supported, it can feel much easier to depersonalise service users. It is particularly hard to engage fully on an emotional level with people who are themselves experiencing mental and emotional distress and it can seem easier and safer to keep our distance and to concentrate on practical or administrative rather than on emotional support.

It is also hard to be emotionally alive and present in our relationships with service users without acknowledging our own emotional reality. An important concept in psychoanalytic theory is 'transference', which refers to the way in which we unconsciously 'project' feelings from other relationships (often from childhood) onto people in our present. A related idea is 'counter transference', which is the exchange of transference between people in relationships. We all run the risk of using the service users with whom we work to locate the uncontained and disturbing aspects of our own personalities, thus not only distancing ourselves from them but also alienating ourselves from the mad, frightened, vulnerable or angry parts of ourselves (Benjamin, 1998). Emotional engagement with the 'other' thus necessarily involves feeling those disturbing parts of ourselves we have disowned. As Robert Adams argues:

> It is necessary to be in touch with our own feelings and understand our own emotional responses in order to relate professionally to others. We have to grasp what our emotional responses signify, for our continuing personal and professional development and for the person with whom we are working. (Adams, 2000: 185–186)

Waddell (1989) testifies to the difficulties in offering oneself in this way and to the challenge of tolerating the 'psychic pain' evoked by this level of interaction. She uses the term 'servicing' to describe the purely practical and administrative activities of social work, which can enable us to distance ourselves from the pain of emotional engagement. Waddell contrasts this with 'serving' which involves helping service users to think about their emotional experiences and so come to know themselves better. Greater self-knowledge, she argues, will enable individuals to acquire a greater sense of control and agency in their lives.

Other writers (e.g., Bateman,1995) have made a similar distinction between 'being' and 'doing' in social work, where the 'being' part of the job refers to the need for receptive and empathic engagement with clients, whereas the 'doing' refers to the practical and administrative part. Bower (2002) argues that both are important aspects of social work and it is the task of the worker to create and maintain a balance between the two. Certainly, there have been occasions in my work with Jane when I have been tempted to take refuge in 'doing' at the expense of 'being'. The personal emotional cost of real engagement has

sometimes seemed very great and yet has been essential to the maintenance of an empathic and supportive relationship. At other times a
focus on practical and administrative activities has been essential in
protecting Jane or in enabling her to move towards greater independence and choice. It is my experience that the creative integration of the
practical and the emotional represents a difficult balancing act, which
demands self-awareness and reflexive engagement with each situation
and which is a defining feature of CBP in mental health.

EMOTIONAL ENGAGEMENT: SOME
THEORETICAL INFLUENCES

The sort of emotional engagement which is being advocated in this
chapter has its roots in social work's long history of psychodynamically
informed relationship-based practice. The challenge to this approach
which arose in the1960s took the form of a radical critique which
emphasised the influence of social context and socio-economic structures on the lives of individuals (Harry Ferguson examines the recent
political history of therapeutic social work in more detail in Chapter I.
See also Cooper, 2002). The focus of much social work, therefore,
shifted from an individualised psychological explanation of personal
distress to a structural perspective, which emphasised social issues as
the central cause of individuals' problems. While the development of
radical sociological approaches made a tremendously important contribution to social work, the emphasis on people's external reality has
often led to a failure to attend adequately to their internal experiences.
As I hope my work with Jane will show, CBP must involve embracing
both the social and the psychological forces which interweave themselves in a very complex way in our lives. The importance of 'being'
and 'doing' is reflected in the need to attend to both the social and the
psychological dimensions of people's experience.

The approach to social work practice being asserted here, which
emphasises the interplay between internal and external forces in the
lives of individuals, can also claim a strong affinity with what is known
in the social sciences as *critical theory*. Put very simply, critical theory
is associated with the work of Theodore Adorno, Max Horkheimer
and other members of the 'Frankfurt School' of the 1930s and 1940s.
Writing against a backdrop of the rise of fascism in Germany, this
group used sociological, philosophical and psychodynamic theories to
understand structures within society and individuals' responses to
them. Members of the Frankfurt school drew particularly on the work

of Freud, the founder of psychoanalysis, in developing their belief that the internal forces to which we are all subject, both shape and are shaped by external social and economic conditions. In order to bring about social (or individual) change, both influences therefore needed to be understood.

One of the aims of critical social work practice is to understand how the 'social' seeps into the inner lives of people, and vice-versa. None of us live in a vacuum. Our relationships with ourselves and with each other take place within a family, social and global context and it is the unique job of the social worker to address both the outer and the inner, the structural and the psychological. CBP seeks to establish how this can be done most effectively.

CRISIS: MY FIRST MEETING WITH JANE

I first met Jane when as an Approved Social Worker (ASW) taking my turn on 'duty' I was asked by her General Practitioner (GP) to arrange an assessment under the 1983 Mental Health Act. As Jon O'Gara outlines in greater detail in Chapter 12, the duties of an ASW include organising assessments with a view to compulsory admission to hospital. So it was that following a process of information gathering about Jane's background and circumstances, I arranged to meet with her GP and a consultant psychiatrist at the flat where Jane was staying. In accordance with the Act, I had informed Jane's nearest relative, her mother, of the forthcoming assessment and she was also to be present.

Jane was officially homeless at the time of the referral, but she had been staying in a friend's flat for two days. She had arrived there by ambulance from a nursing home for people with physical health problems where she had been staying for the previous four weeks. Jane had a diagnosis of Myalgic Encephalomyelitis (M.E) or Chronic Fatigue Syndrome and had been experiencing symptoms of incapacitating tiredness for more than six years. The home however, had discharged Jane on the grounds that they could no longer cope with her high levels of anxiety. For two years before entering the nursing home, Jane had been living with her mother, but she too was now saying that she could not continue to provide the high level of care her daughter needed.

When we arrived at the flat, Jane was extremely anxious and distressed and unable to move around unaided except by crawling on her hands and knees. The Mental Health Act requires the ASW to 'interview the patient in a suitable manner' (Section 13(2)). According to the code of practice accompanying the Act, this includes 'promoting the individual's self determination and personal responsibility' (section 1:1), but Jane's high level of distress and panic made this extremely difficult. I was acutely aware of the powerlessness and shock which Jane must be feeling at the sudden unwanted invasion of her privacy by three strangers. I was also conscious of the temptation I felt to withdraw from 'being' with Jane in her distress into simply 'doing' an assessment of her mental health needs according to the prescriptions of the Mental Health Act.

Jane told us that she had been panicking because her mother had said that she might be 'sectioned'. She said that as a result she had become extremely anxious and her digestive system had gone into spasm. She had become unable to eat and had only managed to drink very small quantities of liquid for the last couple of days. Jane admitted to feeling weaker and more exhausted as time went on; in her words, she was 'falling apart'. She told us that she was terrified about going into hospital and did not feel that it would help her. Jane said that she would much rather remain at the flat with her mother bringing food, which she hoped she would be able to eat when her anxiety subsided.

We spoke to Jane's mother and her friend privately in the kitchen of the flat. They confirmed that Jane had not eaten for two days, that she was drinking very little and was not washing and that she seemed to be experiencing episodes of extreme anxiety and panic. As the friend worked full time Jane was alone for a considerable number of hours each day. Jane's friend said that despite her deep concern she could not cope with Jane any longer and wanted her to leave. Jane's elderly mother was also finding it increasingly difficult to support Jane in the flat as she lived some 20 miles away and was herself feeling exhausted and extremely stressed. She believed that her daughter was experiencing a 'breakdown' and needed to be admitted to hospital. At this point Jane crawled into the room on her hands and knees in great distress and began to beg her friend and her mother, who were both in tears, to allow her to stay. This had become a highly charged situation, which was full of anxiety and deep distress on all sides.

EMOTIONAL CONTAINMENT

For people suffering from mental health problems, Mental Health Act assessments and compulsory admission to hospital are frequently the last resort in the helping process, often following on from unsuccessful efforts to support a person within the community. As such, they often take place in exceptionally fraught circumstances such as those described above. The individual concerned is usually in a state of crisis and their family members are likely to be extremely distressed. As the convener of the assessment, the ASW has a number of clearly defined organisational and practical duties. In addition to these practical responsibilities she also has a significant, yet rarely acknowledged, task of emotional work.

As the person authorised to make the application for compulsory detention to hospital, the ASW is likely to be the focus of powerful feelings of blame, anger, guilt and distress from service users and from family and friends. In Jane's case as in many others, I found myself having to deal not only with my own feelings in a painful situation, but also with the projected feelings of Jane's mother and her friend. The psychoanalytic concept of 'containment' can be helpful in understanding the nature of this task. 'Containment' is an idea which originated in the study of mother–infant relations and in the mother's role in attending to the emotional as well as the physical needs of the baby.

Drawing on earlier work by Klein, Bion (1962) developed a theory that the single most important requirement for healthy infant development was the capacity of the mother to 'contain' the anxiety transmitted to her by her baby, and after processing it, return it to the infant in a more manageable form. He believed that on becoming distressed, and in an attempt to rid herself or himself of these feelings, the infant 'projects' them into the mother who consequently experiences them as her own state of mind (the experience known as 'counter-transference' referred to above). Through the thoughtful acceptance or 'containment' of these feelings the mother transforms them and makes it possible for the baby to take the feelings back into herself or himself in a more digestible form. Bion transferred the concept of containment to the analytic situation, arguing that the analyst acts as a container of the patient's anxieties, thereby freeing him or her to think and to develop. Thompson (2003) in turn suggests that the ASW embodies the concept of containment, by accepting and holding, at least during the brief period of the assessment, the disintegrative forces of mental illness.

The use of the mother–child relationship as a way of understanding a particular aspect of the social work role in mental health may be seen to complicate some of the ideas of equality and service user expertise espoused in this book. We would argue however, that the notion of containment, supported by the potent image of the parent and child, is a way of communicating the significance of the emotional task of the social worker.

The theory of containment offers a way of understanding the practitioner's use of power as authoritative, beneficial and deeply responsive to individual needs. Skilled and appropriate holding of the anxiety of the service user is an element of the sort of skilled, critical practice which creatively and confidently integrates the social and the psychological.

Price (2001) writes about the way in which individuals transfer emotional states to each other on a moment by moment basis in all social interaction. She suggests that we are all 'wired' to respond to each other's emotional communication and that it is actually very difficult to close down the border between ourselves and others. Price describes this as 'psychic work' a term which seems to me to be particularly helpful and relevant to the role of the mental health social worker. Certainly it describes well my own task in containing and responding to Jane's emotional communication as well that of her mother and her friend.

Price further argues that 'psychic work' does not take place in a vacuum, but is coloured by its specific social and cultural context as well as by the particular task being undertaken. This brings us back to the creative integration of the social and the psychological and the importance of both 'being' and 'doing' in social work practice. The mental health assessment process is particularly complex in terms of the power dynamics at play. Jane was disempowered by her physical and mental health difficulties. She was homeless and unemployed and at the point of assessment lacked the means of satisfying even her most basic human needs. She was being interviewed by two male doctors who, by virtue of their gender and their status within society, constituted powerful figures. I too was aware of the potential influence on my own behaviour and decision-making of working with two men of a higher professional status than myself. At the same time I was in a powerful position as a social worker with the statutory power to play a major part in depriving individuals of their liberty for a period of up to six months. In 'sectioning' Jane I was deeply conscious of the fact that I would be taking away most of her rights to participate equally in society.

Critical approaches to social work which advocate anti-oppressive and emancipatory practice can be perceived as sitting uneasily with the use of statutory authority. In this case however, I would argue that it is precisely because I was able to use the authority vested in me and accept the need to be powerful in the situation, that Jane was provided with the help she needed to hold and protect her both physically and emotionally. The empowerment versus oppression dialectic is often more complex than it seems; it constitutes a central concern within statutory work and is of particular relevance in my work with Jane.

EMOTIONAL LABOUR AND THE NEEDS OF THE WORKER

As in the parent–baby relationship, in order for the emotional work of containment to take place the social worker must be open and receptive to the thoughts and feelings of others and must be able to empathise with them and convey an understanding of their situation. But just as the mother exists within a social and family system which has the potential to support or obstruct this emotional process, social workers operate within a societal and organisational context which can either help or hinder their emotional labour. In order to engage with emotional experience the worker herself must feel part of a facilitative environment within a supportive and sensitive organisation which provides good supervision. She must also have the ability (assisted by the supervision process) to acknowledge and understand her own feelings so that she can more accurately understand the feelings evoked in her by the service user.

Jane was experiencing anxiety so great that she felt she was 'falling apart'. She was weak, terrified and desperate and her mother was overwhelmed with feelings of helplessness and guilt. I was aware of feeling a range of emotions myself, albeit of lesser intensity, but which also needed to be managed. I felt frustrated that there were not more resources available to provide Jane with intensive support in the community as well as guilt and inadequacy about not being a more effective helper. I was also aware of a sense of isolation because the support available to me was less than I felt I needed. Underlying these feelings were my own unconscious fears of disintegration – that I would not be able to manage the situation and that it would all prove too difficult and in some way 'fall apart'. Looking back, I can see my fear that the situation would be too much to manage and that due to my own personal failings Jane would die. The responsibility of my role also weighed heavily on me – the decision to deprive someone of their liberty for up to six months of their lives is not one that should be taken lightly. Honig (1996) refers to the 'dilemmatic space' of the public official who is charged by society to act out seemingly unresolvable value conflicts on its behalf, so containing the ambivalence disowned by society. She points out that the cost to the worker is potentially great and if her role is not understood or supported she will continue to experience high-levels of stress. My own anxieties can therefore be understood both in terms of a series of very personal, emotional responses *and* as a consequence of the organisational structure and isolation of my role.

In order to work effectively with Jane, with her family and with my colleagues, I needed to be able to manage or process my own difficult feelings and show that I was not overwhelmed by them. Following on from Carpy (1989), part of the experience of containment is that the client or service user is aware not only that the social worker is affected by the experience but also that she is able to think about and cope with her feelings. It is argued that this constitutes a powerful lesson for the service user who learns, albeit on an unconscious level, that these feelings are in fact manageable after all. In order to carry out the emotional task effectively the social worker needs to be as open as possible to her own feelings as well as those of the service user. Then, ideally with the help of a supportive organisation and bearing in mind the power dynamics of the particular social and cultural setting, the resulting feelings can be managed and even used as a means of communication. Through this careful listening and attending, the social worker can use herself as a tool and in so doing attempt to engage the service user on a very human level. The powerful feelings evoked in me could be seen partly as a vivid form of communication through which Jane was conveying the horror of her predicament. It was therefore vital for me to listen to and reflect upon those feelings. To undertake the emotional labour involved in meeting another person on this level demands attention and energy, but for me it constitutes the heart of critical best social work practice.

AN ONGOING RELATIONSHIP: HOSPITAL ADMISSION

After talking at length with Jane, a decision was made by myself and by the two doctors involved in the assessment, that her situation was sufficiently critical to warrant compulsory admission to hospital under Section 2 of the Mental Health Act. (Section 2 is an order for assessment, which lasts for up to twenty-eight days, as opposed to Section 3 which is an order for treatment). Jane then remained in hospital for four months.

My relationship with Jane has continued throughout the five years since the initial assessment. Sometimes my role has involved 'doing' practical and administrative care management tasks, sometimes it has demanded the receptivity and empathy of 'being' and the emotional labour of helping to contain Jane's anxiety. At other times I feel that I have simply been a source of continuity in Jane's chaotic life. During the five years that we have worked together, Jane has moved from hospital to a residential home, to a supported house, which she shares with four others. This is where she talked to me recently about her experience of being in hospital:

> Jane: I was awful in hospital. In such a state. I needed to be in there but the staff were too busy. I couldn't even get to the phone because I couldn't walk. Eddie (another patient) used to wheel me there so I could phone Mum. And all the other people there were so frightening – strange, with their arms all bandaged up. But I was in such a state in that nursing home. I feel exhausted by it all. Do you know what I mean?
>
> Celia: It was a very difficult time for you. You sound as if it's still having an effect on you.
>
> Jane: It is – I feel so tired from it
>
> Celia: I think when someone goes through those kinds of difficulties it takes a long time to recover their strength again. And you were sectioned. I sectioned you.
>
> Jane: Yes, you did! I hated you – who is this woman coming into my life and taking over? I did need to go into hospital but I couldn't see it then – I couldn't see that anything was wrong with me – you can't can you if you're ill. But it did help. I got really physically well at F.P. [the residential home where she stayed for two years following hospital admission] didn't I – eating and walking about – Dr A said I was doing great. But I didn't feel great inside.
>
> Celia: And your feelings about me?
>
> Jane: Yes, you're still here! It's been 5 years now.

In an ongoing working relationship based on empathy and trust it is important for the service user to be able to express his or her feelings towards the social worker as openly as possible. This is not easy to do, given the often inherently unequal nature of their relationship. However I do feel that giving Jane the opportunity to express her feelings about me and giving those feelings proper consideration has led to a more honest and therefore a more empowering relationship. Although Jane undoubtedly values the consistent support I have offered her and feels warmth towards me she has also experienced a powerful mix of fear and hatred towards me. All service users, particularly involuntary ones, will have complex and often ambivalent feelings about their involvement with social workers. My work with Jane and with many other people experiencing severe emotional distress, supports Ferguson's assertion that 'Much more openness is required about the authoritative role and full acknowledgement of the conflict at the heart of such relationships' (2005: 793).

Rather than denying the existence of conflict and ambivalence, a critically reflexive approach to practice demands that we accept and work with this element of service users' reality. Equally important is an open acknowledgement of our own complex and often ambiguous feeling responses to those with whom we are working. It is only through the candid acceptance of both positive and negative emotional realities that social workers are enabled to exert their authority in a conscious and helpful manner.

AN ONGOING RELATIONSHIP: CARE MANAGEMENT

Within the UK mental health system, the ASW often has no further contact with the service user following his or her admission to hospital. In this instance however, Jane's case was assigned to me and I became her care-coordinator. As such it was my role to work alongside her to assess the level of care she would need on discharge from hospital and to organise this accordingly. Jane and I and the other professionals involved, agreed that she would need some form of residential care, which could address both her physical and her mental health needs. This entailed the very practical process of researching different residential options in the area. Specialist resources are rare, but I was able to find a local residential care home with a therapeutic approach where Jane agreed to stay for a trial period. This necessitated complex bureaucratic arrangements in order to access funding; consequently my focus at this point was chiefly on 'doing' rather than on 'being'.

I was however constantly aware of the importance of keeping Jane's emotional needs in mind. I felt that in her disintegrated and chaotic state she desperately needed a sense of consistent and integrated care and a feeling of being psychologically 'held' until such time as she could muster her own internal resources again. This process of helping service users to build their internal resources is central to CBP. As I would be Jane's 'key worker' when she left hospital, it was important in the interests of continuity that I should engage with the process of building a therapeutic relationship with her while she was still an in-patient, thereby providing some consistency in her chaotic world. I therefore visited Jane on a regular basis during the four months that she remained in hospital.

'Care management', as the words suggest, is often seen as a predominantly technical/ managerial activity, firmly allied to the 'doing' element of social work. However research by Helen Gorman demonstrates the significance of emotional labour to good outcomes for service users. She argues that:

> An analysis of care management from a perspective that acknowledges the significance of emotional labour enables an alternative to emerge that recognises the importance of the skills required for care management that enable quality outcomes to emerge that may be more meaningful for the recipients of services. (Gorman, 2000:155)

It was with an understanding of the importance of maintaining a creative balance between 'doing' and 'being' in my work with Jane, that I continued to visit her regularly during her stay at the residential home. As her care manager I needed to monitor Jane's placement on behalf of the funding authorities. This meant coordinating regular reviews and being aware that as the placement was of limited duration, I would need to help Jane to find somewhere else to live in due course. At the same time Jane continued to feel very vulnerable and seemed to benefit from the consistency and emotional support I was able to give her during this time.

Jane's physical health improved significantly while she was in the residential home. However, although she was more mentally stable than she had been at the point of her admission to hospital, she remained extremely anxious, developing psychotic-like features and engaging in self-harm. During our recent meeting Jane described her time there in this way:

Celia: You say you are feeling better mentally?

Jane: Yes, I feel I have emotional difficulties now, not mental.

Celia: What's your understanding of emotional difficulties?

Jane: Well, I think I was mad in F. P. [the residential home]. Absolutely, it was awful. I lost myself. I remember saying to Mum: 'I can't find Jane, I don't know where she's gone'. I lost my centre. My vision – it was awful – those things I kept seeing – so frightening. I hated it there, but maybe it was because I was so ill. I feel better now – I'm in touch with my centre, my core now – it's still fragile but it's there – it's the stuff around the centre that's difficult between me and the world, but I'm in touch with myself now. So much better.

Celia: What a relief. [I meant for Jane but I suspect, for me as well]

83

> *Jane:* Yes. I feel sad about F.P. sometimes. I feel I wasted it – it's such a lovely place, the woods, the buildings, the tree house … I didn't appreciate it.
>
> *Celia:* You were ill
>
> *Jane:* Yes, I was, I hated it. But I can see it helped me. The activities helped – the candle making, drama therapy, cooking – they held me. I fell apart in between. And the other residents were lovely – R and I used to chat a lot…. it was really good having the woods there – no one could see me – just the trees … . So it was good really, but I've been much better since coming here. [Jane is referring to the supported house].

Jane talks about being 'held' by the structure and activities at the home. The notion of 'holding' is one introduced and often used by Jane in relation to the fear she has of, in her own words, 'falling apart'. She refers to our relationship in the same terms:

> *Jane:* get so worried Celia
>
> *Celia:* About?
>
> *Jane:* About you going. I don't know how I'll cope. I know I don't see you very often but I know you're there and I can phone you and you're good on the phone, you don't tell me to pull myself together, you just listen. It's like I feel held by you. I can't imagine you not being there. It's so difficult.

BEING EMOTIONALLY HELD: CONSISTENCY AND RELIABILITY

The idea of 'holding' links with the concept of 'containment' in that both concern the importance of having one's emotional needs received by another as a fundamental part of human development. The notions of 'holding' and 'containment' echo the pre-verbal stages of individual development and the need by the care-giver to understand how the baby is feeling. Winnicott (1964) believed that the way in which the infant is held, both physically and in the mother's mind, is crucial to the child's development and emerging faith in its environment.

Winnicott used the mother–infant relationship as a model for working with people who are vulnerable and applied the idea of 'holding' to social work in terms of fostering individual development by attention to both feelings and environmental provision. He argued that by being consistent and reliable, social workers can help those they work with to establish a greater level of confidence and trust which can help to facilitate healing and development. I believe that Jane has benefited from the consistency of my contact and my attention to her emotional state. Even though I now only visit her once a month she has a sense that I am able to hold her in mind, not only during my visits, but also during my absences, and this is crucial to her sense of being 'held together'.

It is not always easy to provide this kind of relationship. Sometimes as the recipient of ambivalent feelings which may include frustration, anger or hopelessness it can be difficult to offer the quality of attention and care required. Jane referred to this as we reviewed our relationship:

> Jane: (You've) not given up on me even when I've been horrible and in a state. You didn't give up on me. You kept coming. You've seen me all the way through – you know me – that really helps. The continuity – I don't want to have to get used to someone else.

According to Winnicott, when the holding environment fails, the infant experiences a state of disintegration as a response to 'the unthinkable or archaic anxiety that results from failure of holding in the stage of absolute dependence' (Winnicott, 1965: 61). It may or may not be that Jane's frequent description of 'falling apart' is linked to an earlier, incomplete, stage of development, but whatever its origin she is referring to a terrifying state which requires understanding and holding.

THE PRESENT DAY

My work with Jane continues. She has been living in the supported house for over two years and I still visit her on a monthly basis. The rationale for my involvement on a practical level is to be sure that the placement continues to meet her needs and that she wishes to remain there. Equally significant is my continued provision of a consistent, supportive relationship which helps to address Jane's emotional needs. I am able to conceptualise the organisational and bureaucratic processes as a 'space' within which my emotional work with Jane can be contained. Although it does not always offer me the support I would wish, it does at least provide a legitimated reason for my continued contact. This effective interweaving of the bureaucratic and the emotional is, as I have argued, a key feature of CBP and central to the social work role.

Jane is now more mentally well than she was during much of her stay in the residential home. She says that with the help of the support workers, she feels able to 'hold' herself. However she is currently experiencing incapacitating symptoms of tiredness and spends much of her time in bed. Looking back at the course of her illness, both mental and physical, it seems that when she is physically well, as she was in the residential home, she becomes emotionally disturbed. Conversely when she is mentally well, she experiences inexplicable physical symptoms. In spite of my deep desire to 'cure' Jane she continues to experience much distress.

Despite the best of intentions and the most dedicated work, it is not unusual for situations in which social workers are involved to show little improvement or even to get worse. The way in which we respond to long-term needs such as Jane's may depend partly on our motives for entering the profession. If we are driven by the need for reparation in our own lives for example, we may find it difficult to cope with a situation where there appears to be only marginal improvement or where things break down completely. At times our own emotional needs can become inextricably tied up with the needs of the service user. However, we need to be able to withstand our own, sometimes urgent, desire to find a cure, as well as the pressures placed upon us by the agency for which we work and recognise that recovery proceeds at the pace of each unique individual and not at the pace of the worker. Di Baily (2000) points out that users of mental health services have themselves often articulated their experience of mental distress in the language of 'recovery' rather than 'cure' and argues that critical social work practice must involve exposing and working with such user-led interpretations.

Through this account of my work with Jane I have attempted to illustrate the importance of attending to the relationships we form with service users in all aspects of our work. As social workers we are governed by various legislative, organisational and bureaucratic structures, which aim to deal with welfare issues in a technical/ managerial way. Human pain is a complex and messy business however and requires more than a one-dimensional 'doing' approach to practice. The process of engaging with the psychological and emotional life of service users requires close attention, resilience, courage and a willingness to face our own sometimes painful responses. However it is my experience that through this act of emotional engagement we are able to offer a source of help which can enrich both our own lives and the lives of those with whom we work.

REFERENCES

Adams, R. (2000) 'Developing Critical Practice in Social Work' in Adams, R., Dominelli, L. and Payne, M. (eds) *Critical Practice in Social Work* (Basingstoke: Palgrave).

Baily, D. (2000) 'Mental Health' in Adams, R., Dominelli, L. and Payne, M. (eds) *Critical Practice in Social Work* (Basingstoke: Palgrave).

Bateman, A. (1995) 'The Treatment of Borderline Patients in a Day Hospital Setting', *Psychoanalytic Psychotherapy* **9**(1): 3–16.

Benjamin, J. (1998) *The Shadow of the Other* (New York: Routledge).

Bion, W. R. (1962) *Learning from Experience* (London: Heinemann).

Bower, M. (2002) 'Editorial' *Journal of Social Work Practice* **16**(2): 93–98.

Carpy, D. (1989) 'Tolerating the Counter Transference: A Mutative Process', *International Journal of Psycho-Analysis* **70**: 287–294.

Cooper, A. (2002) 'Keeping Our Heads: Preserving Therapeutic Values in a Time of Change', *Journal of Social Work Practice* **16** (1): 7–14.

Ferguson, H. (2005) 'Working with Violence, the Emotions and the Psycho-social Dynamics of Child Protection: Reflections on the Victoria Climbie Case', *Social Work Education* 24 (7): 781–795.

Gorman, H. (2000) 'Winning Hearts and Minds? – Emotional Labour and Learning for Care Management Work', *Journal of Social Work Practice* **14** (2): 149–158.

Hochschild, A. (1983) *The Managed Heart* (Berkeley, CA: University of California Press).

Honig, B. (1996) 'Difference, Dilemmas and the Politics of Home', in Benhabib, S. (ed.), *Democracy and Difference: Contesting the Boundaries of the Political* (Princeton University Press).

Newman J. and Clarke, P. (1994) 'Going About Our Business? The Managerialisation of Public Services' in Clarke, J., Cochrane, A. and McLaughlin, E. (eds) *Managing Social Policy* (London: Sage).

Price, H. (2001) 'Emotional Labour in the Classroom: A Psychoanalytic Perspective', *Journal of Social Work Practice* **15** (2): 161–180.

Taylor, C. and White, S. (2000) *Practicing Reflexivity in Health and Welfare: Making Knowledge* (Buckingham: Open University Press).

Thompson, P. (2003) 'Devils and Deep Blue Seas: The Social Worker In-Between', *Journal of Social Work Practice* **17**(1): 35–48.

Waddell, M. (1989) 'Living in Two Worlds: Psychodynamic Theory and Social Work Practice', *Free Associations* **15**: 11–35.

Winnicott, D. W. (1964) *The Family and Individual Development* (London: Tavistock).

Winnicott, D. W. (1965) *The Maturational Processes and the Facilitating Environment: Studies in the Theory of Emotional Development* (London: The Hogarth Press).

5 Constructive engagement: best practice in social work interviewing – keeping the child in mind

BARRY COOPER

INTRODUCTION

Interviews are increasingly common experiences for people in the world of work. In the world of *social work* the interview takes on an even greater significance. Few would disagree with Kadushin and Kadushin's (1997: 3) assertion that 'It is the most important, most frequently employed, social work skill.' The interview is often the central means by which social workers make person-to-person contact and a 'constructive engagement' with others in order to begin the process of working together. In this chapter I will be exploring a recorded interview between a social worker and a service user in order to illustrate the expertise involved in making a relationship and working to keep it going. The analysis draws upon 'constructivist' theoretical perspectives as a way of highlighting and understanding the everyday, but mostly unrecognised, critical best practice (CBP) skills of interviewing in social work.

This is the first of two chapters that purposefully sit either side of the 'perspectives' and 'interventions' parts of this book. The intention is to illustrate the point that theory and practice are not separate but integrated aspects of social work practices. Theoretical perspectives can be drawn from practice interventions and vice-versa. Although the focus of analysis is upon 'engagement' in this chapter with 'negotiating and assessing' in the next, these are not discrete activities. In the same way I will argue that relationship making, assessment and negotiation are also indivisible aspects of the social work interview. The analyses of the interview in these two chapters were created through a number of discussions between myself, as author, and Sally, the social worker. Sally is an experienced child care social worker. I was a social worker for

12 years in child care and adult mental health before becoming a social work lecturer. These reflective discussions were important in the writing of these chapters. I have argued elsewhere (Cooper, 2001) that establishing a participative involvement between people is essential for reflective *practice learning* as well as the understanding and analysis of direct practice with service users. There are a number of reasons for this. First, there are many interesting perspectives that could be drawn from just me analysing the interview. However, it would have lacked the practice-based point of view of Sally. I could only speculate about what she meant or what she was aiming to do by saying what she said. Sally could verify and add other ways of looking at it. In other words, my account would have lacked the richness of understanding that Sally could contribute. Exactly the same principle applies to the service user, Adam, as well. However, in writing this chapter, it wasn't possible to involve Adam and this has to be acknowledged as a limitation. Second, the approach to CBP taken in this chapter is one where meanings, understandings and agreements are 'constructed' between those involved. In other words, the extent to which people are enabled and encouraged to participate in working relationships will determine the quality and degree of any subsequent understanding or agreement. Third, it is a 'key role' of social work, as part of the new qualifying degree in the different nations of the United Kingdom, that people are supported to ensure their views are heard. This can only have an impact if people are included and enabled to participate in relationships that prioritise the processes of negotiation and agreement-making. In social work, although there may sometimes be non-cooperation and other limitations to participation, these core social work processes remain constituted through talk and understood through analyses of language.

CONSTRUCTING SOCIAL WORK THROUGH RELATIONSHIPS AND LANGUAGE: WE ARE WHAT WE SPEAK

Relationships are crucial in social work. In social work, perhaps more than in any other professional activity, the quality of the relationship and ensuing communication virtually determines the nature of the work. The effect of this inter-dependence between the character of relationships and communication is often overlooked and needed re-statement 30 years ago:

> What the relationship "means"; how it may influence the person's motivation and behaviour; what its powers are in facilitating or hindering the

person's use of service and resources; in what ways our own feelings, thought, and actions affect that relationship – these are among the particulars we need to learn afresh or re-examine. They lie at the heart of whatever we do in the interchange between ourselves and another person. (Perlman, 1979: 3)

This is not to assume that everybody wants, needs or can achieve the 'counselling ideal' of a secure and trusting therapeutic relationship. However, it is important to recognise the realities of different kinds of social worker / service user, or social worker / colleague, relationships, for different purposes, in different contexts and affected by all sorts of apparent constraints, circumstantial factors and histories. It is a core feature of a CBP perspective (Ferguson, 2003) that the conditions and structures surrounding practice are not necessarily fixed limits. Situations can be construed as either constraining or as opportunities to move forward. An examination of the ways in which social workers approach their work can be illustrative of good practice even in the most difficult of circumstances. CBP, therefore, can be understood as essentially 'constructive' (Parton & O'Byrne, 2000) in being situated in specific contexts and yet amenable to skilled intervention and influence.

A constructivist approach to social work can be found within the key distinction between situational contexts and the different viewpoints of people involved in social situations. From the interplay between the two arises the scope for different 'ways of knowing' (Fisher, 1991) and, therefore, different ways of talking with people, negotiating and constructing definitions of problems and working out future solutions. Creative, constructivist approaches to situational re-definitions can be traced back to the seminal work of George Kelly and his psychology of personal constructs (Kelly, 1991). Kelly's theoretical emphasis, upon the ways in which individuals have unique realities within patterns of commonality and relationships, explicitly highlights and celebrates personal and cultural diversities. It is this recognition of difference and contrast that poses both an opportunity for service user advocacy as well as a challenge to the organisation of professional social work (Hugman, 1996). A core philosophical distinction in the understanding of social problems goes back a long way and is central to a constructivist approach. Fuller and Myers (1941) [cited in Parton & O'Byrne, 2000: 15] argued that 'social problems' are defined by a considerable number of persons as a deviation from some social norm which they cherish. However, such definitions are contestable and subject to change. So:

Every social problem thus consists of an *objective condition* and a *subjective definition*. The objective condition is a verifiable situation which can be checked as to existence and magnitude by impartial and trained observers. The subjective definition is the awareness of certain individuals that the condition is a threat to certain cherished values. (Fuller & Myers, 1941:320)

Subjective definitions are the different 'takes' that different people will bring to social situations. Assessments of social situations cannot be 'objective' in the same way that an engineer would assess a structure or a dentist would assess your fillings. The explanation for this is simple but challenging of 'westernised' ethno-centric assumptions about linear cause and effect. The simple but profound difference between engineers or dentists and social workers is that the boundaries of structures and teeth fillings can be clearly identified and they do not change when they are being assessed. This is not the case with people. Social situations and social relationships are complex and need to be understood holistically (Jack, 2001) within networks of different cultural communities and environments. These networks, in turn, are made up of individual people where each individual will embody a complex set of unique perspectives. These views and perspectives are likely to change through the relationships created by social work processes of engagement and assessment. In other words, processes of assessment are themselves increasingly recognised as constituting an intervention. It is almost an interpersonal impossibility for there not to be changes. What's more, if no changes of view or perception can be discerned in a social work intervention, then questions should probably be asked about its effectiveness or, indeed, its relevance. These processes are essentially constructive (Parton & O'Byrne, 2000). In other words, we are sustained, or constructed, as individuals in our roles and relationships through 'talk'. Talk helps us to locate, negotiate and maintain ourselves and our relationships within a reality that is 'social'.

To argue for the social construction of reality (Berger & Luckmann, 1971) is to identify the importance of a *social* reality in contradistinction from a 'natural world' or concrete reality of external objects. Few people argue about whether or not unproblematic external objects, such as buildings and teeth fillings, actually exist or not. However, the meanings, significance, importance, implications or to re-use a much over-used word in social work, the 'values' that we place upon people and objects are of a different order. These levels of meaning are, in a literal sense, what makes our own world-view, of ourselves and our relationships, 'meaningful'. These meanings arise out of the interactions between people, are both socially *and* personally constructed (Paris & Epting, 2004), and thereby constitute a social reality for those involved in construing those realities. In other words, the processes of making a relationship, sharing perspectives and working towards agreements about different ways of understanding situations, are all ways in which outlooks are shaped and social realities constructed. The difference, therefore, between people and objects is that human beings are inter-active 'others' that, uniquely, change in response to inter-personal processes of contact and communication. This is of crucial significance for making sense of what happens between social workers and service users and for understanding how, together, people can begin to antici-pate and negotiate constructively their options for their future. A robust social work relationship will maintain an awareness and, crucially, an acceptance of the values of different peoples' positions, views and perspectives. These values, in turn, will focus the social work task upon assessing the scope for negotiation and agreement about the ways forward in any future services and interventions. The social worker, as illustrated in this and the following chapter, is on the front-line of such negotiations.

Being 'on duty' or 'intake' in social work are phrases that you often hear in local authority social work agencies in the United Kingdom. The short-hand label describes and reflects a way of organising the initial stages of service delivery and is an important and often unrecog-nised 'gateway' to other services potentially available to agencies and members of the public. It usually involves offering a response to situa-tions that have arisen, or are referred from another part of the welfare network, and that have been initially defined as problematic in some way. This, of course, means not only that the variety of 'presenting problems' can be very wide, but also that the scope for variations in 'problem definition' is similarly dynamic. The opening stages of con-tact or engagement with a situation can take many forms and involve a lot of inter-agency communication and liaison in addition to or before any direct work with service users. Throughout these processes, work-ing rationales are formed to determine whether longer term work may be required. So, duty or intake work can often be a very exploratory activity needing enquiries and investigations and a lot of flexible 'thinking on your feet' in relatively uncharted territories with a strong sense of newness and, because of this, feelings of increased uncertainty. Some writers (Parton, 1998; Beresford & Croft, 2004) have argued that this sense of working with ambiguity captures an important essence of social work and needs to be recognised. For new social workers, this can be a source of anxiety as it involves negotiations and judgements that are necessarily tentative in a process of evolving 'hypotheses' of what is going on in situations. There may be a strong sense in which the reasons and justifications for social work involvement have not yet been fully understood or agreed by either the social worker or the service user. There are likely to be, then, a number of unresolved issues as the people involved start to draw maps of where they are in their working relationship and make sense of where each other is 'coming from'. This sense of exploration in new territories and the potential for creativity that it offers can be a source of great appeal to some social workers. It is a skilful work demanding flexibility, stamina, tolerance of ambiguity and a desire to engage in tussles with people as postions are negotiated and re-negotiated over time. However, the practice requires skill and commitment within an organisational and political context that is not always conducive.

A constructivist approach assumes uncertainty as a pre-requisite for creativity. It prioritises the importance of change through processes of communication and negotiation in social work practice. However, language can be 'taken for granted' (Timms, 1968) despite 'talk' being the very material making up the foundation, building blocks and complex structures and processes of social work. Gregory and Holloway (2005) have recently re-emphasised the argument that language helps to 'shape' our sense of professional identity and, therefore, influence our understanding of what it is we are doing when we 'do' social work. It is what is said; how it is said; why it is said; and when and to whom, that conveys the message and the meaning of social work relationships and agreements. Looking at our conversations therefore offers a gateway to analysis and understanding of how our lives are constructed by what we say (Shotter, 1993). For the purposes of learning about what happens in social work, an investigation of 'talk' offers a way into the under-recognised skills and strengths of the profession.

THE INTERVIEW AND THE ANALYSIS

This interview offers a privileged entrée into the dynamics of an ordinary social work interaction. Social work, for important reasons of privacy and confidentiality, is an activity that is rarely 'open' to examination. The interview is taken from a recording between the social worker, Sally, and the service user, a father, Adam. The interview was recorded, with Adam's permission, as part of a post-qualification, continuing professional development course that Sally was undertaking at University. The dialogue has been produced below as verbatim accounts of what was said, by whom and in response to what. I have also tried to convey some of the important features of how it was said as an illustration of the 'realness' of two people talking and negotiating about issues of great personal and professional importance. You will notice that the grammar and syntax is not perfect; most ordinary people, including social workers, rarely speak 'perfectly' all the time. However, the meaning is nonetheless conveyed in real-life situations. This next part outlines a brief background to the situation that led to the interview.

CASE BACKGROUND

Both the family and the social worker are of White UK origin. The family unit consists of Jane 13; her sister Hannah 8; and their parents Leanne and Adam. The social services duty team for the locality were involved with the family after Jane had run away from home claiming that her father had 'kicked and punched' her. Sally had been part of the early investigation and had helped to draw up a 'written agreement' as a 'contract' for the initial intervention between the agency and the family. The effect of this was to exclude Adam from the family home pending an investigation. However, the family had a pre-booked holiday arranged – so Adam didn't go but stayed behind to look after the family's dog. Sally had met with Jane and her mother since they returned from holiday and this interview is the first with Adam since the incident with Jane and the family's return from holiday. Adam has come into the social services office at Sally's request.

How is she to play this one-to-one meeting? Although Sally was involved in the precipitating 'crisis' before the family went on holiday, there is at this early stage little background relationship to build upon and yet there are duties and professional obligations that Sally needs to pursue without really knowing what Adam's attitude or reaction will be. Sally's opening statement offers her recognition that there have been some difficulties at home.

S   the reason I wanted to see you again today was that I would have had a chance, did have a chance, to talk with Jane, and mum there as well, and Hannah on Friday ... and I realise there's a lot of pressures at home – a lot of 'behaviour' from Jane ...

A   yeah

S   ... that most parents would find challenging ...

A   yep, told you so ... [light laughter]

S   yeah, but umm, ok, we went over this I guess last time, we were saying well there's still thresholds ....

A   yeah

S   ... that you can't go over ....

A   yeah, I understand that

S   ... but it's also about finding ways that might change the patterns at home .... yeah?.

At this early stage Sally is being quite formal and setting out the 'professional line' about 'boundaries', 'patterns' and is establishing a sense of control over the direction, or purpose and aims of the interview. A lot of social work interviewing advice or guidance would confirm this as an important aspect of starting an interview. Trevithick (2005: 140), for example, advises that 'planning and preparation are the hallmarks of a successful interview; failing to plan is planning to fail'. This is undoubtedly good advice although, as this interview demonstrates, in the pressured realities of practice situations there are probably limits to how much practitioners can rely upon planning and preparation. Quite often social workers need to be prepared for the unexpected. In this example, quite quickly, whatever plans Sally may have for this interview seem to be blown off course by Adam's rapid disclosure and implicit 'challenge' to the agenda. He wants Sally to know that things have changed

A   well we had a nice weekend this weekend to be honest with you I stayed over there this weekend! Saturday we had a nice Chinese and all that and watched like Casualty and that sort of thing ....

S   [audible intake of breath] How did that come about Adam? [through clenched teeth]

A   cos she phoned me up said do I want to stay the weekend ...

S   who's she ...

A   Leanne ... and yesterday, well Sunday, we had a nice tea and watched Lord of The Rings, the first one, cos I've got it on DVD, and yesterday evening we all went up town and had a Kentucky meal ... and watched LOTR 2 ... [pause] ... And we had a nice night out.

So, Sally may well have had a professional agenda which she needed to work within but it would be a mistake to assume that she is in control of how this interview will proceed. After all, this isn't a doctor's surgery where there are cultural expectations about how people should behave. In social work there is little, if any, agreed norms about a social work version of the 'patient role'. Adam is not passively going along with Sally's opening gambit! On one level, you might think that Sally has 'had the rug pulled out from under her feet' but it is important for social workers to be prepared for the direction of an interview to change suddenly. Adam has a very different starting point and he is quite able to begin the interview from *his* perspective of what is important. For Adam, it seems essential that a different version of his family's reality is provided, 'things are OK and we're now doing all the things that normal, happy families do … '.

At this point, and throughout the interview, Sally is using the communications between herself and Adam to construct the meaning of what is being said. Fook (2002: 119) describes this as a process of 'constructing a professional narrative' and goes on to make clear that: ' "Workers" own assumptions and interpretations will influence how and what knowledge is selected and what narrative is created. The narrative produced represents the worker's version or perspective on the situation, *which may or may not be used to service users' advantage* [emphasis added].'

Sally has a choice and a dilemma. Does she pursue the approach of 'risk minimisation' that was started with her agency's initial intervention and take a stand at this point by 'confronting' the change/challenge presented in Adam's different version of what is happening – his 'story'? Or does she take a more subtle approach and 'go with' the changed reality as presented by Adam and switch tack by offering a more empathic response that acknowledges Adam's need to demonstrate that he is still a 'good parent'? There is a balance to be struck here and Sally has to make an instant decision about how to react to Adam's response – preferably in a way that maintains a working relationship and yet doesn't jettison the basis for her involvement. Sally has general duties and obligations as a statutory social worker and, to some extent, she may feel that she needs to defend her position; but she also has a very specific responsibility for her 'primary client' in all of this – and that is Jane. As I emphasised in the quote above, and as Sally confirmed in my discussions with her about this interview, it was important to try and keep to a narrative that would eventually work to Jane's advantage. Sally's instinct as a social worker was to acknowledge Adam's story through what Egan (2002) describes as 'advanced empathy'. In other words, Sally's acknowledgement goes beyond a response to what Adam literally said and, instead, ventures into that zone of uncertainty that characterises social work. Sally makes a skilled judgement about the feelings that lay behind Adams disclosure; whilst keeping Jane very much in mind

> S I know Leanne was missing you and more from what, I guessed, Hannah was very much missing you as well …

A yes ...

S uhmm [pause] ... I'm not sure about Jane ... for the future – when she was talking about 'futures' you were always around ....

A she was alright yesterday! ... kissing and cuddling and stuff ...

Adam is still wary of what Sally might be 'getting at'. It is difficult to over-estimate the extent to which, through anecdotal evidence, it is commonly believed that social workers just 'take people's children away'. So there is an implicit challenge within Adam's reaction to, even the possibility of, social work having a privileged 'reading' of a young person's views. This is, perhaps, a 'to be expected' reaction of a parent who would assume to have a far better knowledge and insight into their own child's attitudes towards them than an outside professional. But what is a social worker to make of a father's claims that his 13-year-old daughter was 'kissing and cuddling and stuff' with him? Is this a 'normal' part of *this* family norms and expectations? How can Sally judge this? Would it be based on her own experience of family life? If so, would Sally's experience be applicable to this specific family with whom she may have little or nothing in common? The point of raising these questions is to 'problematise' the tendency for all of us to make judgements based upon sets of assumptions about what is 'normal'. For example, there may appear to be some degree of cultural commonality between the family and Sally in so far as they are both of White UK origin. However, this cannot be the basis for an assumption that issues of working with diversity are not applicable in this case. Social workers have to develop working hypotheses about situations within increasingly diverse, multi-cultural and pluralistic societies. There is unlikely to be one clear, socially accepted, cultural norm or 'objective condition' (Fuller & Myers, 1941) of family behaviour that can be found in child and family-development books. These are real dilemmas of judgement or 'social definition' [*op.cit.*] that Sally is in no position to make right now. Such judgements are the essence of what is meant by being 'critical' in practice and Sally may make a mental note of this as a question to be explored at some point in the future.

A ... speaking to each other and having laughs and everything ...

S yes, [acknowledging this] when she was looking ahead to how she would want things to be, [A – yeah] you were in the picture [A – yeah] ... which I thought was quite significant ...

So, Sally is still carefully weighing her words and maintaining this balance of acknowledging Adam's position whilst keeping her role and professional responsibilities in mind. However, there comes a point in an interview – and this has all happened very early on with little time for deliberation – where it is vital to assert the professional perspective. The reasoning, in plain language, may go something like this, you [Adam] may want to play happy families and forget what happened to precipitate the authorities' involvement – however, you are here in this office because of alleged serious events and you need to understand the social work [and police] agenda as well as social services needing and wanting to empathically understand yours ...'. In other words, there are still, at least, two readings of recent history and at least two agendas. However, Sally didn't explicitly use the power of her position (Hugman, 1991) and speak in the example of 'plain language' above. Skilled best practice in social work is often illustrated through a less 'in your face' confrontational style. In this situation, Sally is working on instinct and calling upon her holistic understanding and appreciation of how best to proceed.

> S   But, I remember her saying to me at the police station – you [Adam] won't stay away and things won't be different ... they'll be different for a little while [A – subdued, yeah] but then it'll be back to what it was. Ummm, so ... this might, in a sense, bear out what she says ...

Sally has achieved two things at this, still early, stage of the interview. First, she has implicitly addressed the fact that Adam has 'broken' the terms of the written agreement made with the agency. This needed acknowledgement and Sally has subtly, and skilfully, achieved this without setting it up as a fixed-position confrontational issue. Second, she has brought the professional reading of the situation back to the top of the agenda and has articulated it through the words and views of the young person, Jane, for whom she has a primary protective responsibility. Moreover, Sally couched the young person's views in the critical terms of how Jane saw the future. It will be helpful to look more closely at these two factors.

First, what is the rationale for using 'contracts'? Written agreements are being used more often in social work and there are compelling arguments both for and against their use. On the plus side, they appear to have an obvious advantage of clarity. If someone has to write down what they want and expect all parties to the agreement to do, then the writer has to think this through and put it into words that are clear and unambiguous. Aldgate (2002: 24) maintains that written agreements are a 'tangible manifestation of working in partnership'. This focus upon clarity and agreement about behavioural expectations is also a central feature of the 'task-centred approach' to social work (Doel & Marsh, 1992). Written agreements share aspects in common with this approach to social work in that there still has to be a judgement made about the viability and utility of their application in particular situations. The following conversation between Sally and myself explores her perspectives on this:

Sally   I think there are some written agreements that, if breached in any way, mean that you are reacting more strongly [than others]; but, some of the rows and some of the patterns I see of risk of family breakdown relationships and risk of family violence when they (young people) are in adolescence ... you are riding with what you've got really. You've got to a certain extent go with what the family gives you ... erm, a teenager will storm out saying they're never going to return, you know, they go and stay with gran until it settles down and then you come back after the weekend to find that the teenager has returned. Families will often have their own pattern and if you're not talking about something as 'heavy' as active sexual abuse then you're not, necessarily, trying to enforce the letter of the agreement – which is not a legal document.

BC   Is there an element of bluff to these agreements?

Sally   No, it's not a bluff. Written agreements have lots of levels on which they can help. They're useful tools. On the most cynical level, which I'd only ever mention last, is that they do cover the agency's back by making clear what the agency's thoughts and actions were ... in a way that the family can't say "no, it wasn't like that" later on ... but that's a management agenda and it shouldn't be the main social work agenda. It makes clear what the risk is and the beginning of what people think the solution is ... why 'a gap' is needed and what needs to be done in that gap. What's gone wrong? What the concerns, risks, immediate plan and outcomes should be. A written agreement, in as simple a form as you can do it for most families, is that. It also emphasises to the family how serious it is ... and it is something that is vital when (perpetrators) minimise the violence or blame the victim.

On the minus side, they can be criticised as being levers of bureaucratic power. It is arguable whether people are really persuaded to change their behaviour or adapt their lives simply through having a 'contract' to sign. Some of these issues were a hot topic of debate around the time of the introduction of this formal approach into social work. The issues have implications for fundamental values about the nature of social work relationships. The exchanges were characterised in terms of questions about written agreements as 'contracts or con tricks' (Corden & Preston-Shoot, 1987, 1988; Rojek & Collins, 1987, 1988).

Second, perhaps the more subtly skilful aspect of Sally's communication is that she has aligned herself with the child. As a child-care social worker she will be mindful of the fact that successive reports, inquiries and resulting guidance, following high-profile child protection tragedies, have emphasised the imperative of remaining focused upon the child as the primary 'client'. [See, as just two examples, the reports into the cases of Jasmine Beckford (London Borough of Brent, 1985) and Victoria Climbie (Laming, 2003)]. However, Sally has not just 'sided' with Jane in an alliance that might run the risk of alienating her father. Sally's chosen way of representing the child's view is an example of CBP in that she has sought Jane's view of the future, *from Jane's own personal perspective*. This emphasis upon an individual's orientation towards the future is a key feature underpinning constructivist approaches to social work. A personal construct-theory approach to working with young people (Ronen, 1996; Butler & Green, 1998) focuses upon the ways in which they construe themselves and others within a view of their future. A focus upon a person's capacity to 'envision' their future also underpins solution-focused brief therapies (De Shazer, 1985, 1988). It is a powerful tool as it offers a way of directly accessing an individual's choices and anticipations about what is important to them in their future. Jane included her father in how she saw her future; but she also felt that things were not going to change and Sally has to convey both these messages to Adam.

However, at this time, as we will see below, he only hears one side and he gets angry at this. It seems that he still needs to defend his position and tries to reassert his perspective and his reading or understanding of what happened and why. But he also reacts to the implicit use of 'empowerment' by Sally. Drawing upon similar principles of advocacy outlined by Dalrymple and Horan in Chapter 9, by acting as a 'representative' for Jane's views, Sally is lending her professional power to Jane's 'voice' and reinforcing her position in what has become a contested area. The 'contest', in this example, is about working towards an agreed version of events. The core battlegrounds are about the *meanings* placed upon what happened; the *understanding* that this supports to explain about what happened; and how any agreement can inform plans for the future. The work of Foucault (Foucault, 1980) offers a helpful perspective in understanding social work as an activity that takes place within networks of power, influence and authority

(Danaher et al., 2000). These networks or relationships are constructed by people within complex social realities, 'the social' (Donzelot, 1988), where individual's meanings and 'versions' of events struggle with each other for acceptance. Adam's reaction to Sally's fairly innocuous observation can be understood in this way. In other words, he recognises the power of Sally's position; he is fearful of what he thinks she might be 'getting at'; and he needs to assert his perspective and version of events,

A   [interrupting] don't you think that could be like a case of Janey like 'spitting venom'? Like she knows she's been given all this opportunity – she knows she had some power and control, innit, she was saying this because she wanted to get me into trouble? … for, because *she* was in trouble? Don't you think that could be the case..? cos she's a clever girl ….

S   I think that prompted it [A – yeah!] I think that prompted it …

A   she's not as stupid as she acts, you know what I mean … ?

S   I will agree with you as far as … if the Police hadn't come looking for her at the place, you know, because she was missing, [A – right] if they hadn't found her somewhere else … *I don't think she would have said what she said at that time* … I don't, you know, I don't think there is any doubt about that …

This part of the interview contains a key statement from Sally and I have italicised the crucial part. It is an admission and agreement with Adam that a full understanding of what was said and why it was said is located in the specifics of situations. In other words, the meaning at a 'deep' level is 'situated' in a previous time and context. Therefore, Sally is acknowledging the potential validity of different perspectives. This is an important and frequently overlooked aspect of inter-personal communication, which is basically what an interview is. There does not need to be a conflict about 'right' versus 'wrong' readings as Adam's is viable to him and Sally can accept some or all of it. As long as she can get Adam to accept some or all of hers, there will be the basis for a negotiation. This process of negotiating, or co-constructing, areas of agreement between versions of events is a vital aspect of the social workers' skill and expertise in situations where there are often conflicting versions. It is not necessarily an insurmountable problem that different versions cannot be reconciled. There can be an agreement to disagree whilst acknowledging that people have reasons for holding to different perspectives.

This process is starting to happen as Sally tries to very tentatively explore the possibility of common territory whilst holding on to her position as a social worker not only needing to work *for* the young person, Jane, as her primary client but also having to work *with* the parent. The respective positions of Sally and Adam have yet to be established in this process and there are still areas that will be contested …

S   ummm … and I guess when she's saying like … the first time she can remember you kind of … . getting *very* angry and physical with her was about, when she was about 11, she wasn't too sure …

Sally is still finding her way through the communication jungle. She cannot easily predict how Adam is going to react to her continued empowerment and representation of Jane's 'voice' as an important perspective. In this respect Sally needs to be both courageous and quietly assertive as she is unable to know that she either has a very aggrieved or determined [or both] parent who is unable at this stage to entertain Sally's [equally determined] counter-reading and interpretation of the situation – and he goes on the assertive offensive …

A   [interrupting] ah, this is crap, this cracks me up, this really cracks me up, I'm being labelled as a child abuser [S – she hasn't said it before] and I'm not – I do no different from what other parents do with their kids.

S   well … I think … .

A   … that's what's the matter in this time and age … people *like you* giving 'em too much 'reins' and giving them the power instead of how it used to be. Look at schools now, kids whacking teachers and stuff like that … it stems from them being given too much power … that's how I look at it … and I said to Janey, at the end of the day, if I comes back or no, if you're told to do something [tapping the table] you've still got to do it … . Whether it's tidy your room or come in on time … . All this codswallop that you keeps on spouting to me about, flippin', giving her more of a free rein, more power, I said to her yesterday, I said 'if you behave yourself this week', there's a new Eminem film she wants to go and see, I said 'I'll take you to see that … . I said, and I'll take you to have a pizza or something and that'll be your present for the week'. She was over the moon at that and said 'I'll behave this week then' … .

S   [emolliently] because she wants to make things right again …

A   yeah, and so do I but you keep on saying … . Look, I wouldn't have been allowed over if Leanne had asked Janey and she'd said 'no I'm frightened of our dad', then I wouldn't have come over. Simple as that and I know Leanne would've asked her.

Adam is aggrieved – he is desperately trying to defend his position and reassert the legitimacy of his perception of how things are. He feels threatened by his perception that Sally is arguing *against* the way that he sees himself and his reading of what happened; that Sally somehow has him 'labelled' (Levy, 1981) as a 'child abuser'. Adam's reaction to his belief that he is being wrongly categorised and misunderstood is to go on to the offensive and verbalise an example of some fundamental differences of perceived standards and expectations. On the one hand he believes that the way he acted is 'no different from any other parent' so he feels he is being unfairly singled out. At the same time Adam challenges the right of Sally [or anybody else] to 'advise' on ways for him as an individual to parent his daughter. He contests Sally's territory of being 'for the young person' and speaking up for her view by referring to how both Jane and her mother had agreed that it was 'alright' for Adam to spend the weekend. Adam's description and explanation of how he had placated Jane by promising 'treats' is a good illustration of the sort of 'parenting strategy' discussion that Sally will want to come back to later in the interview. There would be advantages in negotiating with the family for a longer-term involvement that specifically address 'whole family issues' such as this.

At this time, however, Sally needs to keep in mind and maintain the agency perspective and rationale for their intervention in the past as well as the legitimacy of her current position as constituted by this interview. Adam is not explicitly questioning the 'right' of Sally or social services to be involved. Nevertheless, he is angry and he is challenging the ways in which he perceives he is being labelled along with his perception of social work advice as being 'codswallop'! Sally does not react or respond to any of this. As Celia Keeping explores in Chapter 4, a focus on the emotional dimensions of social work relationships recognises that people often have a need to 'ventilate'. In other words, they have a build up of strong feelings and verbalising them is a healthy way of releasing the tension of these feelings. There is, therefore, in an entirely non-judgemental perspective, nothing wrong with it. It would risk sounding patronising, at this stage, for Sally to actively acknowledge this so she quietly 'contains' the powerful feelings being expressed and stays with the flow of the interview by maintaining her representation of Jane's views ...

S   I think she wanted to make things right again.

A   well so do I. our family works as a unit, we're all like a key member, I can't just stay away like you said for about three months because all my wages are paid in to Leanne's account ....

S   ... and then we were saying four weeks, weren't we because ....

A   ... well even four weeks because I haven't got any bank account of my own or anything like that – I've got no food and I've got to like go to work and stuff .... All my clothes is over there, I can't just stay away, you know what I mean, I can't.

The interview has now begun to move into a different phase. Adam has expressed his angry feelings about how he thinks he is being labelled and he is now expressing a very different set of emotions. Adam's complaint is based within his experience of the implications for individuals and families of major social work interventions into the complexities of people's lives. It is a very 'real' appeal that is addressing the social work 'value' of empathy. How would we feel in his position? The practical and personal implications of a contractual 'agreement' for Adam to be out of the house whilst a risk assessment is undertaken or 'a breathing space' is established makes the situation very difficult to sustain. Adam's powerful plea seems to make the agency's position appear unreasonable. The ways in which practical and ethical realities such as these are handled can have a big impact upon the quality and effectiveness of the relationship between the agency and the service users. These kinds of issues are unavoidable aspects of risk assessment that are bound up with most, if not all, social work interventions.

CONCLUSION

This chapter has explored the first part of an interview that, in real time, lasted little more than ten minutes. And yet enormous amounts of information and powerful perspectives have been unpacked. There have been some important exchanges, the setting of 'positions' from both Sally and Adam, and some groundwork laid to help encourage the fundamental social work processes of negotiation and assessment. This analysis of a small segment of a fairly common interview for social workers has highlighted great complexities as well as some basic human reactions. Sally has had to be focused on her role and her responsibilities to Jane; but at the same time, she has had to be flexible and accommodating to Adam's reactions. She has had to be clear in her communication and has implicitly 'contained' Adam's expressions of powerful feelings by being quietly authoritative but without appearing confrontational. In maintaining this balance, above all, Sally has begun a 'constructive engagement' with Adam and kept open the options and opportunities for further work. These are examples of the often 'hidden' and uncelebrated strengths of skilled social work practice. The following chapter continues a CBP analysis of this interview through a focus upon the constructive processes underpinning negotiation and assessment.

REFERENCES

Aldgate, J. (2002) Family breakdown, in M. Davies (ed.) *The Blackwell Companion to Social Work* (Oxford, Blackwell).

Beresford, P. and Croft, S. (2004) Service users and practitioners reunited: the key component for social work reform, *British Journal of Social Work*, 34(1), 53–68.

Berger, P. and Luckmann, T. (1971) *The Social Construction of Reality* (Harmondsworth, Penguin).

Butler, R. and Green, D. (1998) *The Child Within: The Exploration of Personal Construct Theory with Young People*. (Oxford, Butterworth-Heinemann).

Cooper, B. (2001) Constructivism in social work: towards a participative practice viability, *British Journal of Social Work*, 31, 721–738.

Corden, J. and Preston-Shoot, M. (1987) Contract or con-trick? A reply, *British Journal of Social Work*, 17(5), 535–543.

Corden, J. and Preston-Shoot, M. (1988) Contract or con-trick? A postscript, *British Journal of Social Work*, 18(6), 623–634.

Danaher, G., Schirato, T. and Webb, J. (2000) *Understanding Foucault* (London, Sage).

De Shazer, S. (1985) *Keys to Solutions in Brief Therapy* (New York and London, Norton).

De Shazer, S. (1988) *Clues: Investigating Solutions in Brief Therapy* (New York and London, Norton).

Doel, M. and Marsh, P. (1992) *Task-centred Social Work* (Aldershot, Ashgate).

Donzelot, J. (1988) The Promotion of the social, *Economy and Society*, 17(3), 395–427.

Egan, G. (2002) *The Skilled Helper, 7th edition* (Pacific Grove, CA, Brooks/Cole).

Ferguson, H. (2003) Outline of critical best practice perspective on social work and social care, *British Journal of Social Work*, 33, 1005–1024.

Fisher, D.V. (1991) *An Introduction to Constructivism for Social Workers* (New York, Praeger).

Fook, J. (2002) *Social Work: Critical Theory and Practice* (London, Sage).

Foucault, M. (1980) *Power/Knowledge: Selected Interviews and Other Writings, 1972–77. Edited by C. Gibson* (Brighton, Harvester).

Fuller, R. C. and Myers, R. D. (1941) The natural history of a social problem, *American Sociological Review*, 54(4), 318–328.

Gregory, M. and Holloway, M. (2005) Language and the shaping of social work, *British Journal of Social Work*, 35, 37–53.

Hugman, R. (1991) *Power in the Caring Professions* (Basingstoke, Macmillan).

Hugman, R. (1996) Professionalization in social work: the challenge of diversity, *International Social Work*, 39(2), 131–147.

Jack, G. (2001) Ecological perspectives in assessing children and families, in J. Horwath (ed.) *The Child's World: Assessing Children in Need* (London, Jessica Kingsley).

Kadushin, A. and Kadushin, G. (1997) *The Social Work Interview* (New York, Columbia University Press).

Kelly, G. A. (1991) *The Psychology of Personal Constructs [originally published 1955, New York:Norton]* (London, Routledge).

Laming, H. (2003) *The Victoria Climbie Inquiry*.

Levy, C. (1981) Labeling: the social worker's responsibility, *Social Casework*, 62(6), 332–342.

London Borough of Brent (1985) *The Report of the Panel of Inquiry into the Circumstances Surrounding the Death of Jasmine Beckford*. (London, London Borough of Brent).

Paris, M. E. and Epting, F. R. (2004) Social and personal construction: two sides of the same coin, in J. D. Raskin and S. K. Bridges (eds) *Studies in Meaning 2: Bridging the Personal and Social in Constructivist Psychology* (New Paltz, Pace University Press).

Parton, N. (1998) Risk, advanced liberalism and child welfare: the need to rediscover uncertainty and ambiguity, *British Journal of Social Work*, 28(1), 5–28.

Parton, N. and O'Byrne, P. (2000) *Constructive Social Work* (London, Macmillan).

Perlman, H. H. (1979) *Relationship – The Heart of Helping People* (London, University of Chicago Press).

Rojek, C. and Collins, C. A. (1987) Contract or con-trick? *British Journal of Social Work*, 17(2), 199–211.

Rojek, C. and Collins, C. A. (1988) Contract or con-trick revisited – comments, *British Journal of Social Work*, 18(6), 611–622.

Ronen, T. (1996) Constructivist therapy with traumatised children, *Journal of Constructivist Psychology*, 9, 139–156.

Shotter, J. (1993) *Conversational Realities: Constructing Life Through Language* (London, Sage).

Timms, N. (1968) *The Language of Social Casework* (London, Routledge and Kegan Paul).

Trevithick, P. (2005) *Social Work Skills* (Maidenhead, Open University Press).

Part II

Critical Best Practice: Interventions and Interactions

6 Best practice in social work interviewing: processes of negotiation and assessment

BARRY COOPER

INTRODUCTION

Critical best practice (CBP) perspectives offer ways in which practice interventions can be understood as indivisible from theoretical perspectives. All of the chapters in this book demonstrate elements of this theory-practice integration. In Part I the chapters highlighted various theoretical perspectives that are useful in taking a 'critical' position in social work and conceptualising best practice, while outlining the very practice that was 'critically best'. The book now moves to Part II to build on that by considering CBP firmly from the vantage point of social work interventions and interactions, with theory brought into support the analysis.

In opening the second part of the book, this chapter continues with the interview between Sally and Adam from Chapter 5 and, through a shift of focus, illustrates this continuity of practice and theory. The constructive perspectives of engagement and relationship building continue to be in evidence in this second part of the interview. In building upon these constructive ideas, the chapter has two broad aims. First, to offer an illustration of how processes of negotiation and assessment can be seen to underpin skilled social work interventions. The second aim is to use this focus upon negotiative processes to explore key debates about how assessment in social work needs to be understood as part of complex interpersonal processes but has become increasingly characterised as 'end product' through frameworks and formats.

As the chapters throughout this book illustrate, there is much more to social work than the growing emphasis upon bureaucratic procedures. Within the on-going debates about the future direction, roles and tasks of social work in the twenty-first century, the power of assessment as a key task needs to be recognised, understood and practiced through a mediating prism of professional social work values. For example, it is a core social work value and practice imperative to *involve* people, wherever possible, in the negotiation of working agreements and the creation of plans for services. This is not a simple task. Involving people in meaningful partnerships, in circumstances that are frequently pressured and stressful, necessarily requires a robust grasp of relationships and interpersonal dynamics as well as an awareness of different positions of social power. The negotiation of an assessment therefore entails the creative 'exchange' (Smale & Tuson, 1993) of professional and personal perspectives and the examination of differences as well as areas of agreement. Sally's interview with Adam demonstrates some of these vital social work skills that are so necessary to keep people involved. Before returning to the interview, the next section will outline some background arguments as a way of focusing upon assessment in social work.

THE RISE OF ASSESSMENT IN SOCIAL WORK

I'm governed by a gang of fanatical dogmatists, all determined that everyone shall be continually assessed from the moment of his or her first day at school until the inevitable oblivion of a private nursing home. I don't like it. [extract from a letter from an Elder service user printed in The Independent newspaper] (Platt, 1990: 47).

Assessment is not viewed as a benign process by many of those it is aimed at and in social welfare terms it is a process which seems to happen *to* the social disadvantaged (Middleton, 1997: 1).

It is perhaps 'assessment', more than any other aspect of the work, that distinguishes social work from counselling or therapy (Parton & O'Byrne, 2000: 134).

There is probably no area of social work where debate rages so fiercely as in assessment (Milner & O'Byrne, 2002: 261).

It is significant that these quotes [and they are only an illustrative selection] are to be found at the beginning of their respective sources. They speak to the authors' recognition of the power of assessment for both practitioners and service users in social work. Anecdotal experience suggests that, in recent times, 'doing an assessment' has established itself in the social work vernacular to become an everyday catchphrase for virtually any piece of decision-making intervention. And yet, the social work literature has only just begun to employ the language of assessment in a way that reflects its complexity and influence.

In the social casework literature of the 1960s and 70s, assessment can be found as a key stage within task and problem-oriented frameworks as part of attempts to move away from open-ended counselling approaches and towards a 'systematic, ordered approach' (Reid & Epstein, 1972; Compton & Galaway, 1975; Haines, 1975; Specht & Vickery, 1977). However, assessment was understood at that time as a relatively unproblematic foundation for sequential phases of action and evaluation. In other words, it was assumed that assessment was a quantitative process and that the more information that could be gathered, the better informed would be the assessment and any subsequent intervention. However, the key social work activity of forming judgements and assessments in social situations was not reflected in the UK Government's report into the expansion of personal social services (Seebohm, 1968). At a time of large-scale government expectations for social work, as it became entrenched within the structures and institutions of local authorities, there is no mention of assessment. The next government enquiry into the roles and tasks of social work in the 1980s (Barclay, 1982) again finds assessment only briefly 'named' through cursory passing references. It required the political introduction of marketisation for the profile of assessment in social work to become clearly identified and dramatically increased.

The 1980s saw the advent of 'New Right' political approaches that accelerated the pace of instrumentally driven 'top-down' changes. Substantial changes to the structures of welfare were introduced through new legislation and detailed blueprint guidelines (Department of Health, 1988, 1990a, 1990b). These became known as 'care management' and its effects were felt through increased managerialism and the introduction of competitive 'efficiency and effectiveness' measures. 'Care assessments' were central activities of the new care management regime. However, despite the apparently logical and ordered structures of the guidelines and formats for this new approach, Lloyd and Taylor (1995: 695) argued that social work continued to have its assessments and decisions challenged by the legal profession and castigated in the media with its practices perceived as 'muddled and *ad hoc*'. The problem, as many academic critics maintained, was that assessment in social work was being wrongly conceived and applied. Assessment, they argued, should not be seen as an unproblematic information-gathering activity (Stevenson, 1989) but as a *process* of reflexive interactions that required a critical awareness. Dalrymple and Burke (1995: 123) explain these reciprocal interchanges and negotiation this way: 'As practitioners we must be aware of ourselves in the assessment process and how both we and the service user will inevitably change. That means that we can be in the positions of Participant and Observer which has been described as reflexivity.'

This more sophisticated understanding is becoming recognised within the policy debates for the future directions of social work. At the beginning of a new century, the roles and tasks of social work in the United Kingdom are once more under institutional scrutiny and government review. The profile of assessment within a discussion paper to inform the early stages of this latest debate in England (Blewett et al., 2007), is similar to that found in the review carried out in Scotland (Scottish Executive, 2006). Assessment is cited 40 times in each document and is integrated within complex, conceptual arguments and far-reaching proposals. However, despite the 'new vision' of assessment as a reflexive process and dialogue between partners (Dalrymple & Burke, 1995; Clifford, 1998; Butler & Drakeford, 2005; Cooper, 2006), the pressures of marketisation and increased 'efficiency' continue to prioritise assessment as a 'product' where the end result often shapes the means by which it is achieved.

The past twenty years have witnessed the production of a great many 'frameworks' for assessment in all fields of practice in the United Kingdom. A recent systematic review of English language textbooks and frameworks on assessment in social work found that 'all of the frameworks, and 13 of the 16 textbooks, were written for audiences in the United Kingdom or particular countries therein' (Crisp et al., 2005: 63). The 'social work assessment', as in 'doing an assessment', can often seem to have become solely a task or end-product for social workers to carry out. In other words, there is a tendency for assessments to be defined by the parameters of an assessment procedure or format. Once the form has been completed, the appropriate information gathered, and the criteria for service eligibility ascertained, then the assessment has been done. The tendency towards standardisation and regularisation can lead to a misleading and false simplification that sets out to regularise and standardise some of the complexity. This is often coupled with the espoused aim of being 'comprehensive' and 'fair' (Department of Health, 1988, 2000, 2003) or, in line with the current policy towards integration children's of services, to be as far as possible, 'common' across agencies (Department for Education and Skills, 2005). The underlying assumption often seems to be that progress towards capturing these qualities within policy and procedural guidance will straightforwardly translate into best practice in undertaking assessments. If only things were that simple.

There are clearly some arguments in favour of 'ideal descriptors' and 'good practice guidance'. For example, the recent SISWE guidance in Scotland (2007) makes it clear that assessment is 'a process, not a one-off event'. But there can also be critiques of the effect upon professional practice from the increasing emphasis placed upon regulatory frameworks and standards (Preston-Shoot, 2001; Cooper & Broadfoot, 2006). A problem that arises from procedures for 'best' practice is that set against such ideals, the skills and strengths of everyday practice realities are often not recognised. Or, in comparison, they may be seen as somehow not measuring up. This can lead even experienced workers to doubt their judgement and worry about whether they somehow 'missed something' in an environment where the tacit expectation is that *all* information has to be gathered and *all* factors have to be considered. This can be regarded as not just an unhelpful and unrealistic expectation, but as practically impossible. In my discussions for these chapters (the methodology of how they were prepared can be found in Chapter 5), the social worker, Sally, put some of her worries surrounding assessment like this:

> It's like a performance anxiety – you can feel as though unless you produce some thing very good you don't produce anything at all. I used to worry too much that it had to be 'good'. If it would come to me out of the blue that I had missed one point from a risk factor for a case conference report, even though I had done it, I would want to go back and put it in. And you can't ... that's not a healthy pride in work ... that's a performance anxiety.

Perhaps the most fundamental challenge of the CBP critique, is to the tenacious assumption that seems to underpin Sally's performance anxiety; the belief that there is an objective 'best' practice, somewhere 'out there', separate from the situations and realities of everyday practice, that is being constantly updated by official best practice guidance, and against which social workers have to be judged. The misconception that follows from this erroneous assumption is that the essence of this 'ideal practice' can be captured within increasingly detailed protocols and schedules. It is this belief that underpins Sally's worry that every risk factor has to be covered in order to be 'correct' and measure up to the ideal. This fear of being found wanting and of being left behind by the zeal of 'updating' (Bauman, 2005) is antithetical to the creative approaches to negotiated relationships, meaning-making and knowledge construction taken in this book. In contrast, a CBP approach to social work sets out to identify what social workers do well as a counter-argument to some of the anxieties of measuring up to unrealistic and unattainable performance expectations.

THE INTERVIEW AND THE ANALYSIS

This section illustrates how assessment, as an implicit process of forming social work judgements, can be seen to pervade a social work interview. Sally's interview with Adam from the previous chapter will be
picked up where it left off and the dialogue used to explore some of the
subtle and complex negotiative skills and strengths embedded within
that example of social work practice. Processes of interpersonal
engagement, negotiation and change are highlighted and examined.
We can approach this through Sally's words as she offers one aspect of
her recollections with me about starting this interview:

BC   so, you've invited Adam in to the office having discovered that the
      family had 'merged' in the interim?

S   yes, and I've seen Jane by this point and my agenda isn't, necessarily,
      to get him out ....

BC   because ... ?

S   Jane wants him back – there'd been a lot of 'sorry-stuff', like, you
      know, 'I'm sorry', and sometimes when you find in families where
      they think that they've made their peace and a new start, social
      services have 'had it' on imposition sometimes ....

BC   ... because things have moved on?

S   things have moved on – *they* think ...

Sally's comments in this brief dialogue capture an interesting illustration of some of the key dilemmas of the 'authority role' within statutory social work. The first part reflects the realities of mainstream
social work in the United Kingdom, bounded as it is, by the statutory
duties and obligations enshrined within welfare legislation and complex systems of accountability. These powers can be understood
through Habermas' (1986) model of instrumental, communicative and
emancipatory 'human interests'. Sally's comments reflect the need to
strike a balance between the instrumental powers of her role [the possibility of imposition and 'getting him out'] and the communicative
professional duty to understand the service users' perspective [express-
ing lots of 'sorry stuff']. Through this, almost universal, tension
between the instrumental and the communicative in statutory social
work there remains the potential for the emancipatory. In other words,
Sally needs to try and create a synthesis through her work where the
possibility of change can be created.

The second part of this brief excerpt highlights a related but different
set of tensions. The new frameworks for codes of practice introduced

by the 'professionalisation' of social work through regulatory care councils have emphasised the priority that should now be accorded to service user's views and perceptions. However, Sally's comments reflect a profound difference of view. We saw in the first part of this interview how Adam felt that the 'situation' in his family, from his perspective, had changed. However, Sally is alluding to a common social work assumption in these situations. This is that the 'real' issues, such as any underlying interpersonal family relationship problems that may have led to the 'crisis' and the social work intervention, probably have not moved on at all ['things have moved on – *they* think']. These are difficult issues of professional versus 'lay' perceptions. If a family feels it has gone through a crisis and their way of coping with it is to 'put it behind them' – what is the legitimacy of a social work perspective that interprets this as an avoidance tactic and asserts that families should 'confront' issues or 'work through them'? Some writers have drawn upon the ideas of Foucault and criticised this approach as being indicative of a 'Psy complex' (Rose, 1979) where problems in living are interpreted as an indication of psychological deviation from some assumed normality. On this view, social workers and other welfare workers are seen as 'socialisers' to help people behave within this social norm (Ingleby, 1985). However, a more sympathetic view of the value of professional social work might argue that a modern welfare state has a duty to intervene in private lives where there may be vulnerable people at risk of abuse and in need of protection. The art and skill of social work intervention is to work towards an inclusion of people in fine judgements and assessments about when to intervene and in what ways.

So, in this interview, 'things have [apparently] moved on' and it seems that the ability of the social work agency to 'impose' anything, or to exert any kind of authority or power in this situation, has perhaps also gone?

BC   ... which puts the Dept in a difficult position? Because the last contact you had, formally, was to draw up this written agreement, saying one thing, and life moves on and you're faced with the reality that things have changed. So you have to ... you got Adam back in to renegotiate this ... ?

S   ... renegotiate where we go from here really.

Therefore, the written 'contract' was a formal tool that may only have had relevance to or purchase on the situation *at that time*. It could still be important if the new situation warranted further action based on that approach. However, this is a judgement call that needs to be reviewed; the written agreement may not be so appropriate or useful as the situation has changed. The family appears to be now thinking and acting as though 'things have moved on'. The only real option is to negotiate new readings of the situation and try to engage Adam in a collaborative working relationship. There may appear to be an inevitable conflict about Sally and Adam's positions at this stage. Adam has just made a plea for why he cannot go along with the writ-ten 'agreement' to remain out of the household. Sally could immedi-ately reply to this – and a 'normal' process of conversation might expect this plea to be responded to – but Sally remains focused upon the professional agenda and reasserts the main rationale for a social work agency being involved. That is, an interest in risk reduction and an orientation towards problem-solving. This inevitably entails return-ing to aspects of behaviour that are unpalatable for Adam and to which he may, again, at some point react. Nonetheless, Sally cannot allow these core issues to go unaddressed and chooses this moment to re-introduce them.

> S   But ... what I'm interested in .... is, the next time that there's the reason [A- there won't be] .... For anger and confrontation ...
>
> A   there won't be a next time ....

Adam's immediate and categorical response is the common refrain of 'there won't be a next time'. This is the innocent, if not childlike, appeal to 'an authority' that Adam has 'learnt' and 'will be good from now on'. It is a very human illustration of how people often think and feel and the basis on which many of us wishfully anticipate our futures. However, there are clear boundary issues of the personal and the pro-fessional in this. On a personal level, Sally may feel convinced or want to be convinced by Adam. However, there is an overriding professional issue in that social workers cannot justify an assessment of risk based on one person's statement of intent; however heart-felt and however much that person may really believe it at the time. The temptation to respond to Adam's unequivocal statement has to be resisted, as it is a cul-de-sac. There is no way in this interview that Adam can 'prove' his statement or that Sally could be convinced. Part of the skill of social work interviewing is to recognise these dialogic dead-ends; not to respond to everything that is said, when it is said; but to be free to change the direction of the conversation back to issues that have been raised and yet to be talked about. Adam's immediate and clear-cut reaction leaves little room for negotiation or exploration. So, once again, in order to keep the dialogue going, Sally avoids a potentially unproductive confrontation about Adam's claim at this point and changes tack to an earlier issue.

> S   what I was getting at … coming back to what you were saying earlier, that I was saying 'give her a free rein' ….

This is returning to Adam's powerful 'codswallop speech' in the previous chapter where he put Sally in the position of saying something and holding a view that was not accurate. However, Sally did not immediately confront this at the time. To have done so would have risked getting sidetracked into an argument that was really besides the point; would have been a battle about a parenting values position which would have been too much about her views, regardless of whether it was correct or not; and may ultimately have been counter-productive. Better to let Adam give vent to his frustration about how he felt he was being perceived wrongly. However, Sally 'held it in mind' to return to the issue later in the interview, which is now. Adam has made a claim that there 'won't be a next time' of anger and confrontation, so what will take its place? This is likely to be far more productive as an avenue for exploring positive solutions and ways forward in the future.

> S   no I don't believe that kids should have free rein [A agreeing 'nah'] to make all the mistakes that you don't want them to make, but, [pause] I think sometimes youngsters get into [pause to choose the words carefully] a habit of being contrary [A listening and agreeing 'yeah'] with a parent, a habit of fighting them.

Of course, is what Sally is saying about 'youngsters' also an implicit message about the parents of those youngsters? However, to have talked about 'parents' at this stage would have risked being heard by Adam as being too obviously judgemental about him and his wife as parents. Is there a sense in which, perhaps unconsciously, Sally is 'oiling the wheels of a working relationship'? This is a tacit social work communication and relationship skill; siding with Adam as a parent but at the same time delivering a message about 'youngsters' that applies as equally to Adam as a parent as it does to young people.

> S   So whether it's [A tries to interrupt but Sally carries on] whether they do their room immediately or in their own time …. or whatever it is …. there'll be a reason to push back at them [parents], to fight. And I think sometimes, that can get so that it's almost every day there would be lots of minor things ….

Sally has said this quite slowly and, for the first time, has insisted on having a small amount of space in the interview to make a reasoned judgement that, subtly, is tantamount to a bit of wise advice. The advice is listened to as it is implicitly both validating Adam's experience and offering an explanation. Also, because it has not happened much, and because Sally has exerted a small amount of power by talking over Adam's interruption to 'claim' this small amount of space, and because Sally has made this last statement quite slowly and deliberately, it has the effect of 're-balancing' the interchange. Adam now responds to this and begins to listen to Sally and more enthusiastically contribute to a discussion that is now more open to negotiation.

> A   ... and that's the only set rule she's got. Make sure your room is tidy when you leave it, cos I know what girls is like, try on 10 outfits before they go out and leave 9 on the floor ... that's the only stipulation and to come in on time. Basically she's got free rein in the house apart from that – she can sit in the bath for hours – she can sit up in her bedroom with her music blasting and annoying us down stairs; but we don't stop her as we were all the same and my parents used to whinge to me about music booming – but we know it's part of growing up so we let her go with that ...

'We know'. The 'we know' is not just referring to Adam and Leanne as parents – in this context it is also a 'we know' as in Sally and Adam agreeing together and coming to a shared understanding of the difficulties of growing up and of being parents. The change in the interview is subtle but marked; it can be easily missed and is often only recognisable in reflection afterwards. For Sally the judgement about when to claim some space in the interview and offer advice is almost certainly at the level of intuitive expertise (Atkinson & Claxton, 2000) or what has also been described as unconscious competence. As Adam begins to share his perspectives so Sally responds to keep the negotiation going. Eventually, the beginnings of a disagreement of values and parenting style begin to emerge again in the interview but now it's different as Adam is engaging in an adult exchange of views on the basis of a negotiation.

> S   but one of the things is, sometimes, I think, if we're arguing with somebody a lot, over whether it's room, going out, staying in, what time, ... is to actually say to somebody I've thought about this and I'm fed up with us fighting all the time about this. So we are just going to try it, just going to try it, for one week or two weeks or whatever you're saying, that 'when you're going out you tell *us*; we'd like to know who you're with; [A listening and agreeing – 'yeah'] and where you're going' and what reasonable time you think it is to be back by – whether it be a school night ....

A yeah but I know what she'll say, '10 o'clock', and that's taking the piss, in my eyes, that is taking the piss ... and she'll expect to go out from 4 o'clock, cos we don't do tea til 5 or half-past 5, she expects to go out as soon as she gets home, change, then come in at 10 o'clock, have a bath, have her tea, expect to have a sit down and watch a bit of telly ...

S no 10 o' clock's a bit late to come in and expect to have tea ...

A eight o'clock – half-past eight. I can't see what she wants to do after that time.

S I half agree with you there – the only thing is if she's got other friends about the same age who are all allowed to stay out until half-nine – ten, what it might be setting it up for, if she's the only one in the group having to come back significantly earlier, what it might be setting it up for every so often if she's feeling brave enough or angry enough about something [A listening – 'yes'] or silly enough because we're all .... spontaneous ... at that age [A yes]

'We're all'. The 'we're all' is a reflection back of Adam's words in his earlier contribution and it reinforces an inclusive offer; an invitation for Adam to build upon his personal introduction of childhood experiences in the discussion and join Sally in seeing this from a young person's point of view. The interview continues in this negotiative mode for a further 10 to 15 minutes as perspectives and strategies are shared about the difficulties of being a teenager and being a parent to a teenager. But, there can be a danger of assuming that an interview will continue to progress through predictable phases. From Sally's point of view, this negotiative aspect of the interview is an important indicator of things working well. Encouraging Adam to talk about these issues is one of the main aims of an overall assessment process as it contributes towards Sally's judgement about this parent's willingness to work towards avoiding future crises and potential risk to Jane. However, from Adam's perspective this may present unexpected challenges. Perhaps he feels that he has been skilfully invited into what is for him, and maybe for some men, unusual territory. As a natural part of this sharing and negotiation, Adam has made a number of disclosures about himself and his memories [not all included in the dialogue in this chapter]. He may be feeling a bit vulnerable. He has participated in what can be characterised as a 'feminine discourse' of sharing and he may not be used to this. Perhaps Adam feels that 'the point' of him coming to the office and being interviewed has been lost? For whatever reason, Adam suddenly changes tack and returns to his grievances about how he is being perceived by the social work agency and that, maybe, he feels have not been sufficiently aired or understood.

A   as a social worker you're taking, this is how I feel, I'm the 'bad boy' in all this because so-say I 'abused my child' – which is like grab her, maybe call her a slag which was, at a time when she was covered in make-up and she's 14 not fucking 18 [getting angry at the memory], I said 'get it off, I don't agree with it', stomping around the streets, that's why I called her a slag. I don't agree with me being classed as a child abuser for grabbing her off the sofa and chucking her up the stairs and, as she was running past, kicking her up the backside, that's not abuse. You see adverts on telly where you see blokes throwing their kids down the stairs; coming home from the pub pissed-up and laying in to them; *that's child abuse.*

S   yes, that's an extreme form of child abuse. Yes. I see it as an equation – I don't always look at what happened ...

A   so what would you say, on a scale of 1 to 10, my "abuse" is?

S   well, that's partly still what I'm trying to weigh up ....

Sally chooses this point to reassert the fact that Adam is actually being assessed. An implicit, and usually unspoken, aspect of any social work interview is that the social worker is always developing an assessment. Whatever else may also be going on, the social worker cannot help but use the communication and interaction towards their evolving under-standing of the situation and rationale for moving forward. The apparently innocent 'wondering and weighing-up' statement contains an implicit message of assessment that is all the more powerful for now being voiced as an explicit assumption. It is a key reminder that Sally is in a powerful position as 'the assessor' who has asked Adam in to the office to be interviewed on her territory. However, social assessment can be a delicate balance. If the social worker is in the position of main-taining that there is a 'problem', then in all likelihood they may simi-larly find themselves in the position of being expected to come up with a solution; the description entails a prescription. In other words, Adam has been challenging Sally's reading of the situation, and if he is to accept her problem description then he is likely to expect her to prescribe a solution.

The following dialogue contains the main excerpts from the last part of this interview and it illustrates a number of key issues. First, it contin-ues to show how 'real life' dialogue is not necessarily neat and clear. The discussion is about powerfully personal and important issues, feel-ings and values about how people live their lives and these are not easy to make judgements about or to put into words. Nonetheless, the 'meaning' is conveyed. Second, Adam is expressing a set of values and perspectives that is possibly from a different class and culture to Sally.

It is likely that Adam's comments would provoke reactions from most people. They give voice to common family dilemmas with conflicting expectations about ways of expressing anger, exerting interpersonal power and setting parental limits on growing children. However, taking a clear professional position or making a firm social work judgement in these situations is far from being straightforward. Third, the dialogue provides a further demonstration of how negotiation and assessment processes are integral to these interchanges as both Adam and Sally struggle to be clear about how to go forward and what could be agreed next as part of a plan of future action.

S ... it's not, to me, [speaking carefully and authoritatively] just about, how often it happens, or how hard a blow lands, clip round the ear [that Adam said he got as a child] or kick up the backside [that Adam said he gave to Jane] all those come in to it – to look at what sparked it. There's a whole equation of good and bad going in to the overall experience of the kid as to 'how they might end up', yeah?

A I've been with Leanne for 20 years and I've never hit Leanne. I've never done a clenched fist on Janie; a big poke in the arm or something like that or a clip round the ear hole and 'get up the stairs' or ... I don't think I've even slapped her bum or her legs ... And the 'so-called kick' wasn't like with my heel or my foot, it was like up the side of the back-side like you do with a naughty dog or horse or something like that ...

S I got the impression she was hurt by the kind of feelings that came out doing it, yeah? She was far more hurt by the look in your eye.

A yeah, because I'm angry! [Incredulously]

S and the things you were saying – she was more hurt by you calling her an f-ing slag, or wishing she wasn't your daughter ... that struck deep ...

A yeah, well, ... I know, I shouldn't say those things. It's just like 'heat of the moment stuff' innit, but, I'm being labelled as a child abuser and I fucking don't like it at all. I don't like it. Look where we're living – I must be one of the most mildest and sensiblest people you've had to deal with, yeah? We being truthful or no?

S In many ways ... I haven't seen you as fierce as you can or want to be ...

A You probably wouldn't like it as I can go fucking bonkers, to tell you the truth, but I've never made a fist.

S OK, Leanne wants you around but Leanne was also clearly saying 'I don't like it when it gets like that' ...

A   ... yeah, and I don't want to be like that no more. And that's what it's all boiling down to – I felt I should be the one that's being sorted out by *you*. You should be finding *me* classes, not going on about all this drivel of ... giving her more rein ...

S   no I'm not suggesting giving her more rein ... I'm just suggesting trying to find more sensible ways where the amount of conflict is reduced.

The interview ended shortly afterwards in an, all too real, series of mobile phone interruptions. Adam wanted to finish the discussion with a firm commitment from Sally to provide a 'solution' through anger management classes for him. He appears to have gone some way towards accepting that his angry reactions may be a part of the problem. However, this presented difficulties. Sally was not in a position to make a commitment as such 'parenting classes' are not easily available. Her position as a social worker representing the authorities' intervention into other people's lives has led into a, not unreasonable, expectation from Adam that a 'solution' to 'the problem' should at least be provided. In most circumstances, however, such services are not universally on offer. Sally's last comment is in some ways a fair summary reflection of the realistic aims of her intervention at this point and an appropriate point at which to end the dialogue.

This chapter, like all social work interviews, has to finish. Like most social work interviews, it has raised many interesting questions and provided some interesting, albeit inconclusive, answers. Social assessments are complex processes, for some of the reasons that this analysis of dialogue has illustrated. Sally has demonstrated some high-level skills of fine-tuned and responsive negotiation and done so with particularly uncommon, common-sense insight and diplomacy. In the face of some uncompromising challenges to her position, she has established a viable working relationship with Adam and balanced this with the maintenance of a primary focus upon her paramount duty towards the welfare of Jane. This and many other extraordinarily difficult balancing acts in social work have to be maintained in the face of people's resistance to being assessed. The quote, earlier in this chapter, from the 75-year-old service user's letter about being continually assessed from the cradle to the grave was clear; she did not like it. Adam, as illustrated in the dialogue above, strongly felt that he was being unfairly labelled as a child abuser. His view was categorical; he did not like it. Nonetheless, social workers have to try and find ways to productively work with this very human resistance to being judged. Often they do so very successfully even though the 'outcome' may eventually appear to be unsuccessful. 'Best' practices cannot be defined by a judgement of outcome. Social realities and the nature of social work interventions are too complex and the identification of 'outcomes' too open-ended and ambiguous for this to be a fair or representative measure of social work. Sally's, not unusual but quite everyday, interview is an example of best practice in the uniqueness of that interview. If she could have done better, she would have done. Who is in a position to judge? What implication could you draw from the fact that as Adam was leaving the office he planted a, completely unexpected, kiss on Sally's cheek?

REFERENCES

Atkinson, T. and Claxton, G. (eds) (2000) *The Intuitive Practitioner: On the value of not always knowing what one is doing* (Buckingham, Open University Press).

Barclay (1982) *Social Workers: Their Role and Tasks* (London, NISW/Bedford Square Press).

Bauman, Z. (2005) *Liquid Life* (Cambridge, Polity).

Blewett, J., Lewis, J. and Tunstill, J. (2007) *The Changing Roles and Tasks of Social Work*. A literature informed discussion paper. http://www.scie.org.uk/news/files/roles.pdf

Butler, I. and Drakeford, M. (2005) Trusting in Social Work, *British Journal of Social Work*, 35, 639–653.

Clifford, D. (1998) *Social Assessment Theory and Practice* (Aldershot, Ashgate).

Compton, B. R. and Galaway, B. (1975) *Social Work Processes* (Illinois, Dorsey Press).

Cooper, B. (2006) The Assessment Profession? *Unpublished PhD thesis* (Bristol, University of Bristol).

Cooper, B. and Broadfoot, P. (2006) Beyond Description and Prescription: Towards Conducive Assessment in Social Work Education, *International Studies in the Sociology of Education*, 16(2), 139–157.

Crisp, B., Anderson, M., Orme, J. and Green Lister, P. (2005) *Learning and teaching in social work education: Textbooks and frameworks on assessment* (London, Social Care Institute for Excellence).

Dalrymple, J. and Burke, B. (1995) *Anti-oppressive Practice: Social Care and the Law* (Buckingham, OUP).

Department for Education and Skills (2005) *Common Assessment Framework for Children and Young People* (London, Stationery Office).

Department of Health (1988) *Protecting Children: A Guide to Social Workers Undertaking a Comprehensive Assessment* (London, Hmso).

Department of Health (1990a) *Caring for People Implementation Documents: Draft Guidance CC18 Assessment and Care Management* (London, Hmso).

Department of Health (1990b) *Community Care in the Next Decade and Beyond: Policy Guidance* (London, Hmso).

Department of Health (2000) *Framework for the Assessment of Children in Need and their Families* (London, Department of Health – Social Care Group).

Department of Health (2003) *Fair access to care services* (London, Stationery Office).

Habermas, J. (1986) *Knowledge and Human Interests* (Cambridge, Polity).

Haines, J. (1975) *Skills and Methods in Social Work* (London, Constable).

Ingleby, D. (1985) *Professionals as Socialisers: the "psy complex"* (New York, JAI Press).

Lloyd, M. and Taylor, C. (1995) From Hollis to the Orange Book: Developing a Holistic Model of Social Work Assessment in the 1990s, *British Journal of Social Work*, 25, 691–710.

Middleton, L. (1997) *The Art of Assessment* (Birmingham, Venture Press).

Milner, J. and O'Byrne, P. (2002) Assessment and Planning in R. Adams., L. Dominelli and M. Payne (eds) *Critical Practice in Social Work* (Basingstoke, Palgrave).

Parton, N. and O'Byrne, P. (2000) *Constructive Social Work* (London, Macmillan).

Platt, D. (1990) Assessment and Case Management: Practical Implications of Implementing the Draft Circular in I. Allen (ed.) *Assessment and Case Management* (London, Department of Health / Policy Studies Institute / Association of Directors of Social Services).

Preston-Shoot, M. (2001) Regulating the road of good intentions: Observations on the relationship between policy, regulations and practice in social work, *Practice*, 13, 5–20.

Reid, W. J. and Epstein, L. (1972) *Task-Centred Casework* (New York, Columbia University Press).

Rose, N. (1979) The Psychological Complex: Mental Measurement and Social Administration, *Ideology and Consciousness*, 5, 5–68.

Scottish Executive (2006) Changing Lives: Report of the 21st Century Social Work Review. (Edinburgh, Scottish Executive).

Seebohm (1968) *Report of the Committee on Local Authority and Allied Personal Social Services* (London, Hmso).

SISWE and Scottish Executive's Assessment Working Group (2007) *The Assessment Triangle* http://www.sieswe.org/opencontent/assessment/index.html

Smale, G. and Tuson, G. (1993) *Empowerment, Assessment, Care Management and the Skilled Worker* (London, HMSO).

Specht, H. and Vickery, A. (1977) *Integrating Social Work Methods* (London, Allen & Unwin).

Stevenson, O. (1989) Reflections on social work practice in: O. Stevenson (ed.) *Child Abuse, Public Policy and Professional Practice* (Hemel Hempstead, Harvester-Wheatsheaf).

7 Best practice in child protection: intervening into and healing child abuse

SARAH LEIGH AND ANNE FARMER

Our aim in this chapter is to reflect on the nature and meaning of best practice in child protection. Collectively, we bring to this chapter many years experience of teaching and working with child abuse and protection. Sarah is a lecturer in social work at the University of the West of England, while Anne was at the time of writing a team manager in a social services childcare team. The social worker whose work we critically analyse within a best practice paradigm we have called Miranda, which is not her real name. All identifying characteristics have been changed to ensure anonymity. The case in question was taken from a social work team that dealt with longer-term 'children in need', child protection work and looked after children and young people. Members of this team also carry out Core Assessments using the government's national Assessment Framework for England and Wales (Horwarth, 2000). The team works in a multi-ethnic inner-city area. Team members were from different ethnic backgrounds, of varying ages and experience and both male and female.

ACCESSING AND RESEARCHING BEST PRACTICE

We gained access to the casework of this team initially through a series of focus groups. We began in an introductory session by facilitating a group discussion on the notion of 'critical best practice' (CBP) and gave some reading materials to the focus group members (e.g., Ferguson, 2003). Eight team members participated, although not all attended every focus group. In fact the team was busy with work demands and joined the three different focus groups when they could. At any one time at least four team members attended each one. Our research ethos was that the social workers themselves would be able to define their best practice examples. Within the three focus groups we asked social workers to describe one case in detail where they *personally* felt it was an example of their best practice. We felt the size of the groups and the research process was sufficient to have a rigorous practice discussion with enough continuity to make the choice of the one case valid and democratic.

Interestingly, they all felt that allowing time for this type of case analysis was a luxury, but as one worker commented: 'It's really helpful to focus on one case and be able to concentrate on good professional practice, instead of being driven by statutory functions and targets all the time.'

This view of social work as increasingly bureaucratic is reflected in Jordan's (2000) critical text on the New Labour government's Modernisation Agenda, where he argues that in the late 90s,

> Public sector social work had become locked into a style of practice that was legalistic, formal, procedural, and arm's length .... Social workers were thus primarily involved in allocating services and exercising surveillance through systems of rationing and control that made little use of interpersonal skills. (2000: 8)

Fortunately, the best practice examples we listened to did not mirror Jordan's pessimism. Even in the mêlée of a local authority inner-city office, workers do still truly engage with people on a very human level and there were many examples that emphasised this and echoed the more inspirational social work writing such as that of Jan Fook (2002). Such writing manages to integrate the contextual aspects of people's lives with their individual experiences and links this with the worker's subjectivity. It somehow illuminates the human part of practice and all that is so hard to define. This is astutely summarised by Cooper (2000: 18), who urges us to engage with service users with: 'A commitment to trying to understand their reality and communicating that understanding through responses that emphasise and entail such fuzzy unmeasurables (sic) as sincerity, trust, safety, hope and reassurance.'

The focus group members collectively chose a case study of Miranda's, which highlighted relational engagement, where language and nuance might *make or break* a brittle transaction. We had explained that it does not have to be 'perfect' practice, or have the expected or even desired outcome, but the nature of the values, the engagement and the quality of the language used is where best practice can be found.

BEST PRACTICE EXAMPLES FROM THE FOCUS GROUP MEMBERS

Before getting into our examination of Miranda's case, we want to provide some examples from the focus group discussions of the meanings of best practice. One social worker, a very experienced African-Caribbean woman, described with great passion her work with an angry and violent father who originated from the Caribbean. She explained how she needed to be direct with him, not accept his threats and intimidation, but that at the same time she knew:

> I needed to understand the causes of his anger, violence and distress and give him respect and understanding in his own right – I needed to not allow his angry behaviour to stop me being honest. When he realised this and some trust developed he could then calm himself and start to talk with me, rather than shout at me. Perhaps the fact we were both Black was significant in this encounter? We did acknowledge that perhaps we were not so very far apart in our life experiences. This helped on a human level of the sharing of a common experience. I could look him in the eye …. Perhaps this might be harder for a white worker? It's hard to know?

This example demonstrates the significance of a social worker moving beyond the fear of violence to the forging of a relationship, while doing so in a way, which is still safe for her. Equally it demonstrates that being black in 2005 in the United Kingdom is not an easily quantifiable experience and that this particular worker–user interface should not be approached through formatted responses. It illustrates the human connection between worker and service user can be the path to effective change, as echoed by Walker:

> A depressed black lone parent, for example, could be seen in deficit pathological terms with poor early attachment requiring a 'parental' figure to explore repressed feelings. A whole person approach however would perceive her as a survivor with resilience and positive characteristics despite a racist infrastructure. (Walker, 2004: 170)

Members of the focus group concurred that they had important skills and knowledge but that in effect your chief tool for practice *is yourself*.

127

As one commented, 'you must know yourself at least a little to contribute to building best practice examples'.

This is reflected in Parton and O' Bryne's constructivist text in which they posit an understanding of the 'other' as deriving from:

> The use of self, the nature of and quality of the relationship, the understanding of experience, the search for meaning, the importance of communication and the transactional nature of the relationship between the social worker and the client (sic) and an understanding of and use of language (is) central. (2000: 3)

The focus group agreed that there is frequently a deficit model applied in childcare where attention is generally focused on what went wrong (for example, within the Victoria Climbie Inquiry (Laming, 2003). Our analysis draws from a research literature that has begun to critically appraise this culture, using helpful and accessible frameworks which take us, 'Beyond Blame', the title of Reder and Duncan's book revisiting child deaths (1993) which seems to attempt to understand the complexities, emotions and worker/service users engagement in intervention which has tried to safeguard children. Professional development means we not only need to know what went wrong but we also need access to what went right, and to spend time un-picking the depths of the human interactions. It is a significant gap that there has not been a greater focus on good practice models to help students and practitioners. This is what the following example, drawn from the focus groups, attempts to do.

A helpful lesson in giving unpalatable information to service users, is this: Jed, a recently qualified white male social worker told us:

> I say, 'If I have bad news or difficult things to tell you, how do you best receive bad news? Is it together as a couple? Is it gently over a cup of tea? Is it with your mum there or on your own? Is it straightforward with brutal honesty? There may be things you will not want to hear and I need to know how you can best be prepared for this?'

This type of response has echoes of Barber's (1991) text *Beyond Casework* where he examines realistic methods of negotiated casework with involuntary service –users. Barber asks social workers to 'think aloud' with service- users, thus enabling language to mediate and soften difficult news. 'At least the worker will have demonstrated a willingness to negotiate and a desire to take account of the clients' (sic) right to influence the terms of the relationship' (Barber, 1991: 60).

Other tips on helpful ways to say things can be gained by the nature of open-plan offices, where every telephone call is heard. While we were outside of the focus group sitting in the team room we heard a social worker use a very simple technique of regularly asking, checking and re-checking, which she gave us consent to use:

> Gemma, tell me exactly what you mean by that,' and then, 'so, what you are saying is …' (Summarising and reflecting back) and, 'Let's just go back and see that we both understand where we are.' (Checking understanding) And, 'its not very good for either of us when we don't understand each other … it can sometimes make me feel anxious' (Self-disclosure and sharing commonalities)

Trevithick, referring to the dynamics of such communication and on the use of summarising, comments that 'It can help service-users to clarify their own thoughts and perceptions, and sometimes lead them to look at the issue from a slightly different angle' (2000: 97). Members of the focus groups also thought that guidance for self-disclosure was a tricky area, in relation to which Trevithick observes:

> The general rule is that self-disclosure should not occur unless it is in the interest of the individual seeking help … It can be invaluable to people who feel isolated and alone in their suffering … this can help to break down some of the shame and guilt. (2000: 106)

Equally useful practice advice from a focus group member was that the worker ideally assumes a *position of inquiry* (in an investigation) rather than a *position of judgement or condemnation*. So the kinds of words used might be:

> To the parent (s):'Can you explain to me why you think we are worried?' Or to the children:'have mummy and daddy told you why I come to see you'? 'What have you told your Mum, Dad, Nan and friends about my visits?'

These simple questions check understanding, help people to think through the other's position and role, allow time to stand back and be slightly more objective, and they might begin the engagement in a process of *equality* implicit in best practice. There are key moments when a meaningful working relationship can be forged or can flounder. It is part of building a knowledge base of tips of best practice to enable practitioners to provide careful explanation of 'how you work in your own unique way'. Thus another focus group social worker says to service-users at the first meeting:

> These are the things that I do as a social worker. Sometimes I will write to you, sometimes I may ring, and sometimes I may just call in, and you need to know this. As part of my job it is very important that we talk to each other and that there is honesty, and you need to say if you don't think I am being straight with you.

This indicates that although the social work role is imbued with certain status, authority and power, practitioners can still encourage service users to use their agency creatively, with recognition that resistance is a natural response to feelings of powerlessness (Foucault, 1977). Knowing this only magnifies the complexities of each transaction, but crucially allows us to value social work as *art* rather than *science* (England, 1986) and as a project of life-long learning, noted by one focus group social worker as, 'The more you know the less you know.'

APPLYING A CRITICAL BEST PRACTICE PERSPECTIVE TO MIRANDA'S PRACTICE

On completion of the focus groups we arranged to meet Miranda several times to analyse the work which took place over a period of 12 months to move the case in question from high-risk child protection to reduced risk and finally removal of all three children's names from the United Kingdom Child Protection Register. Miranda is an experienced white social worker with teenage children of her own. We needed to facilitate Miranda's unpicking of the details of what she considered to be an example of her best practice and why. Our task (initially shared with the focus group) was to repeatedly ask: 'Why did you feel this was good practice?', and, 'Could you consider this to be an example of your best practice and why?' We focused on what was actually said, and then encouraged an interpretation of the words used.

Miranda was pleased to gain recognition of her creative, effective, sensitive and professional work with a complex and high-risk case. This mirrors a constructivist approach being literally, 'to build, put together', and to, 'have a useful purpose' (Parton and O'Byne, 2000: 3; see also Barry Cooper's chapters, this volume). The value of 'rediscovering' her practice through the examination of what was *actually* said and *what was actually done* enabled her to illuminate her best practice. This is the 'situated' practice spoken of within a constructivist framework.

LEGISLATIVE FRAMEWORK

Miranda took the case on under legislation determined by the1989 Children Act. Within this legislative framework, two key principles apply: the welfare of children must be of paramount importance, and keeping children within their families and communities must be promoted. Both were key themes that informed her work. Following the child protection investigation (under Section 47 of the Act) and the placing of all three children's names on the Child Protection Register, Miranda's task was to complete a Core Assessment using the Assessment Framework (DOH, 2000; Horwath, 2000). This framework clearly situates the child or children as the central focus for the work. Nevertheless, with very young children, as in this family, the assessment of supportive and protective factors versus adversity and vulnerability factors tends to be gleaned through engagement with the carers/parents. Miranda identified the impact of parental history and the views of relevant professionals and wider family as significant to the assessment (DOH, 2000). She was also adamant that although the father, Andrew, might well be the perpetrator, her ethos was to work with *both* parents and attempt to understand each person's story, their history, to hear their account and record and recognise their feelings.

This child-centred but father-inclusive approach was a tenant of Miranda's practice. She said:

> After all, it is not so hard to plan your visits to coincide with the dad being at home, or to see him separately to begin an engagement, or to at the very least respond to him as a person with an interest in his family his children and the knock–on possible losses, pains and humiliation that he might have to encounter through the process of intervention and assessment.

The importance of working inclusively with all family members, including fathers, in the way that Miranda did, unless there are compelling reasons not is increasingly recognised as best practice (Ferguson & Hogan, 2004). And it is CBP too as it involves an awareness of issues such as gender and power.

FAMILY BACKGROUND

The family lived on the outskirts of the city, and both parents were from educated, middle-class families. The family consists of, Andrew, the father, aged 40 at the time of the investigation, from a comfortably off family, which he experienced as 'cold and unemotional'. Andrew worked as a landscape gardener and had a degree. He had one sister, here called Sheila. Miranda's assessment of his family of origin was that it was, 'high in criticism and low in warmth' (DOH, 1995). Andrew did not feel affectionate or loving towards his parents, but had maintained a good relationship with his older sister.

Sandra, the mother, was 38 years of age at the time of the involvement. She had a Maths degree and worked in finance. She was raised with four siblings in a home she described as, 'educated, had books and there was an expectation that you worked hard at school and went on to university'. She had regular contact with her parents and siblings and felt warm towards them. They had been married for 12 years, and had been unable to conceive children. Sandra had experienced many fertility problems.

RECENT EVENTS IN THE FAMILY

In an emergency the couple were asked to look after their paternal nephew and niece, Matthew aged 4, and Alison aged 2, following a crisis in Andrew's sister's family when her partner left. This had been a violent relationship. Sheila's long-term mental illness became very acute and she was unable to care for her two children. The children had experienced significant physical and emotional neglect and as a result of the child protection investigation and subsequent multi-agency action plan (social services, police and health) it was proposed that the children should be cared for by Sandra and Andrew to keep them within their extended family (Children Act, 1989). Andrew and Sandra were in agreement with this plan and after six months, when it appeared the children had settled and Shelia was in agreement and working with the plan, the case was closed. The children's father had Parental Responsibility under the Children Act 1989 but could not be located despite considerable effort.

The arrival of two traumatised young children sapped Sandra and Andrew's time and energy, but, after caring for the children for six months Sandra became pregnant and Jamie was born healthy and well. At fourteen weeks Jamie was admitted to hospital following a urinary tract infection. Bruises were found on his upper arms and a skeletal survey identified a green-stick fracture to the humerus. The explanation offered by the parents was that Andrew had got up several times during the night, as Jamie would not settle. He recalled he had 'picked Jamie up roughly'. From the multi-agency child protection investigation, the previous social worker's (not Miranda) assessment was that Andrew had begun to feel marginalised because of the time and demands all three children had placed upon Sandra. He told the investigating social worker I feel useless, incompetent and completely exhausted all the time with the kids. It's even worse for Sandra so I feel I shouldn't complain.'

Andrew chose to leave the family while the early assessment work was done, and to allow Matthew and Alison to remain there because professionals thought that they should not be moved again. Support workers engaged with Sandra and the three children daily and practical, tangible help was established for the family. Andrew visited regularly and the maternal grandmother was present during his visits at Andrew's behest, as he had lost confidence in his parenting.

Miranda accepted the case following the initial investigation and began her 'core' assessment. Matthew and Alison had been with Andrew and Sandra for 19 months and Jamie was four months old. Miranda was required to make a thorough assessment of protective and risk factors and she re-emphasised to the focus group that she needed to involve Andrew *actively and positively* from the start:

> Focus is often on the mother but it is equally important to understand fathers or other carers, who are important to the children. I made a conscious effort to ensure I made arrangements to see Andrew as well as Sandra. He was after all in his own trauma, out of the family, under investigation, and possibly at the end of his marriage and family life.

Miranda was therefore, keen to enact her belief that men were often 'discarded' in social work with children, and this angle is reflected in some more recent literature (Christie, 2001). Scourfield (2003) questions the relational aspects of working with men, that because of the dominant way motherhood and fatherhood are socially constructed, men will tend to be excluded on the belief that they are not 'natural' carers whereas woman/ mothers are included in social work interactions and relationships because they are seen in those terms. These ideas are debated within Ferguson's writing as well (2004). Miranda's view was that promoting this work with Andrew and more generally with fathers is vital to twenty-first-century best practice in social work in safeguarding children and promoting their welfare.

Both parents co-operated with the investigation, but felt angry and powerless about its process. Although Andrew acknowledged responsibility for the injuries, he had been hostile to further exploration with the original social worker who was trying to assess his feelings and attitude to his children. This appeared to be a personal feeling, since he then engaged well with Miranda. He also felt angry towards his sister who he felt in some way to have provoked this family crisis. Sandra told her health visitor that she felt isolated and overwhelmed by the demands of the three children, particularly in relation to Alison and Matthew who appeared to have behavioural problems. Andrew had been working very hard building up his own business and could not be at home very much during the day.

The Case Conference had decided that the three children's names should be placed on the Child Protection Register under the category of physical abuse (HM Government, 2006). Given the seriousness of the injuries to such a young and non-mobile baby, and the complexity of the family make-up, Miranda appeared the obvious choice of social worker when the case was transferred. She had understanding of both child protection and children placed in substitute or kinship placements (Triseliotis., Shireman and Hundleby, 1997) and seemed well placed to assess the children and their current family context. The task was to work with the family and reduce the level of risk, thus enabling the children to remain at home. The removal of Matthew, Alison or Jamie was not considered at this stage.

Miranda had a secure knowledge base in the areas of permanency (Triseliotis, 1997), attachment (Howe, 1995), resilience (Gilligan, 2001) and child protection (Corby, 1993). She had prior experience in residential and day care work, which enabled her to communicate with very young children.

Her identification with Sandra, as a woman of a similar age and background, highlighted the tension between possible self-disclosure as a means of engaging with the family and the temptation to over-identify and thus lose the element of objectivity needed when assessing risks to children. She warmed to Andrew, liked his directness and understood his despair and angry feelings towards the authorities (and her) at times. Miranda's intervention with the family lasted for 12 months, during which time the children's names were removed from the Child Protection Register after a period of nine months.

Factors which contributed to this were as follows:

1. The success of identifying protective family members who could provide a network around the children, and support the re-introduction of Andrew. This involved communication and negotiation with Sandra, Andrew, Sheila and key professionals.

2. The social worker also got to know each child individually and hear his/her stories.

3. Andrew asked for counselling through his GP and began to be able to talk about his bleak childhood experiences, which involved physical abuse by his own father, his guilt and anger towards his mentally ill sister and the deep despair he felt for his part in this crisis.

4. Sandra and Andrew were willing to work hard to tackle their problems and wanted to be re-united as a family. They accepted that there was a crisis and that they needed both emotional and very practical help to move on. Andrew accepted he had caused the injury to Jamie and he wanted to learn ways to express his feelings rather than bottle them up.

Thus, the key areas of work for Miranda were as follows:

(a) Initially assessing the dynamics of the wider family and identifying Sandra's key strengths for safeguarding the children while Andrew lived away.

(b) Explaining the system used to assess the family to ensure that Sandra and *Andrew understood the child-protection procedures. In this way Miranda felt she could help* them to channel and explore their resentment and anger by understanding what was happening at every stage.

(c) Supporting Andrew in his return to the family, including close liaison with his GP who had quickly got counselling for Andrew.

(d) Increasing Sandra and Andrew's understanding of Matthew's and Alison's confrontational behaviour, particularly around their past experiences of their mother's mental illness and their father ceasing contact with them.

(e) Coordinating a care package to support the family.

(f) Using her knowledge and expertise in advocating on behalf of Matthew at school, explaining the impact of his early experiences and 'reframing' his behaviour to teaching staff. She involved Andrew and Sandra in all these meetings.

(g) Explicitly using a theoretical framework of loss, attachment theory, social learning theories and an understanding of families as systems.

(h) Having an awareness of the social construction of motherhood and fatherhood and how that might make it easy to exclude Andrew.

This all highlights best practice in using theory in practice to help families to recover. Miranda involved them in this process by 'talking the theory'. For example, by saying to the parents, 'I wonder if the despair you say you feel is because this is like bereavement and you have lost something of your former life. It might help to recognise this loss … . Sometimes saying it out loud helps this process to begin.' This thoughtful and warmly human response to their anguish allowed them both to feel their pain and move on.

SOME PRINCIPLES OF MIRANDA'S BEST PRACTICE

Miranda regarded observation and recording as central to her (best) practice. She recorded what she actually saw (subjectivity recognised) acknowledging her value judgements but recording her professional assessments. She shared this with the family but ensured that she left the family able to function, leaving the children *more and not less* safe after each visit. Miranda placed emphasis on recording not as a 'back-covering' activity but as a means to assess risk. She said to Sandra and Andrew at a particularly difficult time and when the fear was strongest that they may lose the children:

> You need to be part of this process, Sandra and Andrew, and what I write you need to read even if it is painful. I will help you with that pain … these are the expectations the agency has of my role … . It doesn't mean to say you have to be perfect and at each stage we hope to see a way through it. … I will show you the assessment and explain how I have to collect the information I need. I will also show you the assessment forms so you are familiar with how the assessment will be presented to others. You will have a chance to contribute and comment and there are spaces where you can note your disagreements.

This is the voice of a confident and experienced worker, someone who has negotiated these difficult personal and professional boundaries, and who has learned clear and respectful language to perform her job. She also noted that basic courtesy and good manners in the early visits were crucial to developing an ethical relationship, such as waiting to be invited into the home, asking where should she sit, engaging with the children and checking times of day that might be better for family routines. It is best practice because it notes the pain, despair and sometimes apathy than can occur when people feel under siege, and a recognition that threat produces pain.

Miranda also gave us insights into effective 'open' questioning, 'Early on it is better not to express authority, but I use open questions such as, can you explain ... ? Can I ask about ... ? What sorts of things are on your mind at the moment ... ? Tell me why you think I am here?' Such questioning styles can be related to Smale and Tuson's (1993) exchange model. This is where the service user is seen as an expert, at least in their own unique circumstances, and that to draw out the optimum meaning from any exchange the worker asks and listens, using wide questions rather than closing and terminating ones. The nature of such communication attempts to recognise power but to try for equality.

Miranda also needed to find age-appropriate, stage-appropriate and non-frightening ways to explain to the children why she visited mummy (and daddy when he was living at home). She discussed with Sheila, Sandra and Andrew what could be said to Matthew and Alison and they agreed on: 'Sandra and Mummy's friend Miranda is coming to see us today, because Jamie has been ill. I think you are missing your Mummy and Daddy, and Uncle Andrew isn't living here so Auntie Sandra gets very tired.'

Miranda also understood that stressed carers can say things they would not usually say to their children, such as, 'When Miranda comes you need to be good or she might take you away.' Miranda counteracted the knowledge that this could happen by saying to the children,

> No, I am not coming to take you away – I am coming to talk to Auntie Sandra and Uncle Andrew and I go to see your mummy too. I also like to play with you two for a bit. I have to write some things down and this may help you feel a little better. I hope so.

This is clear, explicit and based on much past experience of working with parents and children under threat. While allowing for the fact that the removal of children must always be a possibility in child protection, it also gives hope to those involved. Miranda also felt she brought personal rather than purely professional attributes to this case. Among these attributes were, being a mother herself and knowing what it might feel like to face the possibility of having your parenting challenged. She also felt that her optimistic personality and her 'can-do' belief system helped, although she acknowledged that she had to be wary of being too optimistic and knew of the dangers of the 'rule of optimism' as described initially by Dingwall et al. (1983). This can place some families under undue pressure to cope when they feel they cannot (London Borough of Bexley and Bexley Area Health Authority, 1982).

Miranda's experience and intelligent practice enabled her to be warm in her assessment,

> I felt confident using a professional and evidence-based approach to asking difficult and intrusive questions. I think that this avoids a tick-box approach, which can leave both the family and the social worker feeling awkward – it basically lacks humanity.

And,

> I will try to believe the message that they (service users) are giving me and take it seriously. It comes from basic Rogerian principles, which I use in all my work – that is, it's better to start where people are and to belief there is a profound drive in everyone to try to "right" themselves and achieve what might be called a balanced, stable life. I have read quite a lot of humanistic social work theory and its method is to be warm and non judgemental, and ultimately believe in the person goodness, if at all possible. I was aware that for some parents the reality of family life is different from their expectations. I wanted to give them the opportunity to share this in a safe and non-critical environment.

Miranda was sufficiently experienced and confident to share something of herself with Andrew, Sandra and the children. The danger of *never* sharing personal information, and never taking the risk of self-disclosure can result in social work intervention simply as a one-way process with 'the other' and ultimately heightens the possibility of unwittingly taking our personal agenda into the family. So Miranda said to Andrew and Sandra at the beginning, 'I don't want to talk about myself, but I would like you know that I understand that life can be very difficult as a parent and as a family member.'

THE WORK DONE TO PROMOTE FAMILY SAFETY

Miranda' assessment was multi-professional in that it took account of the range of agency experiences and views and reached the conclusion that Sandra could protect the children with added support. She made this assessment through meeting the parents, the maternal grand-mother and the children, visiting the school, discussing Sandra's moth-ering with health and other professionals, and herself assessing the nature of the attachments. Sandra was able to express feelings of con-fusion and ambivalence towards her marriage, taking in Matthew and Alison and talk about the shock and disbelief at having a baby after all this time. This ability to talk about difficult feelings and emotions lead Miranda to believe that Sandra could be worked with to protect the children. This was based on her understanding of psychological theo-ries of loss, bereavement and the stages that are sometimes necessary to go through before reaching a better understanding of ourselves.

Miranda therefore established that Sandra would be the 'anchor' at this early stage. She would be given practical help involving collecting the children from school, some art therapy for the older two and respite with her own mum (their grandmother) for the Saturday night every week. This respite also allowed Sandra some much needed time with the baby.

Miranda also needed to engage Andrew who was in his own grief, hatred and fear. Arrangements were put in place to see Andrew sepa-rately and while he was having contact with the family. An awareness of Andrew's personal history, understanding of his relationship with Sandra and his attachments to both the baby and to Matthew and Alison were pivotal in determining whether Andrew could return home and on what basis. Miranda, with Andrew's consent, spoke to his GP, both asking her view, and updating her on her assessment. She identi-fied this element of the work as a good example of working with a professional who is often marginalised from day to day social work practice. Miranda, his GP and his counsellor, helped Andrew to look at his emotional responses to situations he found stressful and challeng-ing. Miranda identified this type of inter-agency working as part of her best practice. She felt there was a common understanding of the risks and concerns and an agreed plan of work.

It was essentially Andrew's choice to seek counselling through his GP, whom he liked and trusted. He voiced this very emphatically saying he felt that he wanted the counselling to be 'outside the social services loop'. Miranda decided it was better practice to respect this request as she felt counselling would be ineffective without trust. She equally realised that she had to give Andrew time to understand her role, and that she was not there to 'trip him up' or catch him out. This emotional journey was hard for Andrew as he thought he was about to lose everything. Miranda demonstrated best practice by understanding these processes take time and that Andrew needed targetted help to feel confident to parent again. She also instituted some specialist couples counselling because they said it felt hard to trust each other now. Thus, Andrew began one journey and Sandra another. Miranda and other professionals worked to promote safe parenting through re-building confidence and understanding.

PRACTICAL WISDOM AND SKILL IN BEST PRACTICE

Miranda had used the initial sessions with both parents to allow them to discuss their anger and frustrations. She understood that if people can 'ventilate' their anger it allows them to create psychological space to face reality. She effectively became a 'container' for their stress, anxiety and unpalatable feelings (see Celia Keeping's chapter, this volume). Such application of theory to practice, which was in the interests of helping this couple to face harsh truths, is a poignant example of her best practice.

While at all times theoretically aware, Miranda was clear that social work always requires a skilled, wise practical approach:

> Regarding my visits, I asked them what time was better for the children, for the adults and for my assessment? I visited in the evening at bath time and meal times when the family were tired and could be stressed, thus getting a snapshot of how they dealt with regular stresses of family routine; in the day time when Matthew was at school and Alison at playgroup, therefore seeing Sandra alone with the baby because this enabled me to observe and assess their relationship and attachment. I visited when Nan was there, to assess her role in protection and family safety. And it seemed very important to call when Andrew was there and when he was absent to get a sense of any difference in Sandra and the children's affect. I observed Andrew regularly with all three children, a difficult and inhibiting transition for him, but one where he said he actually gained confidence from my feedback. And finally I made visits to the school to get to know the children a little away from their parents and family.

Further evidence of such practical wisdom lay in Miranda's comprehension of the impact of her presence on the family. She spoke of this to Andrew and Sandra and explained why it was important to acknowledge their ambivalence at times towards her. After all, she was both someone whom they liked, and who demonstrated warmth and empathy, and yet she was also a powerful agent of a state service who could destroy their family life. Miranda suggested, 'I could feel their anger and it was tangible at times but I understood that this was not personally directed at me'. The understanding of such ambivalence has its roots in the psychodynamic tradition whereby the baby experiences both love and hate for their parent, who can feed, cuddle and make them warm and comfortable and can fail to respond to their cries (Froggett, 2002).

Above all, she stayed there when it all felt hopeless and they were angry with everyone. What makes this best practice is that she could *understand* that this anger is a normal part of the process (she understood the theory base). She also understood that working through these ambivalent feelings was an essential part of getting them to move on so that they could keep their children safe from harm. Thus, Miranda described just 'being there' and had the sense that they in turn felt that she had 'gone that extra mile'. This is where the personal and professional blurs to positive effect; where you will never find tools to measure the social work process, but you know it's good when it happens.

MOVING FROM HIGH RISK TO REDUCED RISK

The child protection case conference process under the DOH Guidance *Working Together to Safeguard Children* (1999) determined that review child protection case conferences should be held within 12 weeks and then six monthly intervals following the initial meeting. Miranda shared with Sandra and Andrew the conference reports in advance of the conference and ensured that they were aware of her views and the recommendations to the conference. The recommendation for de-registration after a period of twelve months work was agreed due to the depth of the assessment which had considered all aspects of the family's life alongside the practical and therapeutic supports in place.

Andrew moved back with his family after a year of living away. He now felt he understood where this 'well of anger' sprung from – he had had some frank exchanges with his own parents, who had sadly remained removed from this crisis. His counselling had enabled some old wounds to be spoken of and shared. Sandra saw him as a calmer, more open and a more confident man. She felt more supported and realised they were doing an 'amazing thing' to help to care for Matthew and

Alison. Miranda agreed that a contributory factor in the conference decision to de-register the children's names was Sandra and Andrew's contribution to the case conference process. By sharing her report, allowing them to make their own written contribution and explaining clearly the process of the conference Andrew and Sandra became equal participants. Miranda told us,

> Often parents attend conferences where professionals know each other and know the system, it's not surprising that parents are unable to make a full contribution. By discussing the conference process and making sure they were prepared they contributed rather than feeling this was something for which they were objects of discussion.

The final conference recommended further contact with Miranda for a period of three months and subsequent to this continued support from link workers and community care (practical and emotional help).

ENDING THE WORK – CLOSURE

Miranda saw this three-month period as preparation for her withdrawal, but she had already planned and spoken of this from the start of their encounter. On Trevithick's terms, thinking of endings from the outset constitutes good practice:

> This encourages us to think of our contact with people as complete experiences: as encounters that have a beginning, a middle and an end, all of which should be considered at the planning and preparation stage of the work we are about to undertake. (2000: 107)

One of her final tasks was to attend a meeting at the school to look at supports for Matthew whose behaviour was causing concern. She wanted to be sure that the school could identify a key member of staff to work with Sandra and Andrew. She shared her thinking with Sandra and Andrew. She then came to understand that this family had not grasped that the case was closing which meant that she was going. They 'thought' (maybe not rationally or consciously) that you have a social worker for life. So much of the service-user research of the past 35 years indicates that such misunderstandings are not only common but also often never actually resolved (Mayer and Timms, 1970; Rees, 1978; Howe, 1993; Beresford, 2002; Leigh and Miller, 2004). So, yet another small but vital sensitivity to the 'other' in Miranda's work was in not assuming that the service users had the knowledge and clearing up any misunderstandings.

Miranda also discussed with Sandra and Andrew how she should explain the ending to the children recognising that they too needed an explanation. Miranda wanted to ensure that the 'ending' was positive and seen as part of the family's progress by the children. She chose to visit the children to talk about 'different types of goodbyes', to help them understand the nature of her goodbye. She used Sandra and Andrew's knowledge of the children's relationships and people who had moved through their lives to help craft this final visit. By involving Andrew and Sandra, Miranda did not assume she occupied an 'expert position' in endings but that the family's knowledge and previous experience would be significant in the children making sense of her departure.

CONCLUSION

We started from an examination of what might constitute 'best practice' as defined by the team of workers themselves. This meant that best practice did not mean best outcome, but was an examination of encounters between social workers and their service users, which reflected the use of skills, knowledge and understandings. At the heart of what was seen as contributing to best practice was the quality of the interaction, which influenced the way communication progressed, the language that was used and recognition of the journey of both social worker and family during the process of intervention. How the relationship was defined, the use of self and the recognition of how it can be used to promote understanding between parent and social worker but with sensitivity to professional boundaries and the impact of disclosure was integral to this process.

Not assuming the position of 'expert' and treating the process of assessment as a joint responsibility of the social worker and family seemed important. This needs to be done by finding a careful balance between acknowledging the power behind the role and using a negotiated, 'permission' based approach, such as, 'I would like to talk to the children, what would be a good time?' Challenging the deficit approach to understanding social work encouraged our focus groups and the social worker on whose practice we focused in detail to look critically at their practice with a sense of optimism. We need to lend hope to the present and next generations of social workers who work in childcare, by providing examples of CBP to enhance their work and finally move way from the too-blaming, too-critical models that presently persist.

REFERENCES

Barber, J. G. (1991) *Beyond Casework* (Basingstoke: Macmillan).

Beresford, P. (2002) *System Should Be Shaped by Service Users, Community Care 7 – 13 March.*

Christie, A. (ed.) (2001) *Men and Social Work Theories and Practices* (Palgrave: Basingstoke).

Cooper, B. (2000) 'The Measure of a Competent Childcare Social Worker?' In *Journal of Social Work Practice* 14(2): 113–124.

Corby, B. (1993) *Child Abuse: Towards a Knowledge Base* (Buckingham: Open University Press).

Department of Health (1995) *Messages from Research* (London: The Stationery Office).

Department of Health, The Home Office and the Dept of Education and Employment (1999) *Working Together to Safeguard Children, A Guide to Interagency Working to Safeguard and Promote the Welfare of Children* (London: Department of Health).

Department of Health (2000) *The Framework for the Assessment of Children in Need and Their Families* (London: Department of Health).

Dingwall, R., Eekelaar, J. M. and Murray, T. (1983) *The Protection of Children: State Intervention and Family Life* (Blackwell: Oxford).

England, H. (1986) *Social Work as Art: Making Sense of Good Practice* (Allen and Unwin: London).

Ferguson, H. (2003) 'Outline of a Critical Best Practice Perspective on Social Work and Social Care' in *British Journal of Social Work* (2003) **33**: 1005–1024.

Ferguson, H and Hogan, F. (2004) *Strengthening Families Through Fathers: Issues for Policy and Practice in Working with Vulnerable Fathers and their Families* (Dublin: Research Report for the Department of Social, Community and Family Affairs).

Fook, J. (2002) Social *Work: Critical Theory and Practice* (London: Sage).

Foucault, M. (1977) *Discipline and Punish* (New York: Allen Lane).

Froggett, L. (2002) *Love, Hate and Welfare* (Bristol: Policy Press). Gilligan, R. (2001) 'Promoting Positive Outcomes for Children in Need: The Assessment of Protective Factors' in *The Child's World* by Horwarth, J (ed.) (Jessica Kingsley: London).

HM Government (2006) *Working Together to Safeguard Children* (London: TSO).

Howe, D. (1993) *On Being a Client: Understanding the Process of Counselling and Psychotherapy* (London: Sage).

Howe, D. (1995) *Attachment Theory for Social Work Practice* (Macmillan: Hampshire).

Horwarth, J. (2000) *The Child's World: Assessing Children in Need: A Reader* (London: NSPCC /Dept. of Health).

Jordan, B. with Jordan, C. (2000) *Social Work and the Third Way: Tough Love as Social Policy* (London: Sage).

Laming, H. (2003) *The Victoria Climbie Inquiry* (London: Stationery Office).

Leigh, S. and Miller, C. (2004) 'Is the Third Way the Best Way? Social Work Intervention with Children and Families' *Journal of Social Work* 4(3): 245–267.

London Borough of Bexley and Bexley Area Health Authority (1982) *Report of the Panel of Inquiry into the Death of Lucy Gates – November 1982* (London: London Borough of Bexley).

Mayer, J. and Timms, N. (1970) *The Client Speaks* (Routledge: London).

Parton, N. and O'Byrne, P. (2000) 'What Do We Mean by Constructive Social Work?' *In Critical Social Work* **1**. No 2 Fall, 2000.

Reder, P. and Duncan, S. (1993) *Beyond Blame: Child Abuse Tragedies Revisited* (Routledge: London).

Rees, S. (1978) *Social Work Face to Face* (Edward Arnold: London).

Scourfield, J. (2003) *Gender and Child Protection* (Palgrave: Basingstoke).

Smale, G. and Tuson, G. with Biehal, N. and Marsh, P. (1993) *Empowerment, Assessment, Care Management and the Skilled Worker* (London: HMSO).

Trevithick, P. (2000) *Social Work Skills: A Practice Handbook* (Open University Press: Buckingham).

Triseliotis, J., Shireman, J. and Hundleby, M. (1997) *Adoption: Theory, Policy and Practice* (Cassell: London).

Walker, S. (2004) 'Community Work and Psychosocial Practice: Chalk and Cheese or Birds of a Feather' *Journal of Social Work Practice* **18**(2): 161–175.

8 Best practice in family support and child protection: promoting child safety and democratic families

HARRY FERGUSON

The focus of this chapter is on best practice in child protection work combined with family support. Understandings of the complexities of practice with respect to interventions to protect children have increased significantly through studies which have represented the views of professionals and family members (Farmar and Owen, 1995; Thoburn et al., 1995; Buckley, 2003; Scourfield, 2003). Service provision in family support has also benefited from research and increasing theoretical sophistication (Gibbons et al., 1990; Dolan et al., 2000; Feather Stone, 2004). However, there is still little published work in this area which delineates best practice, where examples are provided of what is being done well and how such best practice can be learned from and developed. Turnell and Edwards' (1999) solution and safety oriented approach is distinctive in its attempt to develop a focus on strengths-based practice in child protection work. In what follows a best practice example of child protection work combined with family support is outlined in depth, critically analysed and offered as a basis for such learning.

THEORETICAL APPROACH AND THE SOURCE OF BEST PRACTICE

The theoretical approach which provides the main basis for my 'critical' analysis of the best practice profiled in this chapter draws primarily on the work of the social theorist Anthony Giddens. He argues that today we live in what he calls 'late modern' society where we all have new choices about how to live and who to be. 'Helping' practices like social work play an increasingly important role in enabling vulnerable people to choose well, and gain control of their lives, which involves learning about and changing the self and one's emotional life. In recent history (prior to the 1970s), people's identities were shaped by very solid social structures composed of the state, family and church which meant that people 'knew their place'. Men and women's roles were quite rigidly fixed as bread-winner and homemaker, respectively. Children were 'seen and not heard'. Heterosexuality was taken as the norm and all other forms of sexual and ethnic identity which deviated from being based around the married, respectable/middle-class, white family were seen as suspect, even pathological. For much of the twentieth century – until the emergence of critical perspectives that began in the 1970s at least – social work in child protection played a key role in enforcing these standards by trying to ensure that men worked and provided, and women kept their homes and children clean and decent (Ferguson, 2004).

Today men, women and children's roles are no longer so rigidly fixed. Women in general, now have the opportunity of a life to plan beyond motherhood, and have acquired rights to protection from abuse. This does not mean that all women get to fulfil such rights to protection and equal treatment to men, but professionals can no longer deny them without justification. Being a good father is now defined as much by being an active carer of your children as providing economically (Burgess, 1997; McKeown et al., 1998). The net effect is a new require-ment for openness and negotiation in intimate relationships: whether to marry or live together and have children; who does what, goes out to work, minds the children, does the housework and so on, all has to be decided by the couple. And as the children grow older, it involves them too. Such negotiation requires men, women and children to come to know and get what they want without denying others their equal rights. This demands self-knowledge and emotional awareness so that decision-making is true to feelings. Thus, for Giddens, the new 'intimacy' is now 'above all, a matter of emotional communication with others, and oneself, in a context of equal relationships' (Giddens, 1992: 139). This is borne out by Featherstone's (2004) work which shows the diversity of 'family' forms that typifies social work and family support work and the importance of using power constructively to work with such fluid relationships in creative, skilful ways.

Giddens argues that intimate relationships are consequently now organised on a much more democratic basis, and that this has given rise to what he calls the 'democratic family' (Giddens, 1998). Opinions vary about the degree to which democratic relations within families are becoming the societal norm (see, Jamison, 1998). In relation to social work, Garret (2003) argues that the evidence for such a change does not exist, and that the dominant pattern is for mothers to continue to be oppressed by social workers who regulate them according to traditional expectations of motherhood, and they carry an unequal share of domestic responsibilities. Holland et al. (2005) argue that state interventions can produce more democratic families to the benefit of children's welfare, but that this is restricted to models of intervention like Family Group Conferences (FGC) (for a detailed account of FGCs, see Dalrymple and Horan, this volume). For Holland, et al. (2005) promoting democracy is difficult to apply to statutory casework interventions by front-line social workers because of how the imposition of power and social control and telling parents and carers what they must do is so central to their function. A different view is taken by Featherstone (2004) and Ferguson (2001, 2003a, 2004), who argue that statutory child protection and family support interventions can and do promote democratic families. Children can now legitimately expect to be heard as well as seen. Social workers can use their powers to enable all family members to have the kinds of relationships within which children, women and men can live safe, more satisfying lives. At the heart of this is a process of 'individualization', and enabling people to shape a 'life of their own' (Beck and Beck-Gernshiem, 2002).

One consequence of this is the extraordinary growth that has occurred in recent years in therapy and counselling. Giddens argues that the essential role of such practices today is 'life-planning', helping people to face the new choices and dilemmas in their lives, and to develop the emotional awareness that is necessary to make relationships work. He refers to this as helping people to achieve 'mastery' over their lives. I shall argue in what follows, that promoting such life-planning and 'mastery' for service users is central to best practice in late-modern social work. This does not mean that there are no limits and controls on what people can do and be. Poverty, racism, sexism, disablism and other social divisions continue to create inequalities which severely limit people's life chances. Yet the perspective I outline here does have much in common with critical social work's traditional concern with issues of equality. It provides the basis for developing critical social work to include significant areas it has tended to ignore, including the 'self', life-planning, the emotions and democratic relations and families.

The case-study used here is taken from a research project which sampled 319 child care and protection cases reported to three Health Board social work teams in the Republic of Ireland over a three-month period and tracked them for 12 months. The research used quantitative methods to produce a 100 per cent sample of all child care and protection referrals made to the teams over the three months, which provided for an analysis of how the system processed cases, from the referral point to long-term outcomes. Qualitative methods were also used to develop a series of case studies in order to establish the deeper meanings of practice from the perspectives of professionals and service users. As many of the key actors as possible who were involved in the selected cases were interviewed, from the professionals, parents and some children, and the case files read. The case selected has been chosen because it typifies the kinds of work that is being done where the best practice involves the provision of combinations of services, in this instance home based (social work and family support worker), clinically based (child psychologist) and care based services (respite care for the children) (for a detailed account of the research, see Ferguson and O'Reilly, 2001). The practice featured here reflects best practice in how child protection and family support were integrated, and child safety, healing and democratic relations within the family were promoted.

THE REFERRAL AND RESPONSES TO IT

The case involves substantiated emotional abuse and neglect in relation to four children. The eldest – here called Joanne – was aged ten at the time of the referral and the three boys seven, five and two years. The family first had social work involvement three years previously due to allegations of physical abuse and neglect by the parents, here called Mr and Mrs Smith. Prior to the referral which set in motion the practice featured in this chapter, the case had been closed. The case-study is based on the interviews with Mr and Mrs Smith (separately), Joanne, the social worker, family support worker and the school principal, as well as the case file.

The referral to the social work department which led to the case being reopened was made by the school and centred on Joanne, whose behaviour at school was alleged to be extremely 'disruptive and aggressive'. According to the principal it was:

> very aggressive and very cheeky and very unusual behaviour. It was beyond what any teacher had to deal with. She would have kicked children in the stomach. I had children that ran away from school because of her ... She was hijacking the whole class and the teacher in her class said to me at the end of this summer, 'I blame her for my breakdown in health'.

The principal asked to meet with Mrs Smith to discuss these concerns and suggested the school seek further help, with Mrs Smith's consent.

He reported the matter to the social work department and also sought psychological support for Joanne – 'It was not just a problem for [Joanne], it was a family problem.' The social worker investigated the case and completed a Child protection Notification Form[1] and felt that there was some evidence of neglect and emotional abuse as: 'Mother shouting, critical and sarcastic with child, to the extent child visibly upset. Mother unaware of child's discomfort and continued laughing at the child. Child got angry and accused of lying by mother. This appears to be a daily occurrence' (case file). There was also concern about home conditions, possible domestic violence and the parents' general capacity to cope.

The children were deemed to be at 'high risk' at the time of referral. During the 12-month research follow-up period the case was re-referred alleging that the mother had hit the child. The social worker completed seven Child protection Notification update forms within 12 months. The overall outcome was 'confirmed emotional abuse'. As the social worker saw it, 'There is definite emotional abuse and it's very severe.' A child psychologist was introduced to develop a behaviour modification programme with Joanne at school and she was assessed as 'depressive and suicidal'. Respite care was also provided for Joanne and her eldest brother. One case conference took place followed by two review case conferences within a six-month period, at the end of which the case was closed for child protection concerns but left open for childcare concerns. Joanne was deemed to be doing well, and was due to be re-assessed by a psychologist.

THE PROCESS OF ENGAGEMENT

It was noted in the case file prior to this intervention that Mrs Smith 'does not like social workers, health board employees'. Initially, both Mr and Mrs Smith were adamant that they did not want social work or any other kind of intervention. They felt this way, in part, because of their past experience with a social worker, who, as Mrs Smith put it, 'never gave me a chance to explain myself. If I tried to say something, she thought I was hiding things and if I didn't say enough, I was still hiding things'. For Mr Smith, 'She was coming down asking questions, questions, but there was nothing coming back.' They felt that the social

---

[1] The Child protection Notification Form is the formal procedure in the Irish system through which cases are designated child protection and are administered and monitored by the Child Protection Notification Committee, a multi-disciplinary group of senior managers.

worker did not explore with the family what she could do to help them resolve some of the difficulties they were experiencing. Things got worse when one of the children was allegedly examined for sexual abuse while undergoing a medical examination. The parents both 'reared up' on the health board. The father said, 'I would not have gone near a social worker again and that is being straight and honest with you. I was very, very, wary and wanted nothing to do with a social worker.' Not feeling able to trust social workers meant that the mother could not actively engage with any formal support system, despite recognising the need for some help: 'I knew my little girl needed a psychologist. I couldn't come in here and say I think she might need someone to talk to. I thought if I do, they'll say I'm not looking after her and then bring me into a social worker.' Thus the parents developed an 'operational perspective' (Cleaver and Freeman, 1995) to child welfare which, while it protected them from undue interference from an oppressive form of social work practice, left them isolated and bereft of the kinds of support they and the children really needed.

While there are many voluntary service users in child care and protection work, intervention with those who did not request the service – 'involuntary clients' – present distinct challenges (Barber, 1991). The Smith case typifies how resistance can arise in some cases from problems with how the service is structured and delivered – the parents' dislike of the style and content of the previous social worker's intrusive, forensic, uncaring protectionist approach (Parton et al., 1997). But it also reveals a form of response and reasons for them which have hitherto been much neglected in the literature of social work and child welfare, where psychological and emotional problems within the client/service user block them from forming meaningful relationships and attachments, with professionals as much as with family and friends (Howe et al., 1999; Ferguson, 2003b). Thus, we need to learn about the best practice involved in the process of engagement of resistant clients in situations where this has succeeded.

Social workers and other professionals have the difficult task in such cases of assessing the needs of the children while at the same time trying to engage a mother and father or other carers who do not want intervention. The social worker recognised that Mrs Smith was 'quite hostile you know, a lot of the time. With the mother very frightened of social work involvement and not trusting, the issues had to be explored very sensitively'. The family support worker found Mrs Smith 'extremely hostile and she used foul language. She did not want to know about social workers'. When the social worker made her first home visit, by her own account, even though she was expected because of the negotiations with the school, Mrs Smith started 'crying' and asked, 'What did I do now?' The social worker did not push the issues too far and arranged to call again the following day. Facilitating this process meant, 'trying to understand where the mother is coming from, and the issues she has gone through. You can actually work when you know where it's all coming from, you're going from what their issue is as well'. This skilled, empathetic approach by the social worker worked well to win over the confidence of the mother, who was adamant that, 'You need someone that is going to sit down, listen to you and not judge you, if you have a problem.'

Even to get to the stage of addressing parenting issues, the family support worker worked hard to build a rapport with Mrs Smith which took some time:

> Maybe two visits a week for about a month until I drank her coffee, smoked her fags and she was quite comfortable with that. She gave me a load of personal stuff which was not really relevant to our work but it gave a bigger insight on her as a woman and as a mother and partner to the father and that was the way we worked it to try and help the mother help the children.

The mother and father's lack of engagement with professionals was viewed within a context which took their feelings about their past experience with social workers into account and which enabled them to express their fears and unhappiness and feel heard. This cleared the air and the process of a more democratic relationship developing in this instance had begun. This is quite different to an approach which would view the Smith's struggle to focus on the problems at hand as a simple unwillingness to engage with social workers and simple proof of their incapacity to parent, which could then lead to a judgemental, unethical approach.

Holding the relationship together required an on-going delicately skilled approach by the social worker:

> When you go in to address an issue, she will try and dismiss it or keep talking about something else, then if you say something the wrong way with her you can get the door. I know her now and know how to say something. She's getting there you know. Before she used to see me and she was so petrified that her mind was racing. She might hear the first sentence and that was it.

The family support worker was also very aware of how Mrs Smith struggles to engage herself in the listening process, and worked to ensure that child protection issues were addressed while at the same time trying to *understand* where the mother is coming from. For example, the family support worker told Mrs Smith, 'When I am talking you are way ahead of me, you are thinking of answers plus another question at the end, so could we just talk today about [this problem] and that would bring her back to parenting.'

At first Mrs Smith found it easier to talk to the family support worker rather than the social worker. Both professionals were aware of this and used it skilfully and strategically to their advantage. As the social worker recounted, 'Sometimes it can be easier for the mother to hear things reinforced from the family support worker. She's less of a threat, so in the beginning she was able to focus in with the mother regarding parenting and stuff.' The mother was however aware of these tactics: 'I was lucky, because the social worker really did work with me, but she sent in the family support worker first and she softened me up to be honest.'

IMPROVING PARENTING SKILLS AND THE PRACTICE OF INTIMACY

Thus a main focus of the work was to promote self-knowledge, emotional health and personal development as part of improving parenting skills. As the social worker said, 'Their parenting is so disastrous that they really don't know how to start or what good parenting is. So it has to be done at a very slow level. It may take up to a year to discuss issues, even the most important issues. One step at a time.' Developing her capacity to help the children and helping her in her own right also meant focusing on Mrs Smith to make her feel better about herself. 'I felt she needed to like herself more, because she did not like herself' (family support worker). Building the woman's self-esteem was done by encouraging Mrs Smith to take care of her appearance. 'She did little things like get her hair cut. She had no teeth and then she went and had her teeth done. She began to look after herself a little more ... it was much more positive stuff.'

The family support worker used small sections of a parenting book in order to address parenting issues. She also actively modelled how to physically care for a child, feeling that the mother, 'was not really aware of the emotional stuff her children needed. She found it difficult to touch her daughter. ... I could talk till I was blue in the face about nurturing and until the mother saw me nurturing it was no good until I left her to think about it'. The family support worker would give the daughter a 'hug' when she met her, in the presence of the mother.

Another example of teaching the practice of intimacy by 'modelling' is apparent in how the school principal observed that, 'There'd be very little affection shown to the daughter by the mother, you know even how her hair looked.' The family support worker agreed with this, 'Her mother was not taking care of the daughter's hair and it took maybe a month and then I went in one day and did the hair' and then told Mrs Smith to 'Go down to the pound shop and get a bottle of oil and treat her hair and you can use half of it yourself.' This was, the family support worker said, 'turning a negative into a positive in a very simple example'. Another such example she gave as: 'The mother would focus on the daughter's "got seven spellings wrong out of ten" and I'd say, "Brilliant you got three right, get four right next week".'

DIRECT WORK WITH THE CHILD

Another feature of the best practice was the direct work the social worker did with the child. She met with Joanne every week for five months, and after that every two weeks. Joanne was allowed to set the agenda about when she would meet the social worker and decide what they would talk about. Strategically, the child's mother or father were not made aware of what the social worker and their daughter talked about, unless it was a child protection concern that demanded limited confidentiality. In common with other children (Butler and Williamson, 1994), Joanne really appreciated this: 'I knew that what I said there was no way it was going to get out … that helped me express my feelings more.' Part of the social worker's aim was to improve parental competencies – or, more accurately, most often *maternal* competencies – by learning what was needed from the child's viewpoint. Joanne, for instance, told the social worker she was embarrassed because her mother was, 'Always roaring and shouting at her in front of her friends.' The social worker discussed this with the mother and daughter and 'a compromise was come too. Mum wouldn't do it, but she expected something from the daughter, that she would respond to the mother, fairly reasonably rather than ignoring her'. A key task for the social worker was to help Joanne get her message across to her mother. As Joanne said, 'She said she was a social worker to help me and things I couldn't say to my mam, she'd help me to say them to her.'

WORKING WITH TRAUMA, ANGER AND OTHER EMOTIONS

The social worker felt that it was Mrs Smith's 'behaviour that causes the problems and if the kids are to remain at home, it's her behaviour that has to change'. Mrs Smith had the same perception: 'The issue was me and my moods and my temper and how that was affecting the kids and how it was affecting my daughter in school.' Intervention was also focused then on how Mrs Smith could control her 'temper', as she explains:

> The family support worker was there to help me with losing my temper and how to cope with what if my daughter came in with a problem. Rather than say, 'Go away and leave me alone', I'd try dealing with it and if I couldn't, rather than shout at her, I'd say, 'Listen, give me five, I'll have a cup of coffee.' Whereas before if she came in, I would have said, 'If you don't go away, I'm going to murder you.' I would have slapped her. I would've lost my head.

Mrs Smith also recognised how the family support worker worked to increase her self-esteem while at the same time teaching anger-management skills, by 'Just words of encouragement, you know, [for example], nobody's perfect. I always thought everything was my fault, I was stupid and silly, the family support worker showed me that I'm a person for meself.' Joanne spoke of how her mother has changed because of this type of work. 'If she was going to say something, she stops. In her mind I'd say she says, "No, I'm not going to shout, the family support worker told me not to do it' and she'd walk out of the room before she'd explode." Moreover, Joanne conceded that she also 'exploded' against her mother and that the social worker helped her overcome this 'problem'.

> She told me, it just wasn't worth it, put your foot down and say, 'you're not going to explode' and just keep your head and think what you're saying even if she's exploding. I'm [now] able to keep control. I'm not as bossy as I used to be.

This is intervention work at its very best: through the therapeutic process the child not only gets support to deal with the impact of her own trauma at being poorly parented and is rendered safer, but she is also helped to learn anger management and emotional literacy. In addition to being helped with her immediate problems, the longer term child protection agenda was secured through this work. As the family support worker notices, 'the daughter has been empowered and if something does happen or she is very unhappy, she, as a child, knows where to go [to get help]'.

A powerful part of Mrs Smith's narrative was an experience she had ten years ago (17 years of age) when she was raped and became

155

pregnant with Joanne. She did not tell anyone at the time, including her partner, who until recently did not know who the biological father of Joanne was. Mrs Smith carried around this 'secret' for over ten years and considers it to be part of the reason why she acted abusively.

> The father didn't know I'd been raped. He didn't know what was making me carry on like this. It was breaking me up, so I contacted the social worker, explained the whole lot to her and said will you work on it with me, yourself and the family support worker. That took so much off my head. I was able [then] to work on other issues that I needed to sort out.

For Mrs Smith, the social worker's totally non-judgemental approach when she told her about the rape made all the difference and 'that made everything seem as if, God, why hadn't I been able to meet this woman ten years ago and tell her this and then it wouldn't have been so bad'. For the social worker, 'Because the daughter is a product of rape, that is underlying a lot of how the mother sees her daughter. Because the mother can love the boys so easily, so as those issues are addressed, that relationship will improve.' The school principal also referred to how she sees Joanne's problems at school as being linked to the family structure. 'In the daughter's case, it's definitely the whole family thing ... the father he's not the daughter's father. And the daughter would talk about that in school.'

The social worker and family support worker gave a lot of support to the parents around this time. As the social worker explains, 'that took, I'd say, about three months from start to finish, between father and mother coping and preparing. He finding out the first time who the daughter's father was and coping with that and moving on to the daughter, to tell the daughter'. In order to facilitate the father in coming to terms with the issues, the social worker and family support worker would call to the house later in the evening when he came in from work, something he very much appreciated:

> Most of the time it's nine to five and if you're not in, good luck! but the social worker and family support worker had never kind of done that you know. If you needed a later time, they'd arrange it. There is very few people who have done that.

The family support worker believes it is important to include men/fathers in interventions. 'If you get the male on board it takes away the threat. It saves the woman from having to say what we talked about or what we can do or what we intend to do.' Getting the father involved in this instance then is seen as reinforcing the work that is being done with other family members. There was a worthy attempt here to develop a father-inclusive practice which was based on a recognition of the man's positive capacities to care for his children and partner, an inclusive approach he – like other men – can greatly appreciate (Hawkins et al., 1995; Dienhart and Dollahite, 1997; Ferguson and Hogan, 2004). However, the man's role is still minimised because he is seen as a supplementary parent to the mother (Milner, 1996; Daniel and Taylor, 1999; Featherstone, 2004). The intervention could have gone further in focusing on how he could assume greater responsibility for the child care and be a greater resource to his children and partner. If there was a cost to Mrs Smith it was that she was left to carry too much parental responsibility (Kelly, 1996; Scourfield, 2003). Yet, it must be stressed that the view within the family, as well as of professionals, was that it was Mrs Smith who was most in need of help. And she got it, which constituted a tremendous gain for her.

HELPING AN ABUSIVE MOTHER

The work done in this case very effectively balanced authoritative child protection, negotiated family support work and informed risk-taking. A year after the initial referral included in this study, Joanne called to the social worker and made a self-report to the effect that her mother hit her and showed the social worker her bruises: 'There was quite serious bruising. This is what she alleged, so I could have gone to the doctor with her and she could have been out of the home.' The social worker did not take this approach: 'I think you just take a risk, I know it's not good enough for the kid to have that sort of beating. Mum spoke about what she did and we all sat down together and the mother apologised and there was hugs and kisses.' The validity of such risk-taking must always be seen in the context of the discretion that social workers have to take risks, which varies from country to country, system to system. In Ireland at this time, what this social worker did could be viewed as sound professional judgement in that, crucially, she did not hide the allegation of abuse or quietly collude with the family, but did discuss the matter in supervision and referred the matter to the police, as she was procedurally obliged to do (Department of Health, 1995) – asking them to hold off their investigation because she and the family support worker were working 'intensively' with the family. The practice here was going on in the context of increased accountability and bureaucratisation of child welfare (Ferguson, 1996; Walsh, 1999), although this had not reached the intensity of managerial and procedural guidance in directing practice typical of the United Kingdom, where almost certainly at the very least a multi-disciplinary case conference would have had to take place (Parton et al., 1997).

The workers were able to shape a form of creative intervention that was tailor made to the specific needs of the mother, daughter and even to some extent the father. In so doing the social worker took into account that the family was experiencing huge financial problems and possible eviction. To help relieve the stress, it was after the abusive incident that respite care was provided for ten days for Joanne and her six-year-old brother. The social worker situates her analysis of abuse by women in a context which takes account of the difficulties of mothering in patriarchal societies, where little support is given to women to parent – especially in poverty – while blaming them (and not fathers) if things go wrong. This is a social worker who clearly and constantly engaged in critical reflection and shaped her practice accordingly to try and promote safety and democratic relationships in families. We see how she has internalised the influence of a theoretical framework based on feminist theory and an understanding of gender and motherhood as social constructs, and how this interacts with individual's identities and emotional lives (Featherstone, 2004). 'She has the main responsibility with the kids all day, so that's why it makes it more understandable.' However, the social worker is also clear that parental culpability rests with the mother because it was she who hit the child which means that the fact that 'The kids are with her all day' is also a social work concern. The social worker made it clear that 'the issue is you can't hit your children' and explained to Mrs Smith that in the event of further abuse she would not hesitate to take the matter all the way. 'So she is aware that the next incident will [result in] a case conference. I think it worked out okay.' Thus, despite – or perhaps more accurately, because of – the openness and trust in the relationship, the social worker was not afraid to take risks and to confront the consequences of child abuse. This is the kind of truthfulness in practice which is essential for promoting child safety and which shows how authoritative child protection can honestly be done in the context of support and healing work.

ACHIEVING MASTERY: PROMOTING CHILD SAFETY, DEMOCRATIC FAMILY RELATIONSHIPS AND HEALING

At the core of the critical best practice in this case was that the workers implicitly understood what Giddens (1991) calls the 'new intimacy' and the role of interventions in helping service users develop awareness and change some key aspects of their lives. Mrs Smith is clear about why she found it hard to care for her children: 'I couldn't help my daughter because I needed help first.' Being able to shed the burden of the rape felt 'great ... things got better with the kids, because it was all off my mind, I can talk to them now, before I shouted at them, because I didn't trust myself. I had all those emotional problems for ten years back'. This process of recovery from the trauma of sexual violence which Mrs Smith had begun is borne out by feminist research and commentary (Herman, 1992). Mr Smith saw how his partner 'is a lot better in herself, because a lot of the pressure that was on her, over that, [rape] was taken off'. Increasing her level of confidence has enabled Mrs Smith to become more intimate with her daughter, to whom the social worker sees her as much more tactile, as she is towards her sons and, 'there'd be a lot more laughs and fun'. According to Mrs Smith, this transformation in her mastery extends to the practicalities of everyday living, 'We go shopping as a family now. I can ... do the shopping without screaming.'

Prior to working with the social worker, Joanne said she herself 'was a really grouchy person and angry always, annoying my ma and just getting in the way. The social worker has just taught me better ways to deal with my problems and that made me feel better. If I was going home, I'd feel happier'. We see at work here child care practice at its best in enabling parents and children to practice the 'new intimacy', in terms of emotional communication and negotiation in the context of equal relationships (Giddens, 1992). They were being assisted to move beyond traditional hierarchical forms of patriarchal relationships and moved towards the creation of a 'democratic family' form, where the children are heard as well as seen and feel safe, women as well as men are treated with respect, and men as well as women are enabled to have expressive, emotional lives and relationships. The promotion of individualisation, self-actualisation and equality for all the family members in terms of the distinct needs and life plans of women, men and children was central to the achievement of best child protection and family support practice.

Best practice in any case or system is always socially constructed and therefore open to debate, and arguably there are always ways in which improvements and different approaches can be suggested for all interventions. For instance, some may not agree with the way the social worker managed the re-referral concerning the physical abuse of the child, whereas others will agree with her supportive authoritative approach. Equally, as I have pointed out, it can be argued that the practice was too mother-centred and not sufficiently focused on the father. The point is not that the practice was perfect – whatever that might look like – or beyond question. What I am arguing is that the practice in this case can in most respects be regarded as taking an exemplary form because of the different levels of intervention that went on, and how the child protection and family support process was managed: From the careful way in which the referral was negotiated by the school with the social worker and the mother, to the sensitive way in which the process of engagement with resistant parents was managed, to the authoritative and supportive therapeutic work which helped the child and parents to confront their difficulties, trauma and emotional lives, all leading to some resolution of their difficulties. In effect, family members were helped to gain an important degree of what Giddens (1991) calls 'mastery' over their lives.

Gaining such mastery is an emotional as well as a practical challenge and achievement. Psycho-dynamic theory provides a crucial means to understanding a key feature of the best practice in this case in how the workers acted as 'containers' for the family members' anxieties, fears, hate and trauma. Through the skilful use of relationship, the workers enabled Mrs Smith, Joanne and to some extent Mr Smith to process their destructive feelings, begin repairing painful experiences and strengthen their internal resources and capacities to cope and love well (see Trevithick, 2003; also, Celia Keeping's chapter, this volume). The mother could not have been more grateful for the help and support she did receive which, she insisted, prevented the children from coming into statutory care: 'Without the family support worker's help, I wouldn't be here.' Furthermore, the social worker refuses to engage solely in avoiding risk, claiming 'I try if at all possible for that child to be reared with its own family [and] when it's possible I really would be willing to go the hard slog with it.' In addition, we see just how much the reflexive action of service users helps to construct the practice. For example, it was the mother who instigated social work support in relation to the rape issue as she was determined to come to terms with the legacy of her past abuse to prevent herself from continuing to repeat it. The best practice extended to the social worker doing direct work with children and parents as well as working effectively as a case manager – here supporting the child and assessing child protection concerns, while the family support worker concentrated on parenting and other therapeutic issues. The clarification of their roles is spelt out by the family support worker: 'I report to the social worker, she has the responsibility of the case.' According to the family support worker attaining this type of relationship, 'has taken a long time and it depends on the social worker, they all have their own personalities'.

The workers could certainly have gone further in challenging the positioning of the mother as primary parent. Yet, it was the mother who was most abusive to the children and initially hostile to the social worker, but she was not assessed solely on her present behaviour. Rather, due consideration was also given to social and psychological factors which contributed to her individual makeup and present behaviour. Feeling positively about social workers represents a complete transformation considering how the parents initially felt about them. This had as much, if not more, to do with how the previous social worker actually *conducted* herself as with the inherently 'stigmatising' and punitive nature of the child protection social work. As the father said,

> The first social worker was all talk and no action. But with this social worker and family support worker it tends to be listen and act. Previously I thought it was all against me and now there's somebody with me. It's more support than what I had previously.

The practice was also refreshingly child-centred. According to the social worker, 'My job is that child. I would work with the child with every case,' which she duly did with Joanne. However, the boys in the family were not engaged in any form of direct work, despite the fact that the social worker said, 'they're probably getting it [abuse] as well'. Not only was the daughter treated as an individual separate from her mother and father – an essential condition of critical best practice (Wise, 1995) – but Mrs Smith was also treated as an individual in her own right and was strategically helped to feel better about herself and towards all the children. This supports Featherstone's (1999) argument that it is in the interests of good *child* protection for professionals to help women to develop their own sense of self outside of the life of their children. This case vividly shows that, as well as with traumatised carer(s), therapeutic/healing work is vital for children in order to help them heal the wounds from the adversity in their lives and gain the emotional literacy which will equip them to grow into adults who are able to practice intimacy in a respectful, healthy way. The language of (best) practice needs to go beyond the limits of 'protection', 'safeguarding' and 'support' to adequately account for the therapeutic processes of self-redefinition, healing and mastery that can be promoted through such creative, skilful, critically aware interventions.

REFERENCES

Barber, J. (1991) *Beyond Casework* (Macmillan: London).

Beck, U. and Beck-Gernsheim, E. (2002) *Individualisation* (London: Sage).

Buckley, H. (2003) *Child protection: Beyond the Rhetoric* (London: Jessica Kingsley).

Burgess, A. (1997) *Fatherhood Reclaimed* (London: Vermillion).

Butler, I. and Williamson, H. (1994) *Children Speak: Children, Trauma and Social Work* (Longman: Essex).

Cleaver, H. and Freeman, P. (1995) *Parental Perspectives in Cases of Suspected Child Abuse* (HMSO: London).

Daniel, B. and Taylor, J. (1999) The rhetoric versus the reality: a critical perspective on practice with fathers in child care and protection work, *Child and Family Social Work*, 4, 209–220.

Department of Health (1995) *Notification of Suspected Cases of Child Abuse between Health Boards and Gardai* (Dublin: Dept. of Health).

Dienhart, A. and Dollahite, D. (1997) A generative narrative approach to clinical work with fathers, in A. Hawkins and D. Dollahite (eds), *Generative Fathering: Beyond Deficit Perspective* (Sage: London).

Dolan, P., Canavan and Pinkerton, J. (2000), *Family Support: Direction from Diversity* (London: Jessica Kingsley).

Edwards, J. (1998) Screening out men: or 'Has mum changed her washing powder recently?' in Popay, J., Hearn, J. and Edwards, J. (eds), *Men, Gender Divisions and Welfare* (Routledge: London).

Farmer, E. and Owen, M. (1995) *Child Protection Practice: Private Risks and Public Remedies* (HMSO: London).

Featherstone, B. (1999) Taking mothering seriously: the implications for child protection, *Child and Family Social Work*, 4, 1, 43–53.

Featherstone, B. (2004) *Family Life and Family Support* (Basingstoke: Palgrave).

Ferguson, H. (1996) Protecting Irish children in time: child abuse as a social problem and the development of the child protection system in the Republic of Ireland, in H. Ferguson and T. McNamara (eds) *Protecting Irish Children: Investigation, Protection and Welfare*, Special Edition of *Administration*, 44, 2 (Institute of public Administration: Dublin).

Ferguson, H. (2001), Social work, individualisation and life politics, *British Journal of Social Work*, 31, 41–55.

Ferguson, H. (2003a), In defense (and celebration) of individualization and life politics for social work, *British Journal of Social Work*, 33, 1005–1024.

Ferguson, H. (2003b), Welfare, social exclusion and reflexivity: The case of child and woman protection, *Journal of Social Policy*, 32(2), 199–216.

Ferguson, H. (2004), *Protecting Children in Time: Child Abuse, Child Protection and the Consequences of Modernity* (Basingstoke: Palgrave).

Ferguson, H. and Hogan, F. (2004), *Strengthening Families through Fathers: Issues for policy and practice in working with vulnerable fathers and their families* (Dublin: Department of Social, Community and Family Affairs).

Ferguson, H. and O'Reilly, M. (2001), *Keeping Children Safe: Child Abuse, Child Protection and the Promotion of Welfare* (Dublin: A&A Farmer).

Garret, P. M. (2003), The trouble with Harry: Why 'the new agenda of life politics' fails to convince, *British Journal of Social Work*, 33: 381–397.

Gibbons, J., Thorpe, S. and Wilkinson, P. (1990) *Family Support and Prevention: Studies in Local Areas* (HMSO, London).

Giddens, A. (1991) *Modernity and Self Identity* (Polity, Cambridge).

Giddens, A. (1992) *The Transformation of Intimacy* (Polity, Cambridge).

Giddens, A. (1998) *The Third Way: The Renewal of Social Democracy* (Polity, Cambridge).

Hawkins, A., Christiansen, S. L., Pond Sargent, K. and Hill, E. J. (1995) Rethinking fathers involvement in childcare: a developmental perspective, in W. Marsiglio (ed.) *Fatherhood: Contemporary Theory, Research and Social policy* (Sage: London)

Herman, J. (1992) *Trauma and Recovery* (Pandora: London).

Holland, S., Scourfield, J., O'Neill, S. and Pithouse, A. (2005) Democratising the family and the state: the case of family group conferences in child welfare, *Journal of Social Policy* 34(1), 59–77.

Howe, D., Brandon, M., Hinings, D. and Schofield, G. (1999) *Attachment Theory, Child Maltreatment and Family Support* (Macmillan: London).

Jamieson, L. (1998) Intimacy transformed: a critical look at the pure relationship, *Sociology*, 33, 477–494.

Kelly, L., (1996), When Woman protection is the best kind of child protection, in Ferguson, H and McNamara, T. (eds), *Protecting Irish Children: Investigation, Protection and Welfare*, Special Edition of *Administration*, 44, 2 (Institute of public Administration: Dublin).

McKeown, K., Ferguson, H. and Rooney, D. (1998) *Changing Fathers? Fatherhood and Family Life in Modern Ireland* (Collins Press: Cork).

Milner, J. (1996) Men's resistance to social workers, in Fawcett, B., Featherstone, B., Hearn, J. and Toft, C. (eds), *Violence and Gender Relations, Theories and Interventions* (Sage: London).

Parton, N., Thorpe, D. and Wattam, C. (1997) *Child Protection, Risk and the Moral Order* (Macmillan: London).

Scourfield, J. (2003) *Gender and Child Protection* (Basingstoke: Palgrave).

Thoburn, J., Lewis, A. and Shemmings, D. (1995) *Paternalism or Partnership? Family Involvement in the Child Protection Process* (HMSO: London).

Trevithick, P. (2003), Effective relationship-based practice: a theoretical exploration. *Journal of Social Work Practice*, 17(2), 163–176.

Turnell, A. and Edwards, S. (1999) *Signs of Safety: A Solution and Safety Oriented Approach to Child Protection Casework* (London: Norton).

Walsh, T. (1999) Changing expectations: The impact of 'child protection' on social work in Ireland, *Child and Family Social Work*, 4, 33–42.

Wise, S. (1995) Feminist ethics in practice in R. Hugman and D. Smith (eds) *Ethical Issues in Social Work* (Routledge London).

9 Best practice in child advocacy: Matty's story

JANE DALRYMPLE AND HILARY HORAN

This chapter will use the story of Matty Collins, a 10-year-old young white person, to focus on best practice concerning the involvement of young people in decision-making meetings that affect their lives. It examines how Joe, an independent advocate, worked with Matty to help him contribute to the assessment of his situation, which was being undertaken by professionals, and to the plans being made for him. Joe's work with Matty was focused on two events – a Child Protection Conference and a Family Group Conference. Matty and his family have agreed that we can use their story, but all names and identifying features have been changed for reasons of confidentiality. The account is jointly written by Hilary Horan, a Children Services Manager working for Barnardos[1], where she has developed and managed several Family Group Conference and Advocacy Services over the past nine years, and Jane Dalrymple, a senior lecturer in social work at the University of the West of England.

The two decision-making approaches that Matty was involved in operate in very different ways. A Family Group Conference (FGC) is a relatively informal way of working that brings together family members and professionals to make safe plans for children (see Wiffen, 2000). An FGC is organised by an independent Coordinator who prepares the family members and the relevant professionals for the meeting. The meeting involves three stages. First, everyone meets together and talks about their concerns for the child and the non-family members explain any available services that the family may find helpful. The professionals then leave the family to have private time in order to work out a plan that will help resolve the problems that have been identified. This plan is then presented to the professionals who, if it is accepted as safe, will support its implementation.

---

[1] Barnardos is a national independent children's charity that provides a range of services for children and young people in need. This project is based in the South West of England.

In the area where Matty lived with his family, FGCs have been used in child welfare decision-making since 1996. However, early on in the project it became apparent that, from a child or young person's perspective, FGCs can just be another adult-dominated decision-making meeting in which they can feel as disempowered and overlooked as they do in more traditional planning meetings. This is because the adult participants concentrate on the young person's welfare from their own perspective – the young person's view is not always sought. As the manager, Hilary felt that it would be helpful for young people to be able to have access to an independent advocate, who is someone who supports young people so that it is easier for them to participate in the process. A small local charity, the Peanut Trust, therefore agreed to fund the provision of independent advocates for any child over five years having an FGC.

We argue that promoting the meaningful involvement of young people in decision-making is central to critical best practice (CBP) and we explore both the advocate's role and that of social the workers in helping to achieve it.

DEVELOPING ADVOCACY FOR CHILDREN AND YOUNG PEOPLE

Advocacy has been described as a useful mechanism to enable people to address the varying power relations that exist between service users and service providers (Braye and Preston-Shoot, 1995; Tunnard, 1997). The role of an advocate when supporting an individual means that,'... where people have their own voice advocacy means making sure they are heard; where they have difficulty speaking up it means providing help; where they have no voice it means speaking for them' (Herbert, 1989: 49).

Advocacy can also make a difference at a systemic level and so has also been described as, 'A political act with consequences for both individuals and the community as a whole, challenging inequality, opposing racism, preventing abuse, or even introducing someone to a new opportunity or social setting – all constituting steps towards a more civil and just society' (Henderson and Pochin, 2001: 15).

In the Cleveland Inquiry into the alleged sexual abuse of children (Secretary of State for Social Services, 1988) it was stated that 'the child is a person not an object of concern'. Through Matty's story we will show how advocacy support is one way of ensuring that children and young people are not treated merely as objects of concern.

The introduction of independent advocates in FGCs was welcomed and valued by children and young people, their families and the service providers involved. Three quarters of children and young people over the age of five who were offered independent advocates chose to use them. As a result the service was expanded so that children and young people over ten years who have a Child Protection Conference are also offered an opportunity, if they want it, to be supported by an independent advocate. Child protection conferences are a more formal decision-making process than FGCs. An initial Child Protection Conference (CPC) brings together family members, and the professionals involved with the child or young person and the family. Its purpose is to

- gather and analyse in a multi-disciplinary setting the information which has been obtained about the child's health, development and functioning, and the parents' or carers' capacity to ensure the child's safety and promote the child's health and development;

- make judgements about the likelihood of a child suffering significant harm in the future; and

- decide what future action is needed to safeguard the child and promote their welfare, how that action will be taken forward, and with what intended outcomes (Department of Health, 1999).

Hilary asked Jane to link with the project when the advocacy service was first set up in order to help develop guidelines and standards for the advocates and establish a training programme. As we have worked together over the years developing advocacy practice in these specific decision-making forums, we have also looked critically at the role of the advocate within social work in order to ensure best practice in the delivery of services for young people. Although advocacy may seem to be a difficult concept to present to children and young people, our research (Horan and Dalrymple, 2003) has shown that young people who have worked with an advocate find it easy to explain – for example, the advice of an eight-year-old to other young people was:

> I would say it is someone who can help you and if you didn't want to say something she will say it for you. Don't be scared, if you were going to be scared of an advocate you won't trust them to talk to, so you will just keep in your mind things that you can't tell anyone except your toys.

A teenager commented

> She would have to say whatever I wanted her to say – she was under my command, which I felt was pretty cool.

For us this is about critical practice, since it involves engaging in meaningful dialogue with young people to help them to tell their stories, so that both their own families and the professionals involved can understand the reality of their lives and develop creative strategies to work with them.

INDEPENDENT ADVOCACY AND CRITICAL PRACTICE

Independent advocacy has developed as a response to oppression and exclusion because children and young people can find themselves powerless in particular situations that affect their lives. This occurs because, it has been argued, they effectively constitute a minority social group whose status in relation to adults is characterised by powerlessness (Mayall, 2002). Mayall suggests three reasons for this view:

1. Childhood is considered by both adults and children as a time of dependency and subordination;

2. Parents and teachers strongly consider that children need socialising (although children also indicate that parents have a responsibility for their moral development); and

3. The experiences of children at home and at school are controlled by adults who use their power to determine the nature of that experience.

Mayall's (2002) research indicates that children have strong feelings about justice, equal shares and participation in decision-making. Often adult power means that participation is shaped and controlled either in the best interests of the child or young person, or because of the claimed expertise of particular adults (in relation to education, health or welfare for example). However, this knowledge is not only bound up with the exercise of power but also expresses 'discourses about society which are themselves expressions of the practices of professional groups' (James et al., 1998). This means that the rhetoric of participation may still deny children and young people voice and political agency. This points to the need for children and young people to have support (advocacy) if they are to effectively participate in decision-making.

While the participation of children and young people in decision-making within various aspects of their lives is enshrined in legislation within all four countries of the United Kingdom, it is often little more than a tick box activity – get the child or young person to complete a proforma and go to the meeting relieved that you have 'done' the participation bit. Empowering children and young people to take a meaningful part in their planning meetings is a complex and skilled task. Consideration of advocacy and critical practice provides an opportunity to think about social work practice in a different way. Rather than focusing on what power it is that adult professionals have, emphasis is placed on recognising the value of listening to children and young people and finding ways of hearing what they have to say. This in turn enables them to have a meaningful experience of participating in the decision-making processes concerning their lives. This is significant, not least because the children and their families may be using complex and expensive services. More importantly perhaps, is the fact that in our work with children and young people we have been stunned by the accuracy of their assessments about their situation and what would work best to improve their situation. Matty's story illustrates this.

MATTY

Matty was referred to the Advocacy Service when a CPC was convened because a number of professionals were concerned that he was being neglected both physically and emotionally. The Collins family had been known to Social Services for over ten years. Matty's two older half-sisters had been on the Child protection Register for three separate periods as they grew up and they left home as soon as they reached the age of sixteen. Mrs Collins is an alcoholic and also misuses drugs. She had tried various rehabilitation programmes and although she managed short periods without drinking, her health had recently deteriorated and her drinking increased. This followed the older girls leaving home and Mr Collins, Matty's father, receiving a substantial prison sentence following a second conviction for drug dealing. Matty had spent several short periods in foster care in the past three years. The concerns expressed by the service providers involved were his erratic and low school attendance, his 'disruptive behaviour' when he was in school, neighbours' allegations that he begged for food and had been scavenging in dustbins and the impact that Mrs Collins lifestyle was having on the care she could offer Matty. Their house was dirty and poorly furnished and had become a meeting place for other heavy drinkers and drug users.

In line with the policy of the local authority, Matty was automatically invited to the CPC. His invitation included a leaflet explaining how an independent advocate might help and that an advocate from Barnardos would be in touch with him to offer him support if he would like it. Mrs Collins was sent the same information. Matty decided that he would like to talk to an advocate. Joe, an advocate who was supervised by Hilary, started by asking Mrs Collins for permission to see Matty and then confirming Matty's agreement that he wanted to hear about the service on offer. Once Mrs Collins had given her consent Joe and Matty met at the family home.

The timescales for the provision of advocates is very tight – there may be only seven to ten days between referral and the CPC taking place. This means that there is likely to be only one, or at the most two, meetings between the young person and the advocate prior to the CPC. In this instance they spent about an hour together. Joe explained his job as an advocate to Matty and that his contact with Matty would only be in relation to the CPC. He ensured that Matty understood that this was a chance for him to choose how, and if, he wanted to take part in the CPC. It was also important that Matty understood the task of the conference, which is clearly set out by the Department of Health (see above) and what decisions can be made. Professionals often have to make difficult decisions about the safety of children and young people, and the aim of the piece of work, therefore, was to ensure that Matty's views and perspectives were part of the thinking and planning mechanisms of the adults involved. However, he would not be expected to take any responsibility for making important decisions about his safety.

Joe then explained to Matty what he had been told about Matty's situation and the concerns for him. This was important as children can assume that adults working with them know all about them. Joe also gave Matty 'permission' to challenge this information – acknowledging that Matty was the expert on his situation and that information held about him might be inaccurate. The project tries to ensure that the advocate knows nothing he cannot share with the child – it is rare for this to be inappropriate. Joe asked open ended questions – if asked whether they know what a CPC is, it seems that most children will say 'yes' in order to not appear stupid, or to please the worker. Joe then talked with Matty about the process of the CPC and what might or might not happen. He made sure that Matty knew who would be attending the conference, so that there would not be any surprises on the day. He also explained to Matty that the CPC is about whether or not his name goes on the Child protection Register and if it does, to make a plan to help keep him safe. Young people often fear they may be 'taken away' at the end of the Conference. The advocate's role involves clarifying what can and cannot happen as a result of the meeting.

A CPC is a formal meeting at which professionals from all the services involved with the family present a report about their contact with the family and knowledge of the situation. It is a key part of the advocacy role that young people get the opportunity to read the social worker's report with their advocate before they decide what they want to say at the meeting. It is unreasonable and unrealistic to expect a young person, full of emotions, to read a report carefully and decide on their response on the day of a CPC. It is an ongoing problem to get the report in sufficient time prior to the CPC. Matty's social worker, however, had made the report available two days before the meeting, which approximates to good practice.

The next stage of the work, therefore, was to show Matty the social worker's report and read it through with him. Reports can be difficult for a young person to read and understand because of their format and the language used. Joe then went on to talk to Matty about what it was like being him: what was good about his life, what upset him or could be improved, if there was anything that he wanted the CPC to know. As Matty spoke Joe made notes and then Matty decided what he wanted in the final version of his 'statement' to the Conference. The information that they shared belongs to Matty and so he also needed to know where his information might go – who will be able to access it in the future? Advocates are expected to be honest about this from the outset of their work. Matty, therefore, understood that what he sent in written format or said at the CPC would be in the minutes and distributed to a large number of agencies and to his parents. Joe made sure he felt alright about the various participants having this information.

Matty and Joe also discussed his attendance at the CPC – did he want to go to the meeting – all of it, or part of it? He was told there might be a part of the meeting he could not sit in because there could be some information confidential to his mother or father. Matty decided to attend for as much of the meeting as he could but he wanted Joe to read out his information as he thought the meeting would be too scary for him to feel able to talk. They also agreed on a special signal between them in case Matty felt that he wanted to leave the room at any time. Joe finished by agreeing to collect Matty on the day of the CPC (with Mrs Collin's agreement). This meant that they had a chance to talk things over again, check over what Joe had written up and to reassure Matty that the Advocate was there and could sit with him before the meeting started. After meeting with Matty, Joe informed the Independent Chairperson of the CPC and the social worker of Matty's decision to attend. He also made sure he had a drink, tissues, paper, felt-tips and some Top Trump cards (Matty's favourite game) ready on the day. CPCs are not child-friendly meetings and a few distractions from the formality and tediousness of the 'hanging around' can make a big difference to the child or young person's ability to cope with the experience.

We can see from this account that the starting point for Joe was to ensure that Matty had a clear understanding of what was currently happening in his life and the 'ground rules' of his work with Joe. It was fundamental that this happened before talking to Matty about what he wanted to say to the meeting. By this time Matty had the information he needed about the conference, the situation as presented by the social worker and what decisions might, or might not be made. Armed with this information Matty was able to use Joe to mull over his situation, what he might want to say to the meeting, his anxieties about the impact of what he wanted to say, his wishes and feelings and suggestions for improving his situation. The quotation we used earlier in the chapter shows that children and young people often feel able to talk to their advocate about 'secrets' they had previously only felt able to talk about to their pets or toys. The majority of these are not child protection 'secrets' but they are issues that have caused the child or young person anxiety and so have felt unable to share elsewhere for reasons of loyalty or to avoid upsetting a parent /carer. The task of the advocate is to 'open up' two-way communication, to the young people and from the young person.

Matty attended part of his CPC and asked his advocate to read his contribution. He had, in fact, written another page of A4 about his situation but, having heard what others at the CPC were saying, he chose to edit his report. He was also fearful that his Mum would be upset at the CPC as he knew that she found such meetings extremely difficult. Joe's original statement to Matty, that he was in charge of his own information, had been adhered to. This 'extra' information is shredded after the CPC or FGC and not recorded elsewhere. This is so that in the future it cannot be accessed for another meeting or procedure. Good practice is clear that the child should be asked for his wishes and feelings at each stage of his 'career' with agencies – his views may alter substantially over time and he might opt to give differing information to different kinds of meetings.

This is what Matty asked Joe to read out at the CPC:

> This is what I want to say: I don't remember some things the report said happened. I can't remember what my Mum was like last year as I was too worried about what would happen to me. It was good when Stacey [his half sister] came back – it is good when someone else is here when my Mum has been drinking. I am sad now Stacey has gone again – I miss her

cos I could talk to her and she did nice things with me like swimming. I still want to live with my Mum.

I know when Mum has been drinking. She sounds funny. She is cheerful when she is drunk but not all of the time and she also gets mad and angry and loud and then tired. I don't know what would help her to stop. When she drinks she lies on the sofa and I put a quilt on her and put her head on the pillow. I make a cup of coffee for her in the morning and make myself a sandwich. I quite often feel upset and I don't know why. I used to go swimming but haven't been able to go for ages. We don't have much money. I wish that I could earn some to help out.

Talking over his feelings of isolation and 'muddles' with Joe, combined with his fierce loyalty to his mother and his fear of being looked after in the care of the Local Authority again, enabled Matty to make sense of his situation and to gain some control. He was anxious and distressed but taking the time to talk about his feelings enabled Matty to negotiate what he really wanted to share at this point with the people involved. For the social worker, actively involving Matty in decision-making to date had inevitably been difficult and she had often had to implement plans that he had not been happy about. When Matty had talked to his social worker twelve months earlier, he had not wanted to be in foster care and was anxious that if he talked to her too honestly this could be the outcome again. Mrs Collins had also seen the social worker as 'policing' their life and her negative views of social services had been passed on to Matty. This meant that Matty's experiences of the social worker's involvement in his life were not positive. Her contact with him had seemed, from his perspective, to be focused on collecting evidence and taking himself and his sisters away from his mother. What had appeared to be coercive and legalistic approaches within his life meant that he had not been able to experience any meaningful involvement in the decision-making processes. By encouraging Matty to be explicit about his situation Joe was able to help him to be involved in the conference.

The material that Matty asked to be read at his CPC gave the professionals involved insight into both his resilience and his vulnerability. He clearly indicated what he thought needed to be included in a plan to improve his situation. This was the starting point of his contribution to the assessment process. He identified that he needed

- to have someone else in the house to share the difficult times;
- to have good quality information about plans being made for him;

- to be able to sort out some of his sad feelings;
- to have some nice activities to enjoy and to go swimming;
- to be able to earn some money;
- his role as a young carer is also identified.

Matty was placed on the Child protection Register under the category of neglect and therefore a full-risk assessment was undertaken by the Social Services Department. It was also agreed that the resource centre worker was given vouchers to take Matty swimming. Matty mentions swimming twice in his account and this is a key piece of information. Making it happen was not expensive for the Local Authority and for Matty it provided an easily available and enjoyable stress-buster. He felt that he had been listened to and that what he had to say was valued. For the social worker, working in an agency dominated by legislation and policy mandates, providing the vouchers was one way of both validating the reality of his situation and recognising his resilience. It is a well-known fact to adults that taking exercise is beneficial and relieves stress.

There was also a recommendation from the CPC that Matty and his family were offered a FGC in order to plan how to support him living at home with his mother. Soon afterwards, however, Mrs Collins was admitted to hospital following an overdose. It was agreed that Matty would stay with his paternal grandparents while the FGC was organised. The Barnardos project gives young people the chance to choose if they would like the same advocate to work with or if they would like someone different. This was another area where Matty could take some control of his situation. He decided to continue working with Joe and they met twice to prepare what he wanted to say to his FGC.

While he was living with his grandparents Matty appeared to be much stronger both physically and emotionally, and, having had a positive experience of involvement in decision-making at his Child protection Conference, he felt able to be more open about his situation. His FGC was attended by eight relatives, his social worker, the head teacher from his school, and Mrs Collins' worker from the Drug and Alcohol team, together with the Coordinator and Joe. Prior to the FGC Joe had talked to Matty about whether he wanted Joe to stay with him during the private family time of the FGC. Matty decided that Joe should be there for the first few minutes and Matty would then decide if he needed him to stay any longer. Again, Matty retained control over his use of the advocate. This is about half of what he wanted to say to the meeting – after hearing what other people had said, he felt it was no longer necessary to say some things. He asked Joe to read this out:

> It hasn't been very nice being me really. I've felt very left out. I don't like going to other people's houses with my Mum so she can get drugs and drink. I've lived in some horrible places and seen some horrible things, people injecting gear, smoking it, falling asleep. I've seen my Dad's mate, Joe, collapse because of drugs, his lips went blue. My Dad called an ambulance but he died so I found out. When my Dad went to prison it was so hard. I cried all the time. I missed him so much. I knew the drugs were killing him – he used to be a big bloke. 12 stone – he lost 4 stone in a year. It was just as well the police arrested him, they saved his life really. If he comes out soon I'll just cry I'll be so happy. My Mum sends me to a different room when she is doing drugs but I know what she is doing. I've been living with Nan and Pops for four weeks now. I feel safe there. I always have breakfast. I have lunch at school and a meal in the evening.
>
> When I lived at Riverside (the homeless families unit) it was really horrible, there wasn't any food. I didn't go to school, I couldn't go. It would get at me, I'd get half way there but I just couldn't go. I wanted to run away.
>
> I want to live with Mum but I only want to live with Mum if she really is clean and we have our own house. Dad says he wants to go and live in Scotland. I just want to live somewhere where there is no drugs. If I can't live with Mum I suppose I would rather live with Nan and Pops – they are the closest people to my Dad. My family are all important to me, they worry about me, they've helped me a lot. I would like to see more of Stacey and Lou [his half-sisters] – I can talk to them a lot. What I really don't want to happen is my Mum and Dad to get back on it, that would be my worst nightmare. My Dad has promised me. He is a lot stronger in the head than my Mum.
>
> I like it at school. It really is nice. I've got loads of mates there. School means a lot. My teachers are nice, my head teacher is really nice, she is always kind to me. I like it at that school, I want to stay there.

Matty's information for his FGC shows starkly the stress and neglect he has been dealing with. Hearing his voice gave the family and professionals a real understanding of what Matty had been through and contained detail that was not previously known to the adults at the meeting. What he had to say was about the reality of his life and everyone really listened and attached appropriate significance to his story. Professional information about abuse is usually given using sanitised language that masks the reality and the pain of the abuse. Best practice means professionals naming the pain and helping service users to do so too. It was, therefore, important that, having worked with Matty to help him to express his feelings, Joe had not changed, altered or interpreted what Matty wanted to say.

The fact that Matty identified that one of the strengths in his situation was a supportive school and friends came as a complete surprise to the head teacher – and not only changed her attitude towards him but also meant that she then actively tried to support him to attend school. The initial referral indicates that not only was he labelled as persistently not attending school but he was also 'disruptive' once there. Such language indicates the theoretical and value perspectives inherent in the referral and reflects the power relations between the school, Matty and his family. However the head teacher was able to understand that the experience of seeing his father's friend die from taking drugs made sense of why his school attendance was so poor: when he was living with his mother, Matty worried every day that he would find her dead by the time he got home. She really listened to what Matty had to say. But she did more – she did something about it. First, she told Matty that any time he felt worried about his mother or what might be happening at home he could go to her office and phone home. This meant that he would be able to get to school and worry less about what was happening at home. This then helped him to concentrate on his work. The head teacher also understood that Matty was not getting the basics of life – (the fact that he mentioned breakfast, lunch and dinner now he is with his grand parents indicates that this was not routine when he was living at home) – and being hungry would also make it hard to concentrate and behave acceptably. She suggested that Matty might like to try out the new 'breakfast club' that was starting at the school.

Matty identifies his reluctance to return to his mother if she is still using drugs. His language is not sanitised – he is describing vividly the experience of neglect. It was hard for both his family and the professionals to hear his information and there were many tears when it was read out. They did more than just listen though. Best practice in terms of participation was about hearing what he had to say and providing services that were relevant to his identified needs. Matty never said that he did not want to be with his parents – his love for them shines through – but he does clearly show that at that point his situation was intolerable.

ADVOCACY PRACTICE

Matty's story enables us to think about CBP in advocacy, but also about the implications for best practice in social work and child care practice generally. First, we will consider the provision of advocacy. Independent advocacy services for children and young people have primarily developed to support children and young people looked after in the state care. The core principles of the National Standards for the provision of Children's Advocacy Services in England (Department of Health, 2002) and in Wales (Welsh Assembly Government, 2003), for example, refer specifically to the need for children and young people in care to understand what is happening to them. Recognition by the UK government of the need for advocacy is demonstrated in the legal mandate for the provision of advocacy for young people making a complaint under Section 26 of the Children Act 1989. While this is an important milestone for children and young people in England and Wales it is still most applicable to those looked after in Local Authority care. However, children and young people who are involved with services through child protection services or having an FGC are usually living in the community and it is particularly challenging to get these children's voices heard.

By listening to children and young people, we can gain the information we need for a fuller understanding of the issues. Butler and Rumsey (2000) suggest that this

> Probably provides the single most important clue as to why there is resistance to meaningful dialogue with children and young people. If we were to really listen to them and hear what they have to say, it would result in the need to radically change many of the services that are currently provided. While these are ostensibly designed to enhance the well-being of children, in practice it could be argued that they are organised around the desire to maintain the current position of children in society and existing power relationships. (p.15)

In this account we have seen that with advocacy support barriers were broken down between Matty and the people hearing his story – barriers which are perpetuated through and act to support the position of adults – and so it has the potential to enable children and young people to have a voice in decision making. This is important because, 'We live in a world dominated by adult values. Children's rights are a political as well as a moral issue and they can conflict with adult authority that oppresses children and denies opportunities that all children should enjoy in safety' (Utting, 1997).

Best practice in advocacy then goes beyond the individual moment to the wider context of practice. Advocates are in a privileged position because they are not constrained by statutory duties, local authority policies of legislative mandates[2]. Matty's social worker was not only committed to working in a child-centred way but was also mindful of her duties as a social worker. For her, then, best practice meant acknowledging that without the support of an advocate the possibility of working in a democratic child-centred way was limited. However, by actively supporting the advocacy service she was able to facilitate Matty's involvement in the process and, together with the head teacher and other professionals involved, to act on what Matty had said, recognising his unique understanding of and insight into his situation.

Joe was aware that the process was Matty's agenda, in which his role as an advocate was to listen and work with Matty so that he could tell his story. Matty's knowledge and experiences were then legitimated, which challenged the traditional authority of professional knowledge (Fook, 2002). Joe's role was to facilitate and utilise Matty's skills (Rayner and Hashagen, 1992). Joe, then, as a critical practitioner, understood the whole context of practice, including an understanding of the power relations that exist in the decision-making situations where Matty needed his support. Feedback from young people using the advocacy service has been that the age, gender or race of the Advocate is not a big issue. The top three identified characteristics are: to be a good listener, have a good sense of humour, and that advocates do what they say they will do.

KEY ISSUES IN THE PROVISION OF ADVOCACY

The experience of Matty highlights practice issues for social workers and other professionals. An important part of the process for Matty was that his information was written in his language. Children and young people can be offered a variety of ways to present their information and Joe was able to ensure that Matty knew that this was an opportunity that he could choose to take, but that there was no pressure for him to say anything. Matty's story shows how he could choose what information he would share in two separate meetings. Other children and young people will make the decision that it is too risky for them to say anything or they may choose to wait and see what information other people are bringing to the meeting before they decide what they want to say. Joe did not interpret what Matty told him nor did he offer his own view. If Matty's story had been presented in any other way it would not have had the same impact.

---

[2] Advocates do, though, work within their Local Authoritie's Child Protection Procedures.

Matty's first language is English so providing an advocate who spoke his first language was easy. However, the Advocacy Service has learned that it is essential to provide the child or young person with an advocate who speaks their first language, even when they may be fluent in their second language. For example, an eleven-year-old girl who had recently been sent to England from the West Indies to live with her father after her mother's death, had an FGC. She asked for an advocate who spoke Patois, although her spoken English was excellent. She told us 'my brain thinks in English but my heart thinks in Patois'. She illustrates perfectly how hard it is to communicate emotions in another language.

Advocacy is traditionally considered as a social work skill (Coulshed and Orme, 1998; Payne, 2000; Trevithick, 2000): it was identified as a central skill by the Central Council for Education and Training in Social Work (CCETSW, 1995) as well as a key element of the social work role identified by the British Association of Social Workers (BASW, 1996) and, more recently, as a key skill for social workers completing the new social work degree[3]. The literature indicates that social workers and other professionals in health and social care can and should include advocacy as part of their required repertoire of skills. This can cause tensions, however, particularly in child protection where there may be a conflict between what the social worker and the child or young person thinks is in their 'best interest'. There will, therefore, be times when young people need the support of an independent advocate (Brandon, 1995, Clifton and Hodgson, 1997, Downs et al., 1997)[4] and this is increasingly being enshrined in policy and legislation in all four nations of the United Kingdom[5]. By recognising the need for an independent advocate Matty's social worker actively considered the possibilities for her own advocacy role. She therefore engaged in CBP by ensuring that Matty's participation in the process was meaningful, and was able to continue working with the family to ensure that the

---

[3] The National Occupational Standards for Social Work in the United Kingdom identify six Key Roles of a social worker. Key Role 3 states that social workers should support individuals to represent their needs, views and circumstances. An element of this role is to advocate with, and on behalf of, individuals, families, carers, groups and communities. (Topss, England, 2003)

[4] The National Occupational Standards recognise the potential dilemmas through indicating under Key Role 3 that social workers should be able to (1) assess whether you should act as the advocate for the individual, family, carer, group or community; and (2) assist individuals, families, carers, groups and communities to access independent advocacy.

[5] For example, the governments in England and Wales have developed national standards for advocacy practice as part of a continued development of advocacy and children's rights services (see, Department of Health (2002) *National Standards for the provision of Children's Advocacy Services*, London, Department of Health publications). The Adoption and Children Act 2002, made changes to the Children Act 1989 and provides children in need and care levers with a statutory right to advocacy when they are intending to make a complaint.

outcomes of Joe's work with Matty had an impact on his life beyond the Child Protection Conference and FGC. Providing a means of empowering young people to participate in decisions made about them is hugely helpful in enabling the adults involved to make the right decisions to help protect young people, build on their resilience and improve their circumstances.

REFERENCES

BASW (1996) *A Code of Ethics for Social Work* (Birmingham: BASW).

Brandon, D. (1995) *Advocacy: Power to People with Disabilities* (Birmingham: Venture Press).

Braye, S. & Preston-Shoot, M. (1995) *Empowering Practice in Social Care* (Buckingham: Open University Press).

Butler, G. and Rumsey, H. (2000), *Hearing children's voices: Myth or Reality? Challenges in Implanting the UN Convention in South Africa and England* (Chichester: University College).

CCETSW (1995) *Rules and Requirements for the Diploma in Social Work Paper 30* (London: CCETSW).

Clifton, C. & Hodgson, D. (1997) Rethinking practice through a children's rights perspective in Cannan, C. & Warren, C. (eds) *Social Action with Children and Families: A Community Development Approach to Children and Family Welfare* (London: Routledge).

Coulshed, V. & Orme, J. (1998) *Social Work Practice: An Introduction* (Basingstoke: Macmillan/BASW).

Department of Health (1999) *Working Together to Safeguard Children* (London: The Stationery Office).

Department of Health (2002) *National Standards for the Provision of Children's Advocacy Services* (London: Department of Health).

Downs, S. W., Costin, L. B. & McFadden, E. J. (1997) *Child, Welfare and Family Services* (USA: Longman).

Fook, J. (2002) *Social Work Critical Theory and Practice* (London: Sage publications).

Henderson, R. & Pochin, M. (2001) *A Right Result? Advocacy, Justice and Empowerment* (Bristol: The Policy Press).

Herbert, M. D. (1989) *Standing Up for Kids: Case Advocacy for Children and Youth, Strategies and Techniques* (Alberta: Office of the Children's Advocate).

Horan, H. & Dalrymple, J. (2003) Promoting the Participation Rights of Children and Young people in Family Group Conferences, *Practice*, **15**: 5–14.

James, A., Jenks, C. & Prout, A. (1998) *Theorising Childhood* (Cambridge: Polity Press).

Mayall, B. (2002) *Towards a Sociology for Childhood: Thinking from Children's Lives* (Buckingham: Open University Press).

Payne, M. (2000) *Anti-bureaucratic Social Work* (Birmingham: Venture Press).

Rayner, S. & Hashagen, N. (1992) *Advocacy for Children and Young People* (Manchester: ASC).

Secretary of State for Social Services (1988) *Report of the Inquiry into Child Abuse in Cleveland. IN 412, C.* (ed.) (London: HMSO).

Topss, England (2003) *National Occupational Standards* (Leeds: Topss).

Trevithick, P. (2000) *Social Work Skills: A Practice Handbook* (Buckingham: Open University Press).

Tunnard, J. (1997) Mechanisms for empowerment: family group conferences and local family advocacy schemes in Cannan, C. & Warren, C. (eds) *Social Action with Children and Families: A Community Development Approach to Child and Family Welfare* (London: Routledge).

Utting, W. (1997) *People Like Us: The Report of the Review of the Safeguards for Children Living Away From Home* (London: The Stationary Office).

Welsh Assembly Government (2003) *National Standards for the provision of Children's Advocacy Services* (Cardiff: Welsh Assembly Government).

Wiffen, J. (2000) *An Introduction to Family Group Conferencing* (London: Family Rights Group).

10 Best practice in adult protection: safety, choice and inclusion

KAREN JONES AND KATE SPREADBURY

The protection of vulnerable adults from abuse as a responsibility of the state is a relatively recent concept and most commentators agree that European policy and practice is some way behind that of Canada and North America (Pritchard, 1999; Juklestad, 2004). In the United Kingdom, the policy framework for practice is only a few years old (DH, 2000) and, despite recent guidance from Directors of Social Services (DH, 2005), best practice in Adult Protection remains a contested and as yet under-researched area.

The protection of adults is an ethically and practically complex aspect of social work, which presents challenging issues in relation to service user autonomy and the limits of professional responsibility. The absence of a specific legal framework for the protection of vulnerable adults can leave service users and practitioners feeling confused and powerless. Misunderstanding about the legal powers of social services departments can also lead to unrealistic expectations on the part of other agencies and individuals, who may have been carrying the emotional burden of risk on a daily basis. At the same time the rights, needs and choices of adults who are being abused, or who are likely to become so are as central and as defining as they are in any other area of practice.

This chapter discusses a situation which a number of professionals regarded as abusive and which illustrates some of the key dilemmas of statutory involvement in the protection of vulnerable adults in the United Kingdom. It is also a story of strength and resilience and describes practice which was not only protective, but also therapeutic, empowering and respectful of the rights and autonomy of those involved.

The chapter was written jointly by Kate, an Adult Protection Co-ordinator, working for Bristol Social Services and Health and Karen, a social work academic. It also draws on interviews with Helen, an experienced social worker in a specialist adult disability team, whose work was central to the *best practice* being highlighted here. The first-person voice within the chapter is Kate's.

MR AND MRS BROWN

Mr and Mrs Brown are both in their early 60s and have been together for 30 years. Ten years ago, Mr Brown was diagnosed as having Multiple Sclerosis. As a result of his illness he finds it tiring to spend more than an hour in a sitting position; he uses a wheelchair, but spends much of his time lying down. Mr Brown has a catheter and needs some help with eating; he communicates slowly and carefully, but seems fully able to make decisions about his life and his future.

THE REFERRAL

Home care workers and district nurses had been visiting Mr and Mrs Brown for just over a year; during this time they had become increasingly worried about Mr Brown's physical condition and alarmed by what they saw as Mrs Brown's expressions of anger and aggression. The workers involved said that they had often found Mrs Brown abusive and threatening and had sometimes felt unable to visit the house except in pairs. The situation came to a head when Mrs Brown seemingly deliberately shut a Home Care worker's hand in the door and told her that she wanted no further visits. Concerns were raised with Social Services and the Adult Protection procedure was initiated.

The particular concerns expressed by District Nurses and Home Carers were:

- **Mr Brown's weight.** He had lost two stones in a year and was now very frail and weak. Mr and Mrs Brown were both heavy smokers and appeared uninterested in food. Mrs Brown did not seem to buy food and there was evidence that much of the couple's money was spent on cigarettes and Mrs Brown's daily bingo sessions. A mobile meals service had been arranged at one point, but this was cancelled by Mrs Brown after a month.

- **Mr Brown's apparent fear of his wife.** He was often passive and would respond to her in ways which seemed designed to placate, such as remaining silent or pretending to be asleep.

- **Mrs Brown's seeming resentment and anger at her husband's illness and dependency.** Mr Brown received respite care locally for two weeks in every six, but his wife was reported never to visit him while he was there. On his return from respite all would be well for about a week before Mrs Brown again began to exhibit anger and verbal aggression towards her husband and visiting staff.

Mr Brown's GP and the District Nurses involved in his care all expressed the view that it was time for Mr Brown to move to a nursing home for his own safety and protection.

Adult protection: legislation and policy

Unlike Child Protection work, which has been subject to a dedicated statutory framework for many years, Adult Protection has had to develop practice expertise within a comparatively general and unspecific legal structure. Misconceptions about the extent of the statutory powers held by social services departments within adult protection situations can lead other agencies and individual professionals to expect immediate, decisive action; in fact, this may be neither legal nor appropriate.

Legislation does exist in the United Kingdom under the 1983 Mental Health Act to protect people with a mental illness as defined under the Act. There are references to the protection of vulnerable adults in much recent UK legislation (Sexual Offences Act 2003, Domestic Violence: Crime and Victims Act 2004, Mental Capacity Act, 2005), but there is no specific law which can be used to protect vulnerable adults who either lack the capacity to protect themselves or who are having to make decisions under duress.

Some commentators have argued for a single piece of legislation to underpin all adult protection procedures, suggesting that the lack of such a law contravenes the United Nations Declaration of Human Rights (Clements, 2000). In fact, the absence of such a framework reflects the inherent practical and ethical dilemmas surrounding this challenging area of practice. The rights of adults to self-determination, sets them somewhat apart from children whose welfare has a statutory position at the centre of current UK child protection legislation (Harbison and Morrow, 1998). Legal and ethical debates in relation to adult protection often centre on the 'capacity' of the adult to make choices about particular areas of his or her life. Certainly in the United Kingdom, the right of those who are judged to have such capacity to make their own choices, remains the dominant principle within policy and practice. As we will see below however, the messy and complex reality of human situations and the equally complicated emotional responses of professionals who encounter them, do not easily lend themselves to principles or prescriptions.

The decision by successive governments not to institute a prescriptive legal structure in relation to adult protection means that *policy guidance* in this area has particular significance for practice. The publication of the 'No Secrets' White Paper in 2000 led to the requirement for those involved in adult protection to develop multi-agency codes of practice in relation to the protection of vulnerable adults from abuse. There are inevitably regional variations in the success with which these codes have been developed and implemented. They have, however, provided an effective starting point for good practice and a site for ongoing debate about that which is *best* in adult protection. It is a debate which should and must continue in the decades to come.

First steps

In common with most allegations of adult abuse made to social services departments in the United Kingdom (DH, 2005), Mr Brown was referred by concerned professionals. Fifty-five per cent of local authorities in the United Kingdom say that the most common source of referral is social services' own or other paid staff. There are comparatively few referrals from either the general public or from vulnerable adults themselves (DH, 2005). The definition given in No Secrets (2000) of a vulnerable adult who may be abused as someone who 'Is or may be unable to protect himself or herself against significant harm or exploitation' highlights the self-evident difficulty that such an adult may face in alerting others to his or her own abuse. The scarcity of referrals from the public may reflect a lack of awareness, and perhaps a historical reluctance to recognise the existence of adult abuse. Recently however, there have been serious attempts to ascertain for the first time, the scope of the problem of elder abuse in the United Kingdom. A large-scale research project, commissioned by the government in 2004 analysed the responses of 109 local authorities and identified 15,089 adult protection referrals for the year 2003/2004. The most common form of abuse reported was physical, followed by financial. About 94.5% of local authorities showed the home as the most common place of abuse with paid carers as the most frequent abusers (DH, 2005).

Helpful and informative as this data is in giving a sense of the scale of adult abuse, no amount of quantitative information can reflect the complexity of the *stories* contained within the statistics or the dilemmas facing the professionals who come into contact with them. No Secrets (DH, 2000) gives social services departments the lead responsibility for co-ordinating adult protection activity in the United Kingdom. As an Adult Protection Co-ordinator, I have learnt that there is no single 'right' way to approach the complex and deeply challenging process of facilitating an abuse investigation. Remaining open to the diverse narratives of those caught up in abuse situations and of the practitioners involved in their lives has however been central to my growing understanding of this delicate role. As Jan Fook (2002: 202) argues, 'The real integration between theory and practice will not come from a ponderous, rigid body of knowledge, but from the humility to learn from practitioner experience.'

Negotiating and co-ordinating a planned response within situations which are inevitably complex and uncertain is hugely challenging. Anne Brechin's (2000: 44) definition of the critical practitioner as someone who is 'skilled and knowledgeable and yet remain[s] open to alternative ideas, frameworks and belief systems' provides a helpful starting point in an area of practice which often involves juggling contradictory perspectives. Brechin goes on to argue that 'Not knowing' and uncertainty need to be valued as an orientation towards openness and a continuing process of learning, even if, at times, it can be essential to act swiftly and confidently (Brechin, 2000: 44). This assertion of critically aware uncertainty alongside the preparedness to act decisively is the essence of what I consider to be good practice in adult protection as well as being central to my own aspirations as a practitioner.

Local authorities across the United Kingdom are at different stages in their development of adult protection systems and procedures. While some have established the equivalent to a police or social services child protection unit (see for example, Linnett, 2001) the geographical area in which I work is at a beginning point in the establishment of effective, shared approaches. While there is an emerging local consensus about best practice, systems for investigating referrals still have to be carefully negotiated in each new situation.

Initial strategy meeting

In Mr Brown's case it was important to listen to the many concerns being raised and to develop as full a picture as possible of the situation before embarking on any other investigative activities. I therefore made the decision in consultation with the other professionals involved, to convene and chair a formal multi-agency strategy meeting.

The initial meeting was large; it was attended by Mr Brown's GP, two District Nurses, two Home Care workers and their manager, two social workers and their team managers and a solicitor from the council's legal department. All those present had recent experience of working with Mr and Mrs Brown, with the exception of the solicitor who was invited to give an expert opinion regarding any proposed use of legislation. Neither Mr Brown nor Mrs Brown was invited to the initial meeting. This decision may appear to be at odds with notions of partnership and openness which are central to critical practice. However, the danger that *any* overt action by practitioners might increase the risk to Mr Brown by threatening the fragile thread linking him to formal services was considerable. In situations of adult abuse the balance of individual rights, risk and the professional responsibility to protect is often precarious. Critical practice in Mr Brown's case involved the fine, situated judgement that his exclusion from the initial strategy meeting was a necessary protective act and one which supported his right not to be placed at even greater risk.

The fact that Mr Brown was not present made it all the more important for his perspective to be recognised and acknowledged as far as possible within the meeting. As chair and co-ordinator of the process I needed to establish at an early stage, how far he was able to make his own decisions and what his wishes were felt to be. As those at the meeting who were closest to Mr Brown began to talk, it quickly became clear that this was a man with the capacity although possibly not the confidence to make informed choices about his own life. I was mindful of the fact that in situations where a vulnerable adult is able to express clear choices, all offers of help and intervention may be refused. As Mike Linnett argues:

> The conference platform ... has to realise that the vulnerable individual may not wish to accept all or any of the care offered and may, as a result, continue to live in a risky situation. The individual has a right to do this unless it is proper to consider formal intervention. (Linnett, 2001: 38)

A large part of the initial meeting was taken up with people talking about what they had seen and how they felt they had failed to protect Mr Brown or engage Mrs Brown. Celia Keeping writes in Chapter 4 about the importance of the psychoanalytical notion of 'containment' in situations of acute mental health crisis. While a multi-professional meeting is a very different situation from the one Celia describes, I am often mindful, as chair of the meeting, of the need to 'hold' or 'contain' the powerful individual feelings of colleagues who have been involved in deeply painful situations. An important part of my role is therefore to enable practitioners to express their anxieties, to feel that they are being heard and acknowledged and to know that they are part of a collective process. In many instances this has proved to be a more important precursor to genuine joint working between professionals than any set of rules or protocols. Nevertheless, agencies and individuals often do have different perspectives on what constitutes abuse, on the appropriate balance between self-determination and risk and on the best course of action in any given situation. Within the often highly charged atmosphere of an adult protection meeting, these views can be expressed with great force and conviction. Another essential aspect of my role as chair of the meeting is therefore to facilitate the sharing of different views without allowing any one person's perception to become a dominant or taken for granted discourse before any investigation has taken place.

While there were differences of opinion, during this meeting about the seriousness and definition of Mr Brown's experience, there was considerable agreement among the professionals that Mr Brown was at risk. The link between his deteriorating health and some of his wife's behaviours seemed undeniable. Mr Brown was losing a dangerous amount of weight and nurses and Home Care workers were witnessing what they perceived as abuse on a daily basis. With such a high level of consensus, there was not only a serious cause for concern and a need to act, but there was also a danger that the construction of Mrs Brown as aggressive abuser and Mr Brown as passive victim, would become accepted and entrenched 'facts' before any more in-depth work could be done. I was also aware that several of those present were beginning to adopt the language of *rescue* and *escape* and to see the *removal* of Mr Brown from his wife as an inevitable next step.

As chair of the meeting, I was aware of the understandable guilt and anxiety of those present. However, I was also mindful of the danger that this collective desire to rescue would cloud out Mr Brown's own needs and wishes. Others' ready-made solutions often fail to address the complexity of distinctive situations and the rights of the individuals who are subject to professional concern, to make their own decisions. Robert Adams suggests that the critical practitioner can move beyond this as she:

> Acknowledges the inherently problematic situation and takes its essence into account rather than pretending it can be simplified and the problem

187

ignored. Thus critical practice is likely to embody the dilemma the conflict holds, rather than ducking or working round it. This is extremely testing for the practitioner, who has to establish a direction for the practice rather than yielding to the temptation to impose a simplistic, often inappropriate solution. (Adams, 2002: 93)

Each of the meetings I chair focuses on individuals within a unique context and set of circumstances. Assumptions about the outcome of an adult protection referral at the initial meeting are generally misplaced, inevitably failing to do justice to the complexity of the situations involved. In all but the most straightforwardly dangerous and abusive situations, an 'open and "not knowing"' stance (Brechin, 2000: 32) is a helpful starting point for investigation. In risky situations such as Mr Brown's, the integration of an open, critical approach with swift protective action is as Adams suggests, difficult to achieve and extremely testing for the practitioners involved.

In Mr Brown's case I had asked a solicitor to attend the initial strategy meeting so that the legal boundaries on any possible action could be established at an early stage. As far as we could tell, Mrs Brown had not committed any criminal act. There were no records of police visits to the Browns' home and no reports of any alleged crime. In spite of the wish of most of those present at the meeting to see Mr Brown move to a safer environment, away from his wife, the view of his GP and others who knew Mr Brown well, was that he was able to make his own decisions; this removed any immediate possibility of utilising mental health legislation. The solicitor further confirmed that there is no legislation allowing a person to be removed from their home against their will in such circumstances and that to do so would in itself be an abusive and illegal act.

The recognition that there was no legal recourse with which to approach Mr Brown's situation immediately increased the anxiety of those present at the meeting, but also made it possible to move to a more constructive planning phase. People again needed time to voice their anxieties and to come to terms with the fact that an alternative approach would have to be found. As the group moved beyond this, they were able to begin to take shared responsibility for planning ways of addressing the risks Mr Brown was facing.

The different perspectives on acceptable levels of risk and strategies for risk management which emerged within the meeting represented yet another layer of complexity within a highly emotive situation. At this early stage, however, it was important to maintain a focus on developing an agreed strategy for immediate protective action towards

Mr Brown rather than attempting to highlight or resolve every difference in professional perception.

The health staff present at the meeting expressed great concern at Mr Brown's recent, rapid weight loss and the immediate risk this posed to his physical well-being. They were also able to confirm that the neglect of his medical needs, which seemed likely if the community nursing team continued to be prevented from entering the house, could quickly become life threatening.

Outcome of the initial strategy meeting

The outcome of the initial strategy meeting was an agreement that Mr Brown's next period of respite care should be used as an opportunity for further investigation. The possibility of extending his respite stay beyond the usual two weeks would be discussed with Mr Brown and separately with Mrs Brown. An extended stay would also provide an opportunity for Mr Brown to receive a thorough medical assessment.

In order for the situation to be assessed thoroughly and fairly, it was essential for effective relationships to be built with both Mr and Mrs Brown. A decision was made to be open with Mr Brown and to let him know that a group of professionals was concerned that he was being mistreated by his wife and that this was a matter of ongoing discussion. We decided to be less honest with Mrs Brown and to tell her that concern about her husband's weight loss and general health was the reason for extending his period of respite care. While this was not untrue, it was also clearly less than the whole truth. The decision was based on our perception that Mr Brown's apparent passivity might lead to him returning home at his wife's insistence, rather than his own, should she become more fully aware of our concerns. Our shared view that Mr Brown's life could be in danger if he were to go home meant that the decision not to tell Mrs Brown the whole truth immediately was collectively judged to be a necessary protective act in this particular case.

This dilemma highlights the complexity of ethical decision-making in social work practice. As Sarah Banks demonstrates in her thorough analysis of ethics and values in social work (Banks, 2006), professional principles and ethical codes are not always sufficient as a blueprint for practice. In complex ethical situations, good judgement, reflexivity and sensitivity to the particularities of a situation are also required.

Relationship building

After the initial strategy meeting, Helen, the social worker began the task of getting to know Mr and Mrs Brown. Establishing a relationship with both parties is particularly important in situations where the person who is allegedly being abused may wish to continue to live with the alleged abuser. Understanding that the unique dynamics of each individual situation are at the heart of effective risk assessment and protection planning is also essential. Helen's role at this stage was to listen and to try to understand as clearly as possible the human story at the centre of a complicated and dangerous situation. This was not only necessary as an act of information gathering in order to inform the next stage of planning and decision-making but it was also a valuable therapeutic activity in its own right. As Nigel Parton and Patrick O'Byrne (2000: 5) argue in their call for a return to language, listening and talking in social work: 'telling one's story and having it heard respectfully is a very necessary ingredient for change to begin to occur.'

MRS BROWN

Helen was able gradually to establish a relationship of trust with Mrs Brown, which enabled her to explain and explore the concerns of the various professionals involved in Mr Brown's care as well as learning more about Mrs Brown's needs. This took time, consideration and attention to the detail of relationship building. Helen later reflected on this process:

> I booked time alone with Mrs Brown when it was convenient for her. It was important not to be late and to give her my full attention; she needed to have some control and to see that I respected her and her environment. She said she was sick of people "just walking in and telling me what to do" and I could really see how it must get to feel like that in her situation. She felt that there were all these people telling her how to look after her husband, but no one was giving her permission to express her own concerns, let alone being concerned about *her* needs.

Part of Helen's skilled practice here was the deceptively simple act of facilitating Mrs Brown to take the lead in expressing and exploring her own and her husband's needs. Helen again expressed this eloquently when she came to reflect on her practice:

> Sometimes you need to jump sideways, it's no good rushing headlong at a person, you need to get alongside them. It wasn't until our second

meeting that I was really clear with her about our concerns. By that point, there was some sort of context – I had listened to her talking about how hard it was for her and also, how much he meant to her. By the time I actually used the word 'abuse', she took it pretty well because she knew I wasn't out to judge her and that we weren't just going to take her husband away from her.

By getting alongside Mrs Brown and not allowing herself to become attached to a preconceived view of her as an abuser, Helen uncovered a moving personal story.

Mrs Brown described a traumatic early life, with long periods of separation from her parents and many episodes of physical and sexual abuse at the hands of male relatives; as a young woman she was involved in a number of violent and abusive relationships. Mrs Brown spoke of her husband as her 'anchor'. His illness and consequent physical neediness hardly featured in her description of him. Instead she characterised herself as physically and emotionally weak and spoke of her husband as 'the strong one'. Mrs Brown talked about her tendency to shout and get angry and the way in which Mr Brown would remain calm and refuse to argue with her. She interpreted this behaviour as further evidence of his strength and ability to cope.

Some of the professionals at the initial strategy meeting had been critical of Mrs Brown for not visiting her husband while he was in respite care. As Helen discovered, this reluctance to go out alone stemmed from a fear of buses, crowds and strange people. Throughout their 30 years of marriage, Mr Brown had organised almost all activities of daily living including any tasks which involved reading or writing as Mrs Brown could do neither of these well. Her aggressive manner masked a deep lack of confidence; she felt that she had to shout in order to be listened to, but often regretted losing her temper. Her supports included cigarettes, which she wanted to give up and gambling. Mrs Brown described her feelings of desperation at her own and her husband's current situation although she refused to acknowledge that Mr Brown was unlikely to live for very long. She was unsure that she could continue to care for her husband, but felt that she could not cope without him.

Helen's good practice in her work with Mrs Brown involved seeking to facilitate the best possible resolution to the situation, rather than attempting to impose a solution. She refused to judge Mrs Brown for her limitations and was able to recognise both the risk to Mr Brown and his right to choice and self-determination. If Mr Brown had been a child, it is unlikely that he would have returned home. In such circumstances the responsibility of the professionals to protect in the face of such evident risk would almost certainly have overridden his right to self-determination. As it was, Mr Brown was an adult, albeit a very vulnerable one, with the capacity to make decisions about his own protection. Helen's role was to *hold* the situation while supporting Mrs Brown and facilitating Mr Brown through the process of making his own choices. As the 'No Secrets' guidance makes clear, the right of the vulnerable person to determine his or her own destiny should be at the heart of all adult protection activity:

> Agencies should adhere to the following guiding principles: ... act in a way that supports the rights of the individual to lead an independent life based on self determination and personal choice ... recognise that the right to self determination can involve risk. (DH, 2000: 21 4:3)

MR BROWN

Mr Brown had already built up a confiding relationship with one of the nurses at the home in which he was receiving respite care. She and Helen worked together to explain to Mr Brown, the concerns of the professionals involved. This was a far more open and straightforward process than the equivalent conversation with Mrs Brown. Mr Brown understood these concerns and acknowledged that life at home was risky and difficult for him. He accepted that some of his wife's actions and more often her inaction had had a serious negative impact on his health. His perception was not of his wife as an abuser however, but as someone who found it hard to cope and on whom he was a calm and stabilising influence. Although Mr Brown was aware that he could remain permanently at the nursing home if he chose to, this was not where he wished to spend the rest of his life. He loved his wife and was concerned about her health, which was far from good. His consistently expressed wish was to return home.

Mr Brown acknowledged that his wife had a temper and that she verbally abused him, but insisted that this was how she had always been and that he was used to it. Mr and Mrs Brown had been married for 30 years; during this time he had developed coping strategies, which included leaving the house when she began to shout. As he could no longer do this, he would simply remain quiet and wait for the storm to pass. In the past Mr Brown had taken an active part in shopping, food preparation and crucially in supporting and motivating his wife in relation to a whole range of daily living activities. His role as the partner in need of care and support was entirely contrary to the past dynamic of their relationship. But while Mrs Brown's reaction was to take out her anger and frustration at this new situation on her husband, Mr Brown responded by becoming increasingly passive and withdrawn.

The findings of a Canadian research project which looked at the experiences of abused and abusing adults strongly echo the apparent dynamics of Mr and Mrs Brown's situation. Nahmiash (1999) found that both parties tended to report feelings of aloneness, self blame, lack of self-worth and depression, while abusers often attempted to empower themselves by abusing the vulnerable other who could then only fight back or remain passive.

These findings may help to explain Mr Brown's extreme passivity, but for the professional involved it was still hard to understand in the face of Mrs Brown's aggressive outbursts. Helen struggled to make sense of Mr Brown's demeanour along with everyone else:

> He's so acquiescent – what's that all about? Is he very depressed or is it because he's so poorly? He's coming towards the end of his life and he needs care, but he's still trying to play the calm anchor – I can see that that's how it is, but it's very hard to accept.

An important skill in Helen's work with Mr and Mrs Brown was her awareness of the complex interplay of power and dependency within their relationship. This was a situation in which the dichotomies of oppressor and oppressed needed to be resisted in favour of a more nuanced and creative understanding. Helen achieved this by building a relationship which enable Mr and Mrs Brown to tell their stories and for those stories to be heard, accepted and understood. She was able to analyse the risks inherent in Mr and Mrs Brown's situation, together with the rights of Mr Brown and the needs of both partners. By refusing to make quick or easy judgements, Helen ensured that the situated truth of the Browns individual experiences and shared lives became the focus of the adult protection activity which followed.

The process of working through his experience with Helen, gave Mr Brown time to consider his future and to make decisions which would help to ensure his own protection. Although Mr Brown's initial response to the suggestion of abuse was to insist on returning home, he gradually moved to the conclusion that a 'shared care' arrangement whereby he could alternate weekly between his own home and the nursing home would be preferable. His expressed hope was that this would meet his own health needs, while regularly diffusing the situation at home and perhaps even helping to make his wife a little more independent.

THE PROTECTION PLANNING MEETINGS

Two protection planning meetings were held after Helen had completed her assessment. The first was a gathering together of professionals involved in the assessment process, at which Helen and others presented their findings to the multi-professional group. The second meeting, which included Mr and Mrs Brown, was set up to plan a package of ongoing protection and support.

Most of those present at the first meeting were vocal in their expressions of concern at the risk to Mr Brown of returning home, even on a 'shared care' basis. Helen did not disagree with these anxieties; the risks involved were too self evidently real. What she was able to do however, was to bring Mr and Mrs Brown's voices to the meeting and to ensure that, their views were represented, in their absence. The idea that Mrs Brown did not visit her husband during his stays at the nursing home, because she did not care for him had become close to a taken for granted 'truth' within the professional group. Helen was able to challenge this and other preconceptions by bringing her knowledge of Mrs Brown's fear of public transport, her lack of reading skills and her anxiety about meeting new people, into the discussion. As the complexity of Mrs Brown's history and experience became apparent, the label of 'abuser', which inevitably carries with it, the desire to punish, became far less relevant. Although some of those present continued to feel uncomfortable about the prospect of Mr Brown spending any time at all at home, a consensus gradually emerged that Mrs Brown needed care and support in her own right rather than blame. It was agreed that a more supportive approach to Mrs Brown was also likely to reduce the risk to Mr Brown and so help to meet both their needs.

It was essential for Mr and Mrs Brown to be involved in the second planning meeting. As Mike Linnett (2001) argues:

> to make plans about individuals without involving them fully in the process, could be considered patronising, possibly in contravention of their rights and likely to be unsuccessful as the best laid plans can only work with the agreement of the subject of those plans. (39)

There is a broad agreement that best practice in situations of child and adult protection demands that participants are fully prepared for their involvement in protection meetings (Linnett, 2001; Pritchard, 2001; DH, 2005). To this end, Helen and I met with Mr and Mrs Brown and a friend whom Mrs Brown had asked to support her, before the meeting. This enabled us to explain what form the meeting would take, to listen to any concerns and talk about what Mr and Mrs Brown should do if they felt they were not being listened to. It also gave us an opportunity to agree ways in which they could stop the meeting if they felt uncomfortable.

Mr Brown was able to tell the meeting clearly in person that he wanted to return home to be with his wife. The focus, therefore, remained much more clearly on his wishes than it had done in previous meetings. For Helen, this was an important validation of the approach she had taken in her work with Mr Brown and of the outcome of her assessment: 'This was a powerful event for me, as finally Mr Brown himself could object to attempts to rescue him and assert his right as an adult to make his own decisions.'

In spite of the effective work that Helen carried out, the presence of Mrs Brown did not make for a calm meeting; her manner was volatile and she repeatedly expressed her animosity towards some of those present. As chair of the meeting I needed to make full use of the previously agreed ground rules in order to ensure that Mrs Brown listened to others and was herself listened to. When she left the meeting at one point, I stopped the discussion until she returned in the hope of reinforcing the message that both the Browns were important to the process and outcome of the meeting. While this did not in itself make the decision-making process easier, it did help to ensure that all those present experienced the meeting as genuinely inclusive of Mr and Mrs Brown's perspectives.

This was a long and sometimes difficult meeting, which both Mr and Mrs Brown found physically and emotionally demanding. Nevertheless, a detailed package of support, which incorporated Mr Brown's wish for a shared care arrangement and Mrs Brown's need for additional support in her own right, was eventually agreed. Helen's final words describe an overall process which was respectful and responsive to the needs of both Mr and Mrs Brown:

> There was a lot of clarity in the process. Professionals were able to share their concerns and have them listened to and so were Mr and Mrs Brown. Practitioners and family members were left clear about what could and couldn't be done. Overall I thought the process of adult protection defended Mr Brown's right to make his own decisions and Mrs Brown's right to be properly listened to. We haven't found the perfect solution – he's still at risk, but the protective factors in their lives are much stronger and there's much more openness about what's going on and how we can help.

CONCLUSION

Mr Brown has recently returned home with a complex package of care and is spending respite periods in the nursing home where he previously received regular respite care. He is physically very frail and still often withdrawn. Mrs Brown is receiving services in her own right as well as support in her role as a carer. She is still at times abusive and neglectful and continues to struggle with her own physical and mental health. The adult protection process was never likely to result in a perfect solution for the Browns. A sensitively co-ordinated procedure and a critically compassionate social work assessment have, however, helped to facilitate a package of care, within which a group of professionals work alongside rather than in opposition to Mr and Mrs Brown. Mr Brown has made his own choices and decided to take risks in preference to a life apart from his wife in a 'safe' but ultimately unwanted environment. He knows that he has the option to leave and people to help him, should he feel he needs to. As a result, both Mr and Mrs Brown are better protected and the overall situation within which services are delivered is less a context of fear and recrimination and much more of partnership and understanding. This approach is essential for the future development of adult protection. Referrals to local authorities will increase markedly in the next five years as professional and public awareness of abuse develops. Situations of abuse are very diverse in nature and in the type of response needed. Some abuses will be perpetrated by unscrupulous people with criminal intent and some by paid carers who may be unfit to work with vulnerable people, but many abusive situations will involve complex histories and dynamics between people who have lived together for many years. Building empowering relationships, protecting rights and ensuring participation and choice, from within a position of openness and non-judgementalism, will ensure best practice in the protection of vulnerable adults from abuse.

REFERENCES

Adams, R (2002) 'Developing Critical Practice in Social Work', in Adams, R., Dominelli, L. and Payne, M. (eds) *Critical Practice in Social Work* (Basingstoke: Palgrave).

Association of Directors of Social Services (2005) *Safeguarding Adults – A National Framework of Standards for Good Practice and Outcomes in Adult Protection Work* (ADSS: London).

Banks, S. (2006) *Ethics and Values in Social Work* (Palgrave: Macmillan).

Brechin, A. 'Introducing Critical Practice', in Brechin, A., Brown, H. and Eby, M. A. (eds) (2000) *Critical Practice in Health and Social Care* (London: Sage).

Clements, L. (2000) *Adult Abuse and the Law* (www.communitycare.co.uk accessed 30.12.05).

Department of Health (2000) *No Secrets: Guidance on Developing and Implementing Multi Agency Policies and Procedures to Protect Vulnerable Adults from Abuse* (London: HMSO).

Department of Health (2004) *The Governments Response to the Recommendations and conclusions of the Health Select Committee's Inquiry into Elder Abuse* (London HMSO).

Department of Health (2005) *Action on Elder Abuse: Report on the Project to Establish a Monitoring and Reporting Process for Adult Protection Referrals Made in Accordance With 'No Secrets'* (www.dh.gov.uk accessed 30.12.05)

Fook, J. (2002) *Social Work: Critical Theory and Practice* (London: Sage).

Harbison, J. and Morrow, M. (1998) 'Re-examining the Social Construction of Elder Abuse and Neglect: A Canadian Perspective', *Ageing and Society*, 18: 691– 711.

Juklestad, O. (2004) 'Elderly People at Risk: A Norwegian Model for Community Education and Response', *Journal of Adult Protection*, 6 (3).

Linnett, M. (2001) 'Hard Care: The Role of an Adult Protection Unit and Coordinator' in Pritchard, J., *Good Practice with Vulnerable Adults* (Jessica Kingsley Publishers: London and Philadelphia).

Nahmiash, D. (1999) 'From Powerlessness to Empowerment' in Pritchard, J., *Elder Abuse Work, Best Practice in Britain and Canada* (Jessica Kingsley Publishers: London and Philadelphia).

Parton, N. and O'Byrne, P. (2000) *Constructive Social Work* (London: Macmillan).

Pritchard, J. (ed.) (1999) *Elder Abuse Work: Best Practice in Britain and Canada* (London: Jessica Kingsley Publishers).

Pritchard, J. (ed.) (2001) *Good Practice with Vulnerable Adults* (London: Jessica Kingsley Publishers).

11 Best practice with people with learning difficulties: being seen and heard

JONATHAN COLES AND PETER CONNORS

INTRODUCTION

Our aim in this chapter is to consider the nature of critical best practice (CBP) with people with learning difficulties. The co-authors of the chapter are Jonathan Coles, who works as a lecturer in social care and has a practice background in education and care with people with learning difficulties, and Peter Connors who is a learning and development manager in an organisation which provides residential and day care for people with learning difficulties, mental health needs and/or physical impairments.

Our experiences in a variety of settings over many years have led us to share Brown and Benson's view that 'Many people with learning difficulties will have experienced both oppression and devaluation in their lives' (1995: 32). In common with other minority groups, a powerful manifestation of this oppression has been a reduced or marginalised voice. Medical or individualised perceptions of disability tend to explain this in terms of personal pathology, locating the *problem* within the individual disabled person, perhaps in terms of their limited use of language or lack of articulacy. We would argue however, that the 'social' (Oliver, 1990; Coles, 2001) or 'disability equality' model (Campbell and Oliver, 1996) offers a fuller and more sophisticated interpretation of the experience of people with learning difficulties, arguing as it does, that the exclusion of disabled people is socially constructed.

It is important to make a distinction here, between 'language' and 'voice'. These are not the same thing. People with learning difficulties did not lose their voice because of their difficulties with language, but rather because of the oppression which flowed from their mass incarceration in 'colonies', asylums and long-stay hospitals. While our focus in this chapter is on people with learning difficulties, an all too similar story could be told in relation to people with enduring mental health needs and many of those with physical impairments. We take as our starting point, an understanding of critical practice as analytical, challenging and disruptive of taken for granted power relations. The practice we are seeking to promote as 'best', therefore seeks to integrate a critical appreciation of individual, personal narratives with a socio-political understanding of the marginalisation of people with learning difficulties.

The project we are going to describe in this chapter and the practice which underpins it is not perfect. It is constrained by time, by resources and inevitably by the skills of the practitioners and others involved. Nevertheless, it is practice which seeks to listen to and promote voices which have historically been silenced and which continue to struggle to be heard. It is the 'best' practice that those of us who were involved, were able to achieve at the time. As such, we hope that it may offer a critical focus for further discussion of the best that *can* be achieved in social work and social care practice with people with learning difficulties.

It is our contention that CBP must involve not only challenging the more and less subtle ways in which the voices of people with learning difficulties are quieted, but it must also seek ways in which those voices may be amplified. This chapter describes the production of a video which seeks to do this in a small way through a series of interviews with service users, most of whom, have learning difficulties and some who have enduring mental health needs. The video seeks to cast the participants as experts in their own situations, as they discuss a range of issues to do with their care and their life experiences.

The finished product is being used as a training resource with social work and social care practitioners. The critical issues which we attempt to address in this chapter, therefore, arise from a number of sources. The editorial and production decisions involved in facilitating and presenting the voices of those who appear in the video raised many questions and dilemmas for the makers of the film. The voices of the participants, which variously have the power to challenge, to enlighten and to disturb, are at the heart of the project, while the responses of those who have watched the video and been forced to question their own values and preconceptions also require critical attention. To this end, we would assert that the intervention we discuss was positive, affirming and creative and hope that as such it will offer some learning to others. Finally, in the name of what we consider to be 'best' practice, we have used the term 'learning difficulties' – the preferred label of the

British 'People First' movement, rather than the more widely used 'learning disabilities'.

WHY INVOLVE SERVICE USERS IN SOCIAL CARE TRAINING?

The struggle of people with learning difficulties in the United Kingdom and throughout the world, for inclusion and equal participation in society, is best understood within the context of the civil rights movements of the twentieth century. Just as women, black people, gay men, lesbians and people with physical impairments have had their voices marginalised or ignored, people with learning difficulties have often been considered unfit to be heard:

> The 'right' to a voice throughout history has been bestowed according to fluctuating perceptions of an individual's ability to benefit from that right. It is only in recent times that the essential personhood of people with learning difficulties has been more widely acknowledged. (Gray and Jackson, 2002: 7)

'People First' is an international network of self-advocacy groups run by people with learning difficulties, which began in Oregan in 1973 (Morgan, 2002) and was quickly followed by similar groups in Scandinavia. People First and similar organisations have done much to promote the civil rights of people with learning difficulties and particularly the right to be heard, through the concept of self-advocacy. As Dan Goodley suggests, this may take a number of possible forms, 'The self-advocacy movement has invited people with learning difficulties to revolt against disablement in a variety of ways, in a number of contexts, individually and collectively, with and without the support of others' (Goodley, 2000: 3).

People First has long argued for a stronger service user voice in the shaping of services which are used by people with learning difficulties and many UK branches make this explicit in their aims and mission statements. (See for example, http://www.peoplefirst.org.aims.html)

In recent years the involvement in service development and provision of those who use health and social care services, has received increasing recognition and support through formal policy initiatives. In the United Kingdom for example, the creation in April 2002 of the patient Advice and Liaison Service (PALS) has required health service providers to demonstrate that local service developments have been informed by patients' views. Also in the United Kingdom, the tradition of service user involvement in social work education has been formalised through the 'Requirements for Social Work Training' (DH, 2002), while the Department of Health now requires service users to be involved in identifying staff development needs and delivering training in all registered care homes (DH, 2003: 93).

In a review of rights-based social policy in relation to people with learning difficulties in the United Kingdom, British Columbia and Canada, Tim Stainton identifies the work of the Australian Advocacy Commission and the UK Whitepaper 'Valuing People' (DH, 2001) as indicative of a more inclusive approach to policy development, 'While advocacy and representation are not new concepts, what is new from a public policy perspective is that the state is increasingly recognising the structural necessity of independent support for articulating wants and needs.' (Stainton, 2005: 294)

While many have welcomed the incorporation of the principles of self-advocacy and empowerment within formal public policy documents, others have expressed a sense of unease about what they see as a policy take over of a radical movement. Dan Goodley for example, argues that self-advocacy cannot be neatly packaged as a service approach without losing the political edge which allows for lack of consensus and change within the movement and within the individuals who are part of it. He suggests that, 'In this sense, self advocacy is more in line with the criticality of the disabled people's movement than it is with the philosophies of policy making and service provision (Goodley, 2005: 341).

As Goodley implies, there is more to the hopes, fears and personal and political ambitions of people with learning difficulties than can be encompassed within the most ambitious social policy initiative. What is needed then is an open and critically questioning approach to user involvement in service development, which actively resists definitions of the *person* in terms of the service they receive.

PRODUCING THE VIDEO

Aspects and Milestones Trust is a Bristol based voluntary organisation, which provides residential accommodation and community support for people with learning difficulties, people with enduring mental health needs and people with physical impairments. It is one of the many voluntary organisations in the United Kingdom which have emerged following the closure of long-stay hospitals from the 1970s onwards. The Trust is working to increase the participation of its service users in the development of the organisation, including the training it provides to its staff. Managers and trainers within the organisation were particularly concerned to ensure that service users had a meaningful voice in the monthly induction training of new staff. While each training session would ideally include personal input from service users, this was proving difficult to achieve in a way which was both representative of those who used the Trust's services and which avoided tokenism.

The idea emerged, of producing a video comprised of interviews with service users from different parts of the organisation. Again our ideal of working collaboratively with service users through the production process was restricted by the limited budget which the trust was able to make available. It was, however, essential to provide careful information in a variety of formats to service users across the organisation and to ensure that time was taken to explain the project and gain meaningful consent from those who volunteered to take part. We also felt that it was vital to engage a skilled and experienced video editor and camera operator. The production of a high-quality product was one way in which we could reflect the importance we were attaching to participants' voices.

In spite of the fact that the project was to be led by professionals, the production team became increasingly confident that the video format could offer authentic ways of amplifying the voices of service users and so support the core principles of self-advocacy. The majority of those who volunteered to take part had been assessed as having some form of communication difficulty. Indeed it seemed likely that several participants would not use expressive language as their main method of communication. The team felt that the use of video might well provide a uniquely helpful medium for facilitating the voices of this group.

Our subsequent experience of making and using the video as a training resource has supported this hope in several ways. For example, the viewer is able to take account of body language as well as speech in interpreting communication, so the 'voice' of the service user is represented by that which is seen as well as heard. This is helped by the potential for rewinding the tape and viewing parts of it a second or third time, so that understanding can be sought with a degree of care and attention which might not be possible in other formats. Interviews were also carefully tailored to the needs of individual participants. While questions covered the same broad areas, we spent time talking with each person before their filmed interview in order to get a sense of the message that they wanted to convey. Our attempts to hold these messages in mind during the filming and the editing processes reflected our belief that 'voice' must be seen as more than language and words. Again the visual possibilities offered by the video format were particularly helpful in this respect. One valuable technique was the use of 'pick up' filming to support the narratives of some participants. For example, Fred's interview, which told of his passion for gardening through words and gestures, was clearly understood by his support worker, but was less accessible to anyone meeting Fred for the first time. We, therefore, filmed Fred in his greenhouse and placed parts of the interview soundtrack over these images, so giving the piece greater accessibility, while also remaining true to his particular message.

The temptation to 'lead' those who were participating in the video or to attempt to put words into people's mouths or shape the message being conveyed through the editing process was often great. Dennis Saleeby draws on the work of the educationalist Paulo Friere to highlight this difficulty and to stress the importance of communication when working with service users on mutually crafted projects:

> This requires us to be open to negotiation and to appreciate the authenticity of the views and aspirations of those with whom we collaborate. Our voices may have to be quieted so that we can give voice to our clients. Comfortably ensconced in the expert role, sometimes we may have great difficulty in assuming such a conjoint posture. (Saleeby, 2006: 14–15)

It was therefore essential to reflect critically on our power as professionals in this situation and to maintain our focus on the 'expertise' (Smale et al., 1993) of the service users with whom we were working. At the same time it was equally important to see ourselves as allies of people with learning difficulties and to acknowledge the positive application of our own power as a means to achieve change (Healy, 2000).

Jane Dalrymple and Hilary Horan, writing about independent advocacy in Chapter 9, argue that facilitating the voices of those who are excluded, marginalised or overlooked is apolitical act. In making the video described above, our critical focus likewise went beyond immediate issues of service provision within a particular organisation. While we intended that participants would express their views about good and bad care and the qualities they look for in support staff, we also hoped to challenge take for granted notions and stereotypes about people with learning difficulties. In order to achieve this in ways which might be positive and empowering for those taking part, it was necessary to attend to the *process* of the interviews and seek to facilitate open and free flowing narratives. As Parton and O'Byrne (2000: 184) argue, 'In order to understand a human situation we must go to the actors themselves and the act of telling their stories not only becomes the focus of the work, but a central way in which their situation can be improved.'

SERVICE USERS' VOICES

Robert Adams (2002) has argued that a key component of critical practice is the situating of people's histories with an awareness of context that brings together past and present. This point is illustrated poignantly in Chapter 3 where a social worker is enabled to understand the needs of an older woman with dementia through the story she tells of her earlier life. Most of those who took part in the video described here, had experienced life in long-stay hospitals with all the marginalisation, enforced dependency and powerlessness that even the most caring hospital regime is bound to create. As Ryan and Thomas point out, 'A hospital is a world divided into two, where the staff dominate the patients and the patients are dependent on the staff for most of their needs.' (1987: 45)

These experiences formed an important part of the lives of those we interviewed and not only featured strongly in their individual narratives, but also sometimes seemed to have a significant impact on how far they were able to engage with the topics being discussed.

For example, several of the participants were asked to talk about staff or staff behaviours that they did not like. This was noticeably difficult for some and produced quite a lot of anxiety. In fact the first three respondents would say no more than that the staff who worked with them were 'nice'. This initial experience prompted us to reflect on the high degree of confidence which would be needed for anyone who had spent much of his or her life in a special hospital or indeed any institution, to be critical of a care provider. It was clear that the interview questions would need to enable people to open up topics in their own way and the interviewers would have to listen more closely if they were to really *hear* the messages contained within individual narratives.

We switched to asking participants if they would like to talk about the 'old days'. This question produced a much more open and expansive response, with several people talking at length about positive and negative experiences of staffing regimes past and present. Another topic area sought to explore people's dreams and ambitions. At first we tried to achieve this by asking people what they would like to be doing in five year's time. While some people gave a full reply to this question, for several others it was a difficult concept to grasp and we were again struck by how challenging it must be for people who have had little choice or autonomy in their lives to imagine different future possibilities. By picking up cues from various responses, we adapted the trigger questions to focus more on what people would buy if they had lots of money. This seemed to resonate much more strongly and received a number of interesting and unexpected responses, some of which will be discussed further.

Nigel Parton and Patrick O'Byrne (2000) have developed what they call a 'constructive' approach to social work, which they describe as 'affirmative and reflexive' and based on 'listening and talking with the other'(186). This was a helpful reference point, which increasingly resonated with our own values, priorities and learning as the video project progressed. Parton and O'Byrne emphasise the importance of people's own life narratives in helping them to 're-author' their stories and so achieve change. We did not have the sort of therapeutic relationship with those taking part in the video to enable re-authorship, nor were we explicitly seeking to facilitate life change. However, our increasing preparedness to 'let go' and to trust people to tell their own stories in their own way, seemed to guide them to greater ownership of their own narratives and may indeed have had a therapeutic value. It certainly led to a more powerful and authentic video as an end result.

The voices on the final video were diverse, often surprising and variously warm, witty and disturbing. It is impossible to do justice here to the range of different opinions, feelings and experiences we encountered, but we would like to give a flavour of some of the common themes which should and can influence best practice with people with learning difficulties.

INDEPENDENCE, CHOICE AND AGENCY

Despite the commonly held view that people with learning difficulties are highly dependent, many of those who participated in the video placed great emphasis on their own usefulness and ability to make a valued contribution.

Dorothy and Betty, who live in a nursing home for older people with learning difficulties, both talked about the satisfaction they get from knitting items for charity to help disadvantaged people in Romania.

Dorothy explained: 'I like to do knitting. Betty casts on for me because I can't cast on for myself.' June said that she enjoyed shopping and helping with household tasks; her words and gestures are supported in the video by film of June laying the table and shopping in her electric wheelchair. Several respondents indicated a desire to help others. When asked what she would do with a sudden financial windfall, one woman said that she would 'buy presents for everyone' another said that she would buy 'presents for my family', someone else answered that he would 'invest it' and use the money to buy a house for his mother.

While these may not appear to be ambitious activities and aspirations, they indicate the importance of recognising the human need to give and provide for others, which can often be denied to people living in institutional care. Christine, who lives in a care home, was keen to assert her current level of independence. She made a series of clear, emphatic statements directly to the camera: 'I make my own decisions. I choose my own clothes. I put them on the bed myself.' The video shows her using the shops independently and chatting to customers and staff. Similarly Doreen talked about cashing her own benefits, doing her own washing, looking after her own room and cooking meals for friends, with the help of support staff.

Again, these may be considered mundane and ordinary activities, but the effect of hearing and seeing often unexpected strengths, together on film is striking. It is impossible not to be powerfully reminded that many people with learning difficulties and many of those who took part in the video in particular, have until recently been denied access to such ordinary activities and consequent feelings of achievement.

LEGACIES OF THE PAST

Not all of the messages coming out of the video are positive or comfortable to take on. When asked what she would do with 'lots of money', June replied that she would like to get married. She went on to talk about the hospital where she spent most of her life and explained that if females were found talking to males they would be put in their bedrooms and not let out until the men or boys had gone away. These comments highlight powerfully, the strength of the eugenics movement at the beginning of the twentieth century and the political determination to ensure that 'mental defectives' should not breed (Ryan and Thomas, 1987; Thompson, 1998). This policy was almost certainly responsible for the gender segregation which June experienced. Importantly, it is a policy which has a profound legacy amongst many middle aged and older people with learning difficulties who may have little expectation that they will experience committed or fulfilling intimate relationships.

The past oppression experienced by people with learning difficulties is starkly evident within the video, as people refer time and again to experiences of being 'locked up' and 'bossed around' in 'the old days'. It would be easy to become complacent or self-congratulatory about current service provision and the lives of people with learning difficulties today. While the circumstances of many have undoubtedly been transformed, a critical approach demands that questions continue to be asked and challenges made. We were aware, for example, that our sample of participants excluded some of those with the most profound learning difficulties, who have no voice or visual representation in the video. Similarly it is likely that those who feel least satisfied with the service they are receiving may have been the least inclined to volunteer to take part. There were also disproportionately few minority ethnic voices on the video. This raises serious issues for the funding organisation and supports Mir and Nocon's (2002) view that voices from these already socially excluded groups are also likely to be excluded from traditional ways of including people with learning difficulties.

Some of the voices on the video reflected dissatisfaction with both past and present service provision. Keith was one of several participants living in care homes who said that he would buy his own flat if he had lots of money and that this would be a place where he 'won't be shifted'. This seems to be the expression of a frustrated desire for autonomy on Keith's part, which service providers have been unable or unwilling to fulfil. However it probably also reflects the experience of many people living in long-stay hospitals, who would be moved from one ward to another with little consultation. When the hospitals closed and community homes were set up, many service users had little choice about where and with whom they would live. Keith's desire not to be 'shifted' may be both a rejection of the lack of agency he has experienced in the past and an assertion of what is currently most important to him.

BEHAVIOUR OF CARE STAFF

Most of the service users interviewed were very clear that they did not want those who work with them to be 'bossy'. This frequently used term often feels like a very mild way of describing some plainly oppressive behaviour and probably indicates a reluctance to criticise, which is itself a sign and symbol of oppression. There was, however, no mistaking the strength of feeling behind Keith's words as he described a recent experience of staff support: 'They took you on holiday and ended up telling you bloody off!' Keith also said that he did not like being 'checked on' and described how such staff actions play on his mind and have the effect of making him feel that, 'you can't be trusted'. This particular interview has prompted some lively and interesting discussions during training sessions. Several people have suggested that for all of us, the way we are treated by others, affects our self-image and many have drawn from this, conclusions which go to the heart of CBP, about the necessity of treating service users with respect and dignity.

A number of those who took part in the video identified positive qualities in the staff who work with them. Some of these are very general, such as 'nice', 'helpful' or 'helps me to do things'. Others are more specific and include a number of variations on the theme of independence, such as 'recognises that I like to do things myself' or 'sometimes I ask the staff not to do things for me … . and they don't'.

Some of the most powerful illustrations of best practice on the video come simply from watching staff members as they support service users during the interviews. Eric, an older man does not speak clearly, but relies on gesture, expression, humour and movement to convey his meaning. Those who have seen the video have found it easy to share the humour as Eric describes various amusing situations. They have also been immediately able to understand that working with Eric is not simply a matter of meeting his personal care needs, but of supporting his enjoyment of slapstick humour. With help from his supporter Eric recalled a time when he ripped his trousers during a cookery class at college. He and his supporter took it in turns to explain the situation, while both laughed warmly at the recollection. Eric also described a time when, as the same staff member was helping him to shower, he turned the shower head on her and got her 'all wet'. Again this was met with a great deal of shared mirth. Support workers are clearly more intimately involved in the day to day lives of those with whom they work than social workers. Nevertheless, this is a moving example of a practitioner who is able to span the usual boundaries between service user and the professional in a way which is appropriate, creative and genuinely empowering (Taylor et al., this volume).

THE PROOF OF THE PUDDING: RESPONSES TO THE VIDEO

Since making the video, we have used it many times in training sessions with staff ranging from inexperienced care assistants to senior social workers. The following observations are representative of many of the comments and responses we have received. One person said: 'These people are the experts on themselves – on their lives' another offered a variation on this: 'They've all got lots to say about what they want – even the ones who don't speak. We need to listen more.' There were also many comments along the lines of: 'They become individuals' and 'their personalities come across really strongly'.

These responses reflect some surprise at the strength and individuality of those whose voices are heard and seen on the video. One of the effects of past mass incarceration and a still limited community presence is the stereotyping of people with learning difficulties as dependent, incapable and unfamiliar or threatening. Social care workers, like everyone else, are surrounded by such assumptions. The video presents individuals with different personalities, strengths and tastes and has unsurprisingly challenged the taken for granted assumptions of those who have watched it.

Parton and O'Byrne emphasise the importance of the narrative voice of service users and the way in which diagnostic labels can so easily become a primary form of categorisation. To see someone principally in terms of their learning difficulty, their mental health need or their impairment can be a means of reinterpreting people's reality and taking control of their stories (Parton and O'Byrne, 2000: 184). However, as so many of the other chapters in this book show, best practice involves the preparedness of practitioners to listen closely to the stories of service users and to challenge their own personal and professional assumptions. It is only on the basis of such close and authentic engagement, that practice can be both empowering and appropriately authoritative.

What we are talking about here is a perspective which does not avoid judgement in the form of assessment, but which places people's strength and capacity at its core. As Saleeby argues:

> The diagnosis or the assessment becomes a verdict or a sentence. Our clients will be better served when we make an overt pact with their promise and possibility. This means that we must hold high our expectations of clients and make alliance with their hopes, visions and values. (2006: 18)

The trainee social care staff who have watched the video, have been surprised by the particular talents, knowledge and enthusiasm of individuals as well as the general competence and independence of so many. Service users are seen discussing and demonstrating their social strengths and a range of creative and technical abilities. Roberts spoke about choosing a holiday destination on the basis of its historical connections, saying that history was his best subject at school. Until that point in the video Robert has seemed distracted, stroking his chin and forehead nervously. As he became engaged in his favourite topic, he became more fluent and animated and looked directly at the interviewer. A senior social worker, who saw the video, felt that this challenged his preconception that service users with learning difficulties do not have academic interests or aspirations.

Observing and listening to practitioners as they watch the video, has offered a striking example of reflection in action (Schon, 1983). Napier and Fook (2000) argue for a reflective approach to practice, which challenges 'top down' notions of theory and effectively induces theory *from* practice. While the video is not a practice intervention as such, it does represent the authentic voices of those at the heart of any practice situation – service users. As people listen, reflect upon and learn from what they see and hear in the video, their understanding of people with learning difficulties is challenged and changed and new theory for practice is created. For many, this is an explicitly *critical* experience, in that the process of reflective analysis 'uncover(s) the ways in which unacknowledged assumptions and discourses construct power relations'. (Napier and Fook, 2000: 12).

Large numbers of people with learning difficulties have achieved a high level of success and satisfaction from their participation in teaching and training sessions. Like many of us however, others will feel that this sort of participation would not be reflective of their strengths or aspirations. The use of video and other more interactive new media technologies offer alternative and creative ways in which the voices of routinely marginalised individuals and groups may be heard. The video described here, was, as we have pointed out, subject to an editorial process, which included only limited service user involvement. Greater participation in the planning and final editing of the video, would certainly have strengthened the end result and should be apriority within similar projects. Nevertheless, it is our belief that the production and use of the video has been a critical and empowering endeavour, which contains key messages for social work practice with people with learning difficulties. In using inventive techniques to amplify the voices of those who are rarely heard or seen, the video challenges uncritical or taken for granted assumptions about people with learning difficulties and promotes best practice through an appreciation of individual strengths. As Saleeby points out, a strengths-led approach, demands the respectful interest and engagement of the practitioner with the authentic voice of the individual service user:

> the social work practitioner must be genuinely interested in and respectful\ of clients' stories, narratives and accounts – the interpretive angles they take on their own experiences ... .clients come into view when you assume that they know something, have learned lessons from experience, have hope, have interests and can do some things masterfully. (Saleeby, 2006: 16)

It is our hope that the video project and our analysis of it in this chapter, have brought into view some of the hopes, interests and masterful abilities of those who took part, with all that this implies for social work and social care practice with people with learning difficulties.

REFERENCES

Adams, R. (2002) Developing Critical Practice in Social Work in Adams, R., Dominelli, L. and Payne, M. (eds) *Critical Practice in Social Work* (Basingstoke: Palgrave).

Brown, H. and Benson, S. (1995) *A Practical Guide to Working with People with Learning Disabilities* (London: Hawker Publications).

Campbell, J. and Oliver, M. (1996) *Disability Politics: Understanding our Past, Changing Our Future* (London: Routledge).

Coles, J. (2001) 'The Social Model of Disability: What Does it Mean for Practice in Services for People with Learning Difficulties?', *Disability and Society* 16 (4).

Department of Health (2001) *Valuing people: A New Strategy for Learning Disability for the 21st Century* (The Stationery Office).

Department of Health (2002) *Requirements for Social Work Training* (The Stationery Office).

Department of Health (2003) *National Care Standards Commission: Regulations and Standards* (The Stationery Office).

Goodley, D. (2000) *Self-advocacy in the Lives of People with Learning Difficulties: The Politics of Resilience*, (Buckingham: Open University Press).

Goodley, D. (2005) Empowerment, Self-Advocacy and Resilience, *Journal of Intellectual Disabilities*, 9 (4), 333–343.

Gray, B. and Jackson, R. (eds) (2002) *Advocacy and Learning Disability* (London: Jessica Kingsley).

Healy, K. (2000) *Social Work Practices: Contemporary Perspectives on Change* (London: Sage).

Mir, G. and Nocon, A. (2002) Partnerships, Advocacy and Independence: Service Principles and the Empowerment of Minority Ethnic People, *Journal of Learning Disabilities* 6(2) .

Morgan, H. 'It's My Choice' in Carnaby, S. (ed.) (2002) *Learning Disability Today* (Brighton: Pavillion).

Napier, L. and Fook, J. (eds) (2000) *Breakthroughs in Practice: Theorising Critical moments in Social Work* (London: Whiting and Birch).

Oliver, M. (1990) *The Politics of Disablement* (Basingstoke: Macmillan).

Parton, N. and O'Byrne, P. (2000) *Constructive Social Work: Towards a New Practice* (Basingstoke: Palgrave).

Ryan, J. and Thomas, F. (1987) *The Politics of Mental Handicap* (Revised edition). (London: Free Association Books).

Saleeby, D. (ed.) (2006) *The Strengths Perspective in Social Work practice* (Fourth edition) (Boston: Pearson Education).

Schon, D. (1983) *The Reflective Practitioner* (New York: Basic Books).

Smale, G. and Tuson, G. with Biehal, N. and Marsh, P. (1993) *Empowerment, Assessment, Care Management and the Skilled Worker* (London: HMSO).

Stainton, T. (2005) Empowerment and the Architecture of Rights Based Social policy, *Journal of Intellectual Disabilities* **9** (4).

Thomson, M. (1998) *The problem of Mental Deficiency: Eugenics, Democracy and Social Policy in Britain, c 1870–1959* (Oxford: Oxford University Press).

12 Best practice in emergency mental health social work: on using good judgement

JOHN O'GARA

My shift on the emergency social work duty desk began at 10.00, one Saturday morning, with a typically terse instruction from the social work team manager: 'There's a mentally ill woman on the seventh floor of Olympic House threatening to throw herself and her baby off the balcony. Go and sort it out'. The implicit faith in my abilities was flattering, but the potential implications of the situation were almost numbing. In this chapter I will use this case example as the basis for examining some of the key issues and dilemmas in performing critical best practice (CBP) in mental health social work. Particular consideration is given to the core ethical dilemmas and tensions that arise from having the intention to work as a critical practitioner in empowering ways which promote service user's choice and self-determination, while being a statutory social worker operating within mental health legislation with the duties and obligations to protect vulnerable people that this brings. What in this context does it mean to use good judgement? In exploring ways to use good judgement and work with the tensions between care and control I will suggest that the discursive use of language (Potter & Wetherell, 1987) is important in all aspects of social work, and particularly in achieving CBP in 'emergency' mental health work. In the case example all names and other identifying details, of service users and professionals alike, have been amended to preserve anonymity. The exception to this is of course my own involvement and where verbatim accounts of what happened in practice are used I refer to myself as 'ASW'.

THE CONTEXT AND SOURCES OF
SOCIAL WORKERS' POWER

Recent Government changes to statutory social care services, in the United Kingdom and elsewhere, have reduced their direct provision function and decentralised intervention, so that assessment has joined, if not replaced, relationship at the heart of much social work. (Stepney & Ford 2000; The 1983 Mental Health Act (hereafter 'the Act'), in England and Wales (DOH, 1983) requires Approved Social Workers (ASWs) to arrange a formal assessment of someone where they feel it is necessary. One outcome of this mental health act assessment can be the legal detention and medical treatment of someone in a psychiatric hospital – against their will – if they satisfy particular criteria set down in the Act. This compulsory admission is colloquially known as 'sectioning' someone, reflecting how some sections of the Act cover compulsory admissions.

Such assessments generally involve two doctors examining the person and deciding whether they are 'mentally disordered', which is considered a matter of medical definition. Although the term 'examining' suggests some medical poking and prodding, it refers more to a question and answer session, together with observations of the patient's appearance and mood. If the doctors believe hospital is necessary, they may complete forms recommending compulsory admission. Based on these recommendations the social worker makes the executive decision whether or not to use the law to detain the person. If they decide to do so they make an application to a hospital for the compulsory admission of the patient, and then have a legal responsibility for ensuring that the person gets into the hospital safely. With respect then to the case study referred to at the outset of the chapter, the manager was asking me to convene a mental health act assessment with a view to determining whether such a 'section' was appropriate in this situation.

The simple presence of mental disorder is not in itself sufficient to necessitate hospitalisation. Crucial to the social work role is balancing the professional offer of expert help with an individual's rights to refuse or limit such help and incorporating an evaluation of the risks attached to either option. The available resources at this time and in the United Kingdom, as across the western world, tend to be medically focussed: hospital and nursing care, and licensed medications. Because statutory mental health social workers use primary legislation to guide them, it is impossible to avoid consideration of legislation (on these legal aspects of the work, see Brown, 2006). However, the law simply provides the framework within which decisions are made and our main focus here is on the professional and ethical tensions involved in practice. For example, empowerment is a core value of social work and underpins many of the intentions of social workers. Nonetheless, this espoused value to enhance and maintain user control is seriously compromised when exercising a legal power to take that very control away from the user. Similarly, this can lead to conflicts between social workers and other professional groups due to their different expectations and perspectives. Thus, the statutory social work role must be understood in terms of the ambiguity and ambivalence that are at its core and how the work routinely evokes a challenging mixture of the uncomfortable and the satisfying. A CBP perspective (Ferguson, 2003; see also Chapter 1, this volume), involves uncovering and embracing these dilemmas and setting out how they can best be theorised and creatively worked with in everyday social work practice.

THE COMPLEXITIES OF GATHERING AND INTERPRETING INFORMATION

Let us return to Justine, a white British woman aged 29, and her six-week-old baby Emma on the balcony of a tower block. Several questions spring to mind about it, aside from the immediate one of how to try to prevent deaths. An important question concerns the way in which such situations come to our professional attention in the first place; and how far the details given to us are accurate? The manager has asked me to go and carry out a mental health act assessment to determine whether this person needs to be treated for an apparently overwhelming psychiatric problem. The first step is to establish what is reliably known about the situation. After a deep breath to gather my wits, a call to the manager revealed that a member of the public had seen Justine on her balcony and alerted the police. They already had trained negotiators on hand trying to secure the safety of the child and the mother, and had then contacted the Social Services Department.

A difficulty in interpreting situations such as this is that comments made by most of us are viewed figuratively. If I say in anger (say, about a naughty teenager), 'I'll kill him,' no-one takes this literally. Put these words into the mouth of someone deemed mentally distressed, like Justine here, and the exact opposite applies. We need, therefore, to attain as precise an understanding as possible of what has been observed and said. Was Justine in the very act of hurting herself and/or Emma? Was she simply stating she would do so, but not carrying out the act despite having power to do it? Was she threatening someone else with this act, to coerce them into doing something? What was her intention? Questions arise as to whose needs are paramount here and for whom? More than one person's welfare is involved, reminding us that people do not exist in a social vacuum. The ethics of intervention in this case are complicated by the situational context of 'mental ill health' and, even more pressingly, by a child's vulnerability. An extreme libertarian ethical stance (Szasz, 1974) would argue that adults have the right to harm themselves, but those rights would not extend to damaging another person, particularly a child's safety. Achieving a reflexive understanding of this situation then, has to include scrutiny of the social worker's own perspectives, professional codes of ethics (GSCC, 2002), and the assumptions that are brought to an assessment (Glover, 1990).

The professionals at the scene agreed that it was imperative first of all to secure the safety of Emma and Justine. Only once these objectives had been achieved could we move to the assessment of her well-being itself. The role of the trained police negotiators was crucial here and it would have been naïve and potentially fatal for me or the psychiatrists to have attempted to step into this role. Fortunately, the police persuaded Justine off the balcony, managing to get hold of Emma and a child care social work colleague took her to be cared for by Justine's mum.

Gaining some sense of how the person is from those who know them is crucial and I decided to immediately take the opportunity to engage with Justine's mother. Dilemmas arise for families in their choices about what to pass on to professional workers (Shardlow & Doel, 1996). For some families getting access to professionals is difficult, and once they have this attention they are reluctant to let go without giving a full story as they perceive it. That can involve telescoping a long history of actions into a single event. This is not in any way to diminish or belittle the family's anxieties, but it is easy to come away with an impression which conflates everything into the present moment. One effect of this is to increase the perception of urgency to a situation. A key task of the social worker then is to take account of the history and to see the present crisis on its own terms, not confusing it with the past.

Justine's mother told me that Justine had been in psychiatric hospital before, some ten years earlier. I would need to try and get a sense of how life had been for Justine during the intervening ten years and whether this current development is an entirely new phenomenon. Her mother said that the previous difficulties had arisen when Justine was a student away at college, and had been dumped by a boyfriend. She linked this to the present situation by saying that the father of Emma abandoned Justine on learning of her pregnancy. A critical approach seeks to make explicit the assumptions and motives behind and forming such accounts. I tried exploring Justine's mum's reasoning about identical cause–effect chains applying now as then:

ASW:	So you are saying that a similar event has (re-) triggered the same problem ... ?
Justine's mother:	Of course.
ASW:	Did she threaten to harm herself or anyone else before ... ?
Justine's mother:	No.
ASW:	If events were running along the same course might she have done something immediately he abandoned her, or waited ... ?
Justine's mother:	Hmm straightaway I suppose ...

It seemed clear that Justine's mother wanted her daughter put into hospital, and was trying to persuade professionals of the need for this. When one line of argument seemed unpromising, she changed tack. Although paying explicit respect to professional expertise in assessment and diagnosis, families often 'warn' an assessment team about the interviewee.

Justine's mother:	Justine's very clever, she's pulled the wool over the doctor's eyes.
ASW:	What do you mean?
Justine's mother:	She's very good at pretending there's nothing wrong. She'll tell you she's fine.
ASW:	*What would show us she wasn't?*
Justine's mother:	She hasn't slept this week, even when the baby's gone off – she's been pacing in her room at night, arguing with ... somebody.
ASW:	Somebody there ... or who wasn't there?
Justine's mother:	*No* – with her voices. She's psychotic.

In raising my own suspicions, I asked Justine's mother a leading question (Trevithick, 2000), though I do not seem to have put words into her mouth. Her use of a technical psychiatric term was more typical of families and users who have a greater previous connection with services than was the case here. However, she had been looking things up on the internet, and acquired the jargon. What is included in and omitted from someone's account, besides the slant of how things are presented in their narrative, is often done with impression management in mind (Billig, 1997). All parties to what is a 'crisis' in a family's life will have their own accounts, in the sense of having their own angle on events, and varied motives. There are often several overlapping and not necessarily compatible narratives which social workers must integrate. Such perspectives and assertions can be explored explicitly with users during the formal assessment interview. The CBP acknowledges this plurality of accounts, whilst also gently questioning them all (including one's own developing views as a practitioner) in order to elicit hidden assumptions and intentions.

THE ASSESSMENT

Although the views of people like her mother assisted in making the assessment, Justine's own perspective was obviously paramount. This was done in conjunction with the other professional present, while it is the social worker who is responsible for coordinating an assessment and for arriving at an individual professional decision. Clarity of language matters greatly here in framing actions. The ASWs go out to do *assessments*, not to do 'sections', which are merely one possible outcome. The independence of their role is set out in the legislation and it is important that they make a decision that is both within the law yet in the best interests of the patient or client. For emergency mental health assessments, ASWs need to find two doctors to attend with them at short notice, although there is some latitude over who this should be.

Like all decisions, such choices need to be influenced by what is in the best interests of ensuring services users having the best expertise available and are treated fairly. Critical practice involves being aware at all times of the influence of social divisions such as class, race, gender, sexuality and religion on people's lives and how they are responded to by services. For example, African-Caribbean males are compulsorily detained proportionately more than white males (McGovern & Cope, 1987). Black men are also viewed as much more dangerous and violent than their white counterparts, or women (Walker & Beckett, 2004: 47). The poor reliability of predictors in the field of mental distress caution us against accepting findings unquestioningly, and sensitise us to the need to seek to incorporate safeguards of critical thinking to protect peoples' rights.

One approach towards minimising this discrimination is to seek to match the user's social background with the professionals'. As being myself a white British man, had Justine been from a black or minority ethnic group I would have sought to correct for that in any way possible. For example, one would try to involve an advocate from a black users' group if possible, or at least one doctor from a similar ethnic background. In this case I was unable to get a female doctor, but ensured a female police officer was present for Justine. It was she who informed us that Justine had been persuaded to step inside from the balcony of her own accord.

An assessment normally begins with introductions by the assessing team and an attempt to explain their framework, aims and intentions. This worked here, although with some people, especially those in a very manic or angry state, it can be all but impossible to achieve this effectively. It is also vital to maintain a distinction between mental distress and criminal behaviour. It can do unhappy or confused people little good to additionally feel under threat of being criminalised. The presence of the police in uniform has powerful symbolic connotations for people when they are feeling vulnerable.

> ASW: Justine the police aren't here today to arrest anyone, their job is to keep everybody safe and so they will stay whilst we talk to you ...
>
> Justine: You're going to lock me up in hospital aren't you? They always hunt in packs of three.

The last comment appeared to be an aside made towards the wall of the flat.

> ASW: There might be a range of options, from doing nothing at all and leaving you to get better on your own, through someone coming to talk to you, through to a short period in hospital ...

Though the aim of the assessment is to find out how best to help someone, immediately mentioning the possibility of detention can be both alarming and undermining. However, many people, just like Justine, are perfectly aware of these options, particularly 'sections'. Best practice means careful use of conversational and interviewing skills (see also Chapters 5 and 6, this volume).

The doctors will spend some time questioning the person, usually moving fairly swiftly to the known or suspected concerns, seeking for signs typical of mental disorders. However, it is crucial for those involved in an assessment not to be drawn into a 'psychiatric reductionism' which primarily sees people as being defined and categorised solely as a set of symptoms. Despite these symptoms, the person retains some degree of motivation and intent which needs acknowledging, as well as strengths which might be harnessed (Ryan & Morgan, 2004).

The team sought some understanding of the sequence of events, but Justine, although not outwardly visibly distressed by Emma's removal, refused to discuss this and resorted to rocking in her chair. After some fruitless repetition of questions about her intentions on the balcony, the doctors became blunt:

Dr Smith:	Do you hear voices?
Justine:	(Cupping her hand to her ear) I can hear you.
ASW:	No do you hear voices when no-one else is around?
Justine:	Yes I have the TV on most of the time, and the walls of the flat are so thin I can hear the neighbours arguing.

This sort of linguistic judo is typical of most of us when we want to avoid a particular line of discussion. However, someone in Justine's position persisting with it in what is a serious situation suggests a lack of grasp over the likely consequences of the strategy. Doctors can be persuaded that this kind of 'recklessness' may be a sign of more general mental dysfunction. The discussion thus far appeared to be accompanied by a clearly resentful stance from Justine. For the critical practitioner, this could be seen as a perfectly rational response to the invasion of her privacy. Besides acknowledging this explicitly, good practice involves using subtle shifts in register to get beyond the resistance:

Dr Jones:	When you're on your own with the telly off and the neighbours are quiet, do you hear voices telling you to harm yourself or other people?

This approach sought to construct a sense of mutuality and get underneath the resentment, with its informal reference to the 'telly'.

Justine:	No. Course not. Duuh.

At a certain point, however, one must confront matters head on. I suggested that we had some third-party evidence from her mum that this was in fact happening. After initially trying to maintain that it must have been another neighbour's TV, Justine either ran out of persuasive alternative accounts, or the energy to continue this line.

Justine:	Well yeah sometimes. They drive me mad …
ASW:	Do you think we might be able to work out with you some better ways of dealing with the voices?

Having come close to establishing a possible constructive engagement, it was an important part of the assessment to observe Justine looking over to the corner of the room and seemingly involved in some kind of discussion with no-one. On being gently redirected to focus on us, she was less willing to continue in positive mode.

Justine:	I don't want help from you people. I don't even know you but your sort just messed my head up before.

Despite our collective entreaties, including a warning/ threat reminding her of the decision we were likely to come to without further contributions from her, Justine began pacing up and down and muttering quietly to herself while repeatedly looking to the same corner of the room. Despite being similar in age to the professionals present, Justine could be said in some ways to have regressed to an adolescent level of behaving towards these three male authority figures, and so it seemed worth trying to shift this and emphasise a different self-identity, that of a caring and competent mother:

ASW:	Justine you have been looking after Emma for 6 weeks now, and being a new mum is never easy. But everybody says how well she has been cared for.

But after a short dialogue in which this was underlined, it was also necessary to keep in touch with the reality of today's dramatic events.

ASW:	Given what you were threatening earlier, you must see that you could do with some help with all this …
Justine:	I just went a bit mad for a minute. I'm fine now … I just need some space from this lot.
Dr Smith:	Who do you mean Justine? Who is "this lot"?
Justine:	Them! They make me do things.

A critical perspective leads us to explore the intentions and the meanings behind peoples' utterances, while taking full account of the power dynamics existing in the encounter. It is particularly hard to achieve in this kind of circumstance. Our own sense of external reality is so strong that it is hard to conceive of someone really believing that they can hear voices which do not exist. One almost has to laugh at it, perhaps feeling they are playing games with us and having us on. The shock to someone when voice-hearing first happens must be tremendous, but of course by the time professionals become involved the person may have got quite used to it.

Having a knowledge base on which to make sense of such behaviours is crucial to CBP. Over the past century or so, the theoretical focus about mental distress has been on medical symptoms and syndromes (e.g., 'schizophrenia') based on brain dysfunction, leading to a qualitative distinction between normal' and 'abnormal'. Recent work (Bentall, 2003) has sought to develop a coherent theory with a different unit of analysis, taking cognitive constructs as human variables ranging in prevalence. Approaches at the psychological level may shed more understanding than does a biological perspective on the importance of hallucinations and delusions. For the latter, the content of what 'voices' say is taken as meaningless (Boyle, 2002). Critical thinking (Adams et al., 2002) invites us to re-contextualise an assumption that, say, to hear voices automatically necessitates hospital, and drug treatment. Coleman and Smith (1997) report successful ways of working with people in sustained self-help groups to manage the effects of voice-hearing, although as yet in the United Kingdom this resource is limited. Voice-hearing of itself certainly does not necessarily imply impaired competence, as Romme and Escher (1996) demonstrate.

At the immediate point of an assessment however, the issue of what caused the problem may become secondary. For whatever reason, a person's rational faculties and sense of social reality may have shifted in directions posing increased risks to their welfare. Like a kayak rider who has tipped over, unable to self-right their craft, discovering this was caused by a large wave is no consolation. It appeared then, that Justine's voices were compelling her to behave in dangerous ways. Our urgent priority was to decide whether and how she could be helped to manage any destructive commands to reduce the risks to herself and others. It was vitally important then for us professionals to make sense of Justine's voices: who 'they' are, and what they communicate. This had to be done in the knowledge that we did not have time to forge therapeutic relationships with her in the current crisis, and the perceived risks appeared to remain too great for us to leave her alone at home.

It is ethically vital for the assessing team to try to persuade someone to genuinely accept help on a voluntary basis. This requires some evaluation, since there are inevitably those who agree just to get professionals out of their house, or because they realise they will be detained otherwise.

In these cases help is sometimes defined as acceptable if it is to happen later and the person may try to avoid a specific contract about this. It is almost easier when people categorically refuse, since at least professionals know where they stand. Justine had retreated into herself and would no longer engage in discussion with us. Appealing to her responsible side was not working, and so we stepped outside to form a plan.

THE PROFESSIONALS' DECISION

Following an assessment interview, the team of professionals often withdraws to discuss their views out of the hearing of the user. At this point the perceptions of the different professional groups are pooled in a negotiation over what should happen next. A continuous range of factors has initially to be distilled into a single decision: are we going to section the person or not? Practically, this involves evaluations of perceived risk and how it might be managed, though at a level of meta-theory the discussion may be seen as an 'empirical window ... into power structures' (Nikander, 2003: 114).

Some people feel it best to have this discussion in the presence of users, though doctors often prefer otherwise. That may be due to fears of further upsetting already-distressed users, or of their probable disagreement or hostility. Some social workers worry that it is used by doctors to emphasise numerical medical advantage and persuasive power over the social worker. Generally these discussions are honest, concerned exchanges. The patient's mental state is considered on the basis of the language used by them in the interview. The parties involved also use language of course, to put the most favourable light on their own preferred outcome. Views are sometimes expressed with little thought for contradiction.

> Dr Jones: Well she's obviously sectionable.
>
> Dr Smith: She clearly needs to come in.

Evaluations may prioritise various negative dimensions of people's identity (Edwards, 1997) – such as specific symptoms, capacity and risk, at the expense of competences and strengths.

> Dr Jones: She is hallucinating ... and seems unable to resist the voices telling her to harm the baby ...
>
> ASW: She seems not to be sleeping at all, and has put her child at serious risk ...

For social constructivists such as Edwards (1997) and Burr (1995), language constructs situations – a stronger claim than to say it merely reflects them – and social workers must keep in mind the large differences in meaning which can come from slight changes of phrasing, as Adams et al., (2002: 3–4) demonstrate succinctly. With slightly more success in reaching Justine, we could have examined options such as allowing her to stay at home and involving a crisis or assertive outreach team with her. We could have clarified what risks we were prepared to take, and what strengths we could build on (Ryan & Morgan, 2004).

However, on this occasion it seemed that despite all efforts there was little clear hope of securing a reasonable arrangement to keep Justine safe at home, and so I agreed with my medical colleagues that a 'section' was required. Hospital could provide a safer environment for exploring her distress. Inevitably, there will be occasions when both the doctors feel compulsory admission is essential but the ASW refuses (see Gatefield & McGarry, 2005). The ASW has to balance the risks posed by admission and non-admission. Moreover, whilst having powers to detain her, the organisation of emergency mental health social work in the United Kingdom and separation of increased assessment from subsequent service provision (Milner & O'Byrne, 1998) meant that I had no control over the kinds of help she received in hospital, which could be drugs or electro-convulsive therapy (ECT). Thus, besides the obvious risks from doing nothing, attention must be given to risks posed *by* the treatment (Pilgrim & Rogers, 1997), which include the psychological consequences of forced loss of liberty (Campbell, 1996),plus the role of anxiety in professional decision-making (Ferguson, 2005).

However, increased mutual respect between doctors and social workers means that happily we have moved on from the days when a doctor said to me 'well if she dies it will be your fault', which was an unconstructive response some years ago to my refusal to detain someone. Professionals are now more willing to act coherently and cooperatively to develop an alternative care plan to admission, notwithstanding the fact that differences of opinion, reservations and uncertainties often accompany decision-making.

The doctors and I returned to the room and advised Justine that we felt our only option was to 'section' her, and went on to explain what this entailed. This decision often leads to people becoming more amenable to earlier, previously rejected suggestions, such as voluntary admission, causing one to question one's judgement. However, sometimes they stop trying to 'hold it together' and a string of bizarre thoughts and feelings may be released. A social work practice which prioritised liberty would view this outcome as a negative one, but I had no qualms about the decision as I felt our assessment to be fair and comprehensive, because of how it was based on sound knowledge, skill and critical thinking. The risks of leaving Justine at home were too high and so the protection we provided was the best practice under the circumstances.

SAFE JOURNEY

Once such a decision has been made, a hospital bed is organised through the medical and nursing channels. However, one remaining task for the social worker is to ensure that the person gets there safely and effectively. Conveying psychiatric patients can be problematic for ambulance crews. People in car crashes or who have heart attacks are not normally unwilling passengers, but this can be problematic when it comes to mental health detentions. There will be some risk of the patient deciding not to go, and crews vary over how far they are willing to lay hands on someone as a form of encouragement, although the ASW has the power to delegate legal rights to them to do so.

There is a degree of calculation often undertaken by the patient. What are the odds here? What's the balance of power? Are they really going to compel me or can I sit tight and maybe they will go away? Justine seemed to be stalling for time by insisting 'OK OK but I'm dirty. I need a bath before going to hospital,' a delaying tactic that is not uncommon. It was met by Dr Jones saying 'Have one at the hospital. It'll be less of a rush then, a bit more relaxing.' In this case of course there were more serious considerations than merely delay, as we had concern that she may self-harm if allowed to lock herself in the bathroom. Justine then stated she needed to go to the toilet. I asked the policewoman if she could remove the lock, which proved simple enough. She also looked through the bathroom cabinet and removed some razor blades. Justine was then invited to use the toilet, which she no longer wanted to do.

Inevitably, urgent medical cases will take priority for the ambulance service and so there can be long delays over transporting psychiatric patients, as proved in the case here due to a traffic pile-up. In situations where the ASW and possibly a doctor wait at the person's home for an ambulance without police support, the sort of power struggle noted above is less clearly in the professionals' favour. In addition, if the person is in genuine distress a wait of several hours can only exacerbate this. We considered alternatives.

One was for me to take Justine in my own car. However, although nearly every ASW I know has taken a detained person to hospital this way at least once, it is generally unwise. Even when seating someone in the rear, with seat belts and child locks, and one or two escorts, there is still a chance that a reluctant passenger could try and leave. This is not to characterise them as unpredictably insane or wild, but merely to emphasise that moving cars are inherently dangerous objects, and any untoward events inside the car can easily lead to accidents. At Justine's flat, we did have a further option, which was to request transport in a partitioned police vehicle, which the police prefer to one of them travelling as an additional escort in an ambulance, as it gives them more control over situations. For maximum road safety they generally seek to use handcuffs, which I sought to avoid. Beyond the social stigma attached to Justine being publicly taken away in a police car, I feared it would increase her apparent feelings of degradation and restriction of liberty. It was also likely to enhance false public stereotypes equating madness with dangerousness (Muijen, 1996). I was able to engage Justine sufficiently to ask her and she said she preferred conveyance by police now rather than ambulance later. We were able to negotiate sufficient police staffing plus myself to convey her safely to hospital without handcuffs. Overall, it felt that a difficult situation had been resolved effectively through good communication and with the cooperation of several disparate professional groups.

INTER-PROFESSIONAL WORK AND SKILL RECOGNITION

As will be clear, an important aspect of this work is that it is inter-professional and one does not act alone. As we saw here, doctors and social worker, ambulance crew, police and others may all play some part in the overall process. Besides holding powers of detention, the ASW has the ultimate responsibility for pulling together the different inputs from these specific professional roles. Psychiatrist's skills centre on evaluating the relevance of the patient's comments and mood to their mental state. A catalyst here is what used to be known as 'bedside manner', or the way in which they deal with the patient on a human level. In social work, we stress the importance of 'relationship' and our ability to forge an immediately trusting relationship with service users. As we have seen, this sometimes needs to be made to happen in coercive situations. Ambulance crews know how best to encourage relatively unwilling and resistant passengers to go along with them. Police are trained to maintain physical control over situations in the least damaging way.

Like those of actors, set designers and make-up crew in a theatre play, these disparate skills need to be combined effectively by someone, in order to make the whole performance work. Like the director of a play, the ASW is the axis on which hinges the success of the enterprise as a whole. Acknowledging and respecting their colleagues' skills, ASWs have to have an overview of the various roles and tasks involved, and coordinate their deployment appropriately. This requires a degree of authority to be assumed for the duration, which can lead to difficulties with other professionals, who act according to their own sets of rules and authority structures, and some of whom are not used to being told what to do. At times they have to be gently directed by the ASW, someone who is outside their own organisational culture, and possibly perceived as being below them in status. As on the stage, resentment and resistance can occasionally arise. CBP involves avoiding taking any tensions personally, while skilfully maintaining a focus on the task in hand.

USER PERSPECTIVES, PREVENTION AND COMMUNITY SUPPORT

Through it all, we must not forget that the key participant in the enterprise is the service user at the centre of it all. The past 30 years have seen increasing acceptance in social work that users have important inputs to make in resolving their own crises in the way they want to do, potentially diminishing the professional expert role (Campbell, 1996b). The status of users has increased, they are viewed more as experts on their own situation, and responsibility for solutions is more often than not a widely-shared matter. This is generally less true in medicine, and as mental distress is still characterised as being a medical matter, can lead to doctors, ASWs and users having conflicting takes on the meaning of a given situation. This in turn can make for difficulties in coming to agreement on a widely-shared responsibility for resolving problems and managing risk. The ethic of user-empowerment is embedded within a nexus of values rather than being paramount to all inter-professional work. Recently in mental health work we have seen the increasing use of advance directives (MIND, 1999), whereby individuals can specify, when well, the kinds of treatment they wish to receive, or avoid, in case of future illness, although these are not binding on professionals.

The service user 'voice' may refer to more or less representative opinions given by bodies of service user groupings. There is little apparent willingness by government to listen to such voices in the mental health field – planned legislation is characterised by prioritising public safety over user rights (DOH, 1999a and 1999b). Further, users make the criticism that even such service-led initiatives as do exist diminish their views through tokenistic listening. Hodge (2005) argues that structural inequities such as poverty are ignored politically and airbrushed out of debates, meaning such wider perspectives are excluded from policy-making.

This is all at a public policy level however, and does not deal with the views of individual service users at the point of service delivery. How do users feel about the process and outcome of mental health act assessments? Some answers have been collated by Rogers et al., (1993); (see also, Keeping, this volume). Other writings suggest that demonstrating respect (Repper et al., 1997), and clear communication to service users, whilst not overcoming the loss of power entailed (Campbell, 1996a), are crucial factors. Inevitably, it is difficult to make general conclusions as some people I have detained have been very angry, even years afterwards, either refusing to speak to me or becoming aggressive. Others have ruefully acknowledged that I may have been right to take the action I did. As one put it to me: 'I was really out of it by that stage, wasn't I?'

In fact, a year later I bumped into Justine, shopping with Emma, then a toddler. We were both quite embarrassed, but she did express gratitude to all the people who had helped her get better at that time, and how awful it would have been to have been allowed to harm her daughter. She had remained in hospital for three months, the last two voluntarily, and had been helped by a combination of medication and talking through the various stresses on her.

One frustrating aspect of emergency duty work is that it is not always easy to carry out any follow-up. Sometimes one does not even know what happened to the person later. Human rights legislation in terms of privacy of information further complicates the issue, since the end to professional involvement with someone means one has no continuing rights to information on their welfare. It is nice to know what happened, partly for reassurance, but also to be able to reflect in an informed way over how one acted, since it is hard to develop one's practice without accurate feedback.

Doing emergency duty work of this kind is also problematic from a more general point of view in that it focuses on immediate individual crises, often losing sight of the preventative aspects. Consideration of compulsory admission is the end of the line, and should only be necessary when all other options have been exhausted – not being simply a 'plea-for-removal crisis' (O'Hagan, 1986) through ignorance of possibilities. Prevention covers both individual and community levels, and can involve statutory and voluntary bodies. However, 'preventive work' is often viewed in statutory social services as a luxury option, a managerial carrot offered to staff to maintain their enthusiasm, but the first thing to be cut when workloads increase.

As long ago as the 1890s, the eminent social reformer Beatrice Webb remarked that 'social workers … only pull people out of the swamp, instead of draining it'. While assessments are necessary, this does not preclude ASWs working more generally to enhance community resources, that is helping to drain the swamp which contributes to mental ill-health. Facilitating a local voice hearers group, for instance, can be seen as a step towards empowerment at the group, or collective level (Dominelli, 2002: 18), as part of a critical practice. User run services such as (in the UK) the Hearing Voices Network could be invaluable for Justine. It is crucial to stay aware of the locally available resources and projects (Johannessen, 2004) which help provide community support and avoid the need for hospital admission. A distinctive contribution of critical social work is that it highlights user views and group action (see MHF, 2001; Duggan et al., 2002), perspectives which need to be developed at the training level (Bainbridge, 1999; Jordan & Parkinson, 2001). Such a critical approach enables individually focused practice to remain embedded in the social conditions which contribute to what people are and the interventions and supports that can help them.

CONCLUSION

This chapter has examined the dynamics of practice in conducting an emergency mental health assessment and the ethical dilemmas which flow from the use of statutory powers to protect vulnerable people. While all cases are individual and different, the core issues involved are quite typical of such practice. It is particularly important not to form the impression that all mentally ill people are dangerous to themselves or others. This is not so – most are simply extremely distressed and keen to get the help which is often lacking. The question of compulsory admission is only considered for a small percentage of cases, not the majority. The key point is that the very act of having, considering the use of such powers and using them raises profound ethical dilemmas which cannot be reduced to simple formulas of 'good' or 'bad' practice or outcomes. Using statutory powers to detain them, as this chapter has shown, is often precisely what vulnerable people need. It should not be framed as an inherently oppressive thing to do, but a course of creative action which can ultimately help to put people on the road to recovery. In individual cases, many factors need to be considered with each user before decisions can be made: sometimes people get detained, sometimes not. The same is true of outcomes: sometimes they get well again, sometimes not, and these two are not always linked. Happy endings are not always guaranteed in social work, yet the difficult decisions must still be taken, even in the light of imperfect information. The central message is that social workers must continually question all aspects of their practice and where they believe that restricting liberty may be the appropriate option, awareness should be maintained of the person behind the symptoms – a person with intentions, struggling to make meaning out of their own distress.

REFERENCES

Adams, R., Dominelli, L. & Payne, M. (2002) *Critical Practice in Social Work* (Basingstoke: Palgrave Macmillan).

Bainbridge, L. (1999) 'Postmodernism and Mental Health Education' in Pease, B. & Fook, J. (1999) *Transforming Social Work Practice: Postmodern Critical Perspectives* (London: Routledge).

Bentall, R. (2003) *Madness Explained* (London: Allen Lane).

Billig, M. (1997) *Arguing and Thinking* (Cambridge: Cambridge University Press).

Boyle, M. (2002) (2nd ed.) *Schizophrenia: A Scientific Delusion?* (London: Routledge).

Brown, R. (2006) *The Approved Social Worker's Guide to Mental Health Law* (Exeter: Learning Matters Press).

Burr, V. (1995) *An Introduction to Social Constructionism* (London: Routledge).

Campbell, P. (1996) 'Challenging Loss of Power' in Read, J. and Reynolds, J. (1996) *Speaking our Minds* (Basingstoke: Macmillan).

Coleman, R. & Smith, M. (1997) *Working with Voices!! Victim to Victor* (Merseyside: Handsell Publications).

Department of Health (1983) *Mental Health Act* (London: HMSO).

Department of Health (1999a) *Safe, Sound and Supportive: Modernising Mental Health Services* (London: HMSO).

Department of Health (1999b) *Mental Health Act 1983 Code of practice* (London: HMSO).

Dominelli, L. (2002) 'Values in Social Work: Contested Entities with Enduring Qualities' in Adams, R., Dominelli, L. & Payne, M. (2002) *Critical Practice in Social Work* (Basingstoke: Palgrave Macmillan).

Duggan, M. et al., (2002) *Modernising the Social Model in Mental Health; A Discussion Paper* (Social perspectives Network spn@toppsengland.org.uk).

Edwards, D. (1997) *Discourse and Cognition* (London: Sage).

Ferguson, H. (2003) 'Outline of a Critical Best Practice Perspective in Social Work and Social Care', *British Journal of Social Work* **33** (8), 1005–1024.

Ferguson, H. (2005), 'Working with Violence, the Emotions and the Psycho-social Dynamics of Child Protection', *Social Work Education* **24**(7), 781–795.

Foucault, M. (1980) *Power/Knowledge: Selected Interviews and Other Writings 1972–1977*, Colin Gordon et al., (trans.) (New York: Pantheon).

Gatefield, J. & McGarry, D. (2005) 'Doctors' Orders Overruled', *Community Care* 22–28 Sept. 2005.

GSCC (2002) *Code of practice for Social Care Staff*, accessible from www.gscc.org.uk

Glover, J. (1990) *Causing Death and Saving Lives* (Harmondsworth: Penguin).

Hodge, S. (2005) 'Participation, Discourse and Power: A Case Study in Service User Involvement', *Critical Social Policy* **25**(2) 164 –179.

Johannessen, J. (2004) 'The Development of Early Intervention Services' in Read, J. & Reynolds, J. (1996) *Speaking our Minds* (Basingstoke: Macmillan).

Jordan, R. & Parkinson, C. (2001) 'Reflective Practice in a Process for the Re-approval of ASWs: An Exploration of Some Inevitable Resistance', in *Journal of Social Work Practice* **15**(1) 67–79.

McGovern, D. & Cope, R. (1987) 'Compulsory Detention of Males From Different Ethnic Groups with Special Reference to Offender patients', *British Journal Psychiatry* **150,** 505–512.

Mental Health Foundation (2001) *Something Inside So Strong: Strategies for Surviving Mental Distress* (London: MHF).

Milner, J & O'Byrne, P. (1998) *Assessment in Social Work* (Basingstoke: Palgrave Macmillan).

MIND (1999) 'Advance Directives' in *OpenMind* **99** (London: MIND).

Muijen, M. (1996), 'Scare in the Community: Britain in Moral Panic' in Heller, T. et al. (eds) (1996) *Mental Health Matters* (Basingstoke: Macmillan).

Nikander, P. (2003) 'The Absent Client: Case Description and Decision-Making in Interprofessional Meetings' in Hall, C. et al. (2003) *Constructing Clienthood in Social Work and Human Services* (London: Jessica Kingsley).

O'Hagan, K. (1986) *Crisis Intervention in Social Services* (Basingstoke: BASW-Macmillan).

Pilgrim, D. & Rogers, A. (1997) 'Two notions of risk in mental health debates' in Heller, T. et al. (1997) *Mental Health Matters* (Basingstoke: Palgrave Macmillan/Open University).

Potter, J. & Wetherell, M. (1987) *Discourse and Psychology: Beyond Attitudes and Behaviour* (London: Sage).

Read, J., Mosher, L. & Bentall, R. (2004) *Models of Madness* (Hove: Brunner-Routledge).

Repper, J., Sayce, L., Strong, S., Willmot, T. and Haine, M. (1997) *Respect* (London: MIND).

Rogers, A., Pilgrim, D. & Lacey, R. (1993) *Experiencing Psychiatry: Users' Views of Services* (Basingstoke Macmillan: MIND).

Romme, M. & Escher, S. (1996) *Hearing Voices* (London: MIND).

Ryan, P. & Morgan, S. (2004) *Assertive Outreach: A Strengths Approach to Policy and Practice* (Edinburgh: Churchill Livingstone).

Shardlow, S. & Doel, M. (1996) *Practice Learning and Teaching* (Basingstoke: Macmillan).

Stepney, P. & Ford, D. (eds) (2000) *Social Work Models Methods and Theories: A Framework for Practice* (Lyme Regis: Russell House).

Szasz, T. (1974) *Law, Liberty and Psychiatry* (London: Routledge Keganpau).

Trevithick, P. (2000) *Social Work Skills: A Practice Handbook* (Maidenhead: Open University Press).

Part III

Critical Best Practice: Practice Settings and Cultures

13 Partnership working as best practice: working across boundaries in health and social care

PAT TAYLOR AND KAREN JONES WITH
DES GORMAN

INTRODUCTION

In the preceding chapters, we have presented some of the underpinning theoretical concepts which inform our idea of critical best practice (CBP) and drawn on these to explore its meaning in a number of different practice contexts. This chapter and the two which follow seek to develop the idea of CBP by focusing in greater detail on the organisational and cultural context of social work.

The concept of 'crossing boundaries' is introduced in the current chapter as a way of both conceptualising and achieving best practice through partnership working with service users, their families and with other professionals. Practice, which embraces the notion of crossing boundaries, involves not only an explicit rejection of hierarchies of power but also a generosity in the sharing of professional expertise and in the promotion of service user and carer participation and empowerment. We examine these issues by looking in detail at a social work response to the needs of an older person whose age and health made him vulnerable to crisis and to the possibility of unwanted life change. The practice described also illustrates a central theme of our chapter – that social workers within multi-professional settings are uniquely equipped with the skills and values necessary to promote and develop effective cross-boundary partnerships.

The chapter is a collaboration between Des, a social worker within an Intermediate Care team, and Pat and Karen, who are both social work lecturers with research and practice experience in the areas of 'partnership' working and adult social work. The practice described and the reflections on it come mainly from Des, while the accompanying analysis has emerged from discussions between all three authors.

We will begin by unpacking the concepts of 'partnership working' and 'working across boundaries' and offering an account of our own understanding of these terms and as a basis for further discussion.

PARTNERSHIP WORKING

Partnership working is a key concept within current European public policy agendas and extends to widely varied areas of public life. It is a term which expresses the (sometimes remote) aspiration of avoiding duplication and overlap in service provision by encouraging different organisations to work together in order to respond more flexibly to identified needs. Partnership is perhaps best understood as much by reference to what it *is not* about (competition and conflict) as what it *is* about (co-operation and collaboration). Tennyson offers the following helpful definition, 'a cross-sector alliance in which individuals, groups or organisations agree to: work together to fulfil an obligation or undertake a specific task; share risks as well as benefits; and review the relationship regularly, revising their agreement as necessary' (Tennyson, 1998).

The Audit Commission (1998) suggest that partnerships must involve a minimum of two agencies or agents, who have at least some kind of common interest or goal in an association which requires a degree of trust, equality or reciprocity. Other commentators (Sullivan and Skelcher, 2002) make a distinction between partnership as a form of organisation – as described above – and partnership as a method of individual working, sometimes referred to as *collaboration*.

The term 'partnership' as it is used in this chapter incorporates ideas of organisational trust, reciprocity and common goals, alongside individual and group, collaborative methodologies. It also goes beyond these definitions to include two distinct *applications*. The first is that of working in partnership with service users and their families in a one to one relationship and the second is that of working in partnership with other professionals and organisations to achieve better outcomes for service users and their families. Critical social work practice requires the bringing together of these two meaning of partnership as the practice example later in the chapter seeks to demonstrate.

WORKING ACROSS BOUNDARIES

Contained within the concept of partnership and essential to making partnerships work is the notion of 'working across boundaries'. As Robert Adams points out, boundaries have always been pivotal to the social work role, 'social workers occupy boundary positions between people and diverse views of their situations and different choices about what they could do next' (Adams, 2005: 100).

Sometimes it is the relatively clear boundaries between different professionals and organisations or those between service users and professionals, which demand to be crossed. At other times social workers need *leaking* boundaries (Adams, 2005: 99) simply in order to exercise the imagination and ingenuity required to deal with the complex uncertainty of people's lives. This ability to work across a range of boundaries, demands a high level of critical awareness and a commitment to understanding and bringing together different perspectives, in order to facilitate a common goal or way forward.

PARTNERSHIP ACROSS BOUNDARIES WITH SERVICE USERS AND THEIR CARERS

For most social work practitioners the reality of working in partnership with service users and carers means working with an individual and his or her network of relatives, friends and contacts within the wider community. The activity of networking and relationship building has always been central to social work practice, but there is now cause for real optimism at the way in which partnership with service users has become an accepted concept within health and social care policy in the United Kingdom. Users of health and welfare services are increasingly recognised within policy directives as having expertise through experience and as being able to make a vital contribution to the development and evaluation of services (DoH, 1996, 2001a, 2005).

Barnes et al. (2000) suggest that the notion of partnership in welfare policy has emerged in recent years from other, less helpful approaches to conceptualising user involvement. They suggest that service users were first seen as 'consumers' within a 'care market' much as we are regarded as consumers of different brands of soap powder. The problems associated with this model relate to the difficulties of creating real choices in services catering for very vulnerable people. Resource constraints inevitably restrict the purchase of complex services and so limit the freedom of the 'market'; furthermore, it is often unrealistic to

237

expect those who are vulnerable due to ill health and incapacity, to act as effective consumers. Barnes and his colleagues also consider the 'empowerment' model. While accepting that empowerment remains a helpful notion in general terms, they reject it as unrealistic in situations of health and welfare provision, where service users have less than perfect choice and where their vulnerability makes power differentials significant. The third model – that of 'partnership' – seems to the authors of *this* chapter to best describe the way in which social workers work effectively across boundaries with service users; it is also favoured by Barnes et al. as the approach which best allows the recognition of different contributions, 'we consider partnership a more realistic concept because it acknowledges differentials in power without demanding equality. Instead it requires a negotiated agreement about roles and responsibilities and an understanding about where power is located' (Barnes et al., 2000: 90).

Effective partnerships which allow boundaries to be questioned and crossed in social work practice with service users and their carers, demand a critical social work perspective. Critical practice, with its open recognition of power relations, is central to an understanding of the different meanings, levels and layers of partnership working with service users. In other words, the ability to reach across and where necessary to disregard boundaries in treating service users and their families as experts in their own experience, is at the heart of CBP. As our case example below demonstrates, critical, anti-oppressive partnership working requires a commitment to really listening to the perspectives being expressed and careful reflection and appraisal of the possible ways forward. As such, it is the antithesis of taken for granted or uncritically accepted 'off the peg' service solutions.

PARTNERSHIP ACROSS BOUNDARIES WITH PROFESSIONALS

What we are calling 'partnership across boundaries' sits alongside terms such as 'inter-professional' or 'interagency' working (Ovretveit, 1997; Harries, 1999; Barrett et al., 2006): as well as looser expressions like 'working together' (Leathard, 1994; Harrison et al., 2003). In spite of some differences in emphasis, this group of ideas all refer to collaboration between different professionals, services or support networks, with the aim of ensuring that service users receive co-ordinated and comprehensive attention to their needs. It is our contention that social workers are as well equipped, by their skills and experience, to work effectively across traditional *professional* boundaries, as they are to work across boundaries with service users.

Recent social policy initiatives in the United Kingdom (DoH, 2001b, 2000a) have emphasised partnership working between health and social care professionals as a fundamental aspect of the government's agenda for modernising services. The notion of 'joined up' working has repeatedly been emphasised as crucial to the delivery of more effective services. (DoH, 2000b) In adult care, the newly introduced 'Single Assessment' process is, as its name suggests, an attempt to reduce duplication and ensure that different professionals contribute to the needs of individual older people in a co-ordinated and effective way. (DoH, 2002) Single Assessment also recognises the stress involved for vulnerable service users in having to relate to a stream of professionals, each assessing a different need according to their own area of expertise. The 'best' assessment in such situations may be one carried out by a single carer, who is prepared to go beyond professional boundaries, drawing on the knowledge and skills of others where necessary.

As the government acknowledged in its formal guidance on Single Assessment, social workers possess skills which lend themselves particularly well to this wider co-ordinating role in health and social care services:

> social workers have expertise and experience in working with older people who are experiencing health and social care difficulties. They have to understand these difficulties in the wider context of the older person's family, social, financial, housing and other circumstances ... they play an important role in contributing to, or co-ordinating, assessment and care planning where a number of agencies are involved. (DoH, 2002: 1)

In order to be truly effective, this form of partnership across professional boundaries requires social workers and others to be generous with their knowledge, imaginative in their engagement and open to new learning, in their dealings with other workers. If individuals are to be encouraged to venture out of their professional silos, then different contributions and perspectives need to be respected and new alliances carefully negotiated. Inter-professional partnership working, therefore, extends the focus for core social work skills such as engaging, promoting and enabling, beyond direct work with service users, to include work with other professionals. Critical practice in this context requires social workers to understand the complexity of each practice situation and, therefore, the complexity of each partnership. This means resisting the imposition of easy solutions, based on assumption or

239

established patterns of service provision and making a reality of listening and valuing the views of service users and carers, as well as the expertise of other practitioners. As we will see in the practice example below, this may require the social worker to 'hold' a situation while working co-operatively to arrive at a truly shared consensus.

THE PRACTICE CONTEXT: 'INTERMEDIATE CARE'

The past decade has seen growing concern about the financial cost of hospital care in the United Kingdom and increasing evidence to suggest that older people, in particular, do better if they can avoid going into hospital. National policies such as The Health and Social Care Act (2001), The National Service Framework for Older people (DoH, 2001b) and the Whitepaper on the future of adult social care (DoH, 2006) have all given attention to this issue. In order for unnecessary hospital admissions to be avoided, it is seen as essential for health and social care agencies to work together. To this end, the UK government has made specific funding available to encourage health and social care agencies to set up localised joint services. 'Intermediate Care' is the term given to a range of joint services developed over the past ten years to help to ensure that adults do not spend time in hospital unnecessarily. Sometimes provision takes the form of short-term, but intensive rehabilitation or social care services to help people adjust to new circumstances and ultimately be able to resume their lives at home. In other situations, high-level support is put in place quickly to help prevent people from going into hospital in the first place.

In Bristol the Intermediate Care Service has grown rapidly over the past five years. It is funded jointly by the local primary care trust and the local authority adult social services department and jointly resourced by health and social care staff. The service consists of a number of different multi-professional teams, which deal with people in a range of circumstances. The majority of the 250 front-line staff are nurses and community rehabilitation workers, with additional support provided by therapists, specialist mental health nurses, social workers, pharmacists, managers and administrative staff. This new way of working requires staff from different organisational cultures to work closely together and to explore new and flexible ways of responding to people's needs. The fact that all of these Intermediate Care services are provided within a single organisation means that service users should be able to move between the various forms of provision as they need to with the minimum of bureaucracy or delay.

The social workers in the service work across all the different teams. In so doing, they occupy a cross boundary position within the structure of the organisation. Social workers are, therefore, well placed to build partnerships with service users, helping them to articulate their needs and acting as advocates where necessary. At the same time, they are in a position to work creatively alongside a wide range of fellow professionals and to draw on a broad base of expertise and varied service provision.

MR GREEN

Mr Green was an 88-year-old man who had been living in sheltered accommodation since his wife's death five years earlier. Although his mobility was limited by the effects of a stroke, he seemed well settled in his flat and had developed good relationships with other residents and staff. Mr Green enjoyed light gardening in the communal grounds of his home and was well known in the local area, where he regularly shopped for himself and for his neighbours. His daughter and her family lived some distance away, but were regular week-end visitors.

When Mr Green developed a chest infection he was admitted to the 'Safe Haven' unit within the Intermediate Care Service. The 'Safe Haven' beds provide very short-term (usually no more than ten days) accommodation with nursing care, in a residential unit, with the aim of preventing admission to hospital. The warden of the housing scheme in which Mr Green lived had been concerned for some time about his increased levels of confusion. She described his tendency to 'wander' at night and a recent incident when Mr Green became disorientated during a visit to the shops and had to be returned home by the police. Shortly after Mr Green's admission to the Safe Haven bed, the warden contacted his daughter to say that she felt it would be impossible for him to return to his flat. She argued that Mr Green's confusion, coupled with the fact that the scheme did not employ staff to cope with wandering at night meant that he was likely to be a danger to himself.

When Mr Green's daughter visited her father in the Safe Haven unit to discuss the warden's concerns, he denied that he wandered at night and argued that the incident at the shops was an isolated one, which might happen to anyone of his age. Mr Green was adamant that he wanted to return home; it was bad enough he said, leaving his old home after his wife died, but moving again would 'finish me off'. Not surprisingly, both father and daughter became very distressed during this encounter.

The team in the residential unit decided to ask Des – one of the Intermediate Care social workers to work with Mr Green in helping to find a long-term solution.

MEETING MR GREEN

Des met with Mr Green shortly after receiving the referral; he later reflected on his initial thoughts:

> What was really apparent during that first meeting was how much this man wanted to return to his flat. He spoke warmly about the warden and the other staff and seemed bemused by their apparent rejection of him ...

> I could see immediately that this was a complex situation. Working in partnership with Mr Green was going to involve representing his views and supporting his choices, but these were in direct conflict with what looked like an emerging consensus among the professionals, that he now needed 24 hour care. So part of my job at that point, was to make sure that the options remained open. There were still lots of unanswered questions about the nature of Mr Green's confusion. For instance: was it permanent or was it linked to his chest infection or some other cause? What were the potential risks if he were to return home and were there other agendas embedded in the different perspectives on his situation? Ideally, I needed time to make sure that these issues were worked through thoroughly, but I was conscious that Mr Green's stay in the Safe Haven unit was only for 10 days and that I needed to work quickly.

THE PLANNING MEETING

Des decided to call a planning meeting involving Mr Green, his daughter, the warden (who arrived with her manager), a community mental health nurse from the Intermediate Care Service and a nurse from the residential unit. It became clear during the meeting that most people thought it would be too risky for Mr Green to return to his flat and that residential care would be the better and safer option. Mr Green seemed to have recovered from his chest infection, but the nurse from the unit reported that he was still 'wandering' during the night. The warden and her manager outlined in strong terms the risk to Mr Green of not being supervised at night and the disruption his behaviour was likely to cause to other residents. The community mental health nurse talked not only about the support that he and his team could offer but also of the near impossibility of arranging night-time care within the community. Mr Green's daughter spoke of her growing concern for her father's safety, her uncertainty about what was best for him and her need for advice from the professionals involved in his care.

In their analysis of inter-professional talk, Taylor and White (2000) argue that case discussions and planning meetings are often charac- terised by movement towards agreement on a particular version of a situation. They suggest that 'Inter-professional talk about cases works to construct and maintain particular client/patient identities. These identities become more fixed and durable over time and with multiple and collective recitations of the case' (Taylor and White, 2000: 138).

Des sought to resist the process of closing down by which a particular version of events can take on the status of 'truth' before all options have been explored. He was able to bring to the meeting, some of the potential benefits of a return home, as well as supporting Mr Green in his strongly communicated desire to go back to his flat. There was a danger that Mr Green's voice would be lost as a collective professional account of the need for change emerged. Des was able to ensure that Mr Green was given space to talk about the importance of his home and neighbourhood and to draw on their earlier conversations as a way of helping him to express his wishes. In fact Mr Green communicated his views to the meeting with considerable clarity and determination, which helped to ensure that the discussion remained open. The meeting ended without a firm decision being made about Mr Green's future, but with the agreement that Des would speak to Mr Green's GP who was thought to be quite supportive of his wish to return home. Des also agreed to explore the possibility of temporary residential accommoda- tion until a long-term decision could be made.

In Des's view this outcome still gave rise to concern:

> It was right that no definite long-term decision was made during the meet- ing. I was still worried though, that we were moving too quickly towards an inevitable conclusion that was more about our needs as professionals try- ing to run a service, than about what was best for Mr Green. I knew from past experience that another temporary move might confuse Mr Green further and make it even more unlikely that he would ever get back to his flat. Although he was 'over' his chest infection in formal medical terms, I felt that Mr Green was still in the process of recovering his independence and

sense of self. I could see that my colleagues were genuinely concerned for Mr Green's welfare and that there seemed to be mounting evidence that he would be seriously at risk on this own at home. At the same time, I was aware that part of the agenda of those working in the Safe Haven Unit was to move people on after 10 days, so that beds could be made available to the next person in urgent need. I was also troubled by the warden's repeated assertion that it was 'impossible' for Mr Green to return to his flat and her refusal to discuss any other option. I couldn't help feeling that a fuller and more open discussion must be possible.

Des's skilled practice here is demonstrated not only through his empathetic engagement with Mr Green's experience but also by his critical awareness of the role responsibilities and priorities of his colleagues. In order to move forward as fairly and as honestly as possible, Des now needed to strengthen his partnerships with everyone currently involved in Mr Green's world while continuing to work in partnership with Mr Green himself.

CROSSING BOUNDARIES AND BUILDING PARTNERSHIPS

The GP

Des had agreed to contact Mr Green's GP – the only professional involved in his care who had been unable to attend the earlier planning meeting. The GP had treated Mr Green for his chest infection at home and in the Safe Haven Unit. She expressed surprise at the warden's decision and seemed convinced that Mr Green's confusion was connected to his illness, which she thought had been affecting him over several weeks. She was rather dismissive of the warden's position and felt that with the correct treatment for his chest infection Mr Green would be able to return home and resume his normal activities.

Taylor and White (2000: 134) describe the way in which doctors often hold a dominant position within inter-professional groups; they suggest that 'It is often treated as an inevitable "given" hierarchical arrangement in which doctors somehow 'gain' and others are exploited and "lose"'.

Des was aware of the potential power of the GP within the decision-making process; however, in this case she had provided vital information:

> The GP's belief that Mr Green's confusion was short term did really boost my hope that he might be able to return to his flat after all. Her

view of Mr Green's medical condition was very significant within the overall assessment, but I needed to use it alongside, rather than in opposition to the views of my colleagues. Doctors can sometimes exert a lot of power because of their professional status, but the warden and the nurses caring for Mr Green in the Safe Haven Unit were the ones with 24 hour experience of his confusion and they were still very concerned.

The Warden

Des decided to visit the sheltered complex to talk to the warden directly. In doing so, he not only established a more honest and open relationship but also gained new insight into her perspective:

> I become aware that the warden was under a lot of pressure from her manager to stick to newly developed guidelines about levels of confusion among residents in the complex; this was almost certainly the reason behind the manager's unexpected appearance at the planning meeting. Management guidelines were not the warden's only problem however, she was also having difficulty finding and keeping care workers, all of whom were recruited from private agencies. Care staff at the unit, were poorly paid and received little or no specialist training in the needs of confused older people. The warden blamed this on poor wages; she told me with much feeling: 'My window cleaners get more an hour than these people do to care for extremely vulnerable older people, it's a disgrace.'

> We also talked about the fact that agencies are increasingly recruiting staff, who have recently arrived from abroad and so have limited English. The warden recounted several situations where communication difficulties between tenants and staff had led to residents in the complex making racist comments. She confided in me that as a black woman who had experienced racism and worked her way through many difficult situations to progress in her career, she often found herself in very uncomfortable situations.

Des later reflected on the way in which different forms of oppression were impacting on one another in the warden's experience:

> I understood from this conversation that the warden was in a relatively powerless position within her agency. As well as responding to the demands of her manager, she was struggling to meet the needs of residents and to be sympathetic to care staff who were themselves often vulnerable and disempowered.

When the conversation moved to Mr Green, the warden spoke of how much she had enjoyed working with him. She told Des that if it was left to her, she would try to look after Mr Green for longer. It would be difficult to get her manager's agreement if Mr Green continued to need night-time care, she said, but, 'We really should be able to look after him – he gives a lot to this place and this is his home after all.'

The conversation between Des and the Warden broke through some of the usual professional boundaries and enabled Des to understand the complex factors underpinning the warden's cautious perspective on Mr Green's future. It also revealed a different and much more optimistic viewpoint than the one expressed by the warden in the presence of her manager and it opened the possibility for greater frankness and honesty in their future conversations.

Nigel Parton and Patrick O'Byrne, in their book on 'constructive' social work, argue for the need to move beyond the formality of the professional social work role and to use *informality* as a method. In other words, best practice requires fluid boundaries between the formal and the informal:

> Social workers are differentiated from workers in other services mainly by their willingness to forsake the formality of their roles and to work *with* ordinary people in their 'natural' settings, using the informality of their methods as a means of negotiating a solution to problems rather than imposing them. Imposed formal solutions are a last resort in social work, whereas they are the norm in other settings. The more social work moves from this situation, the more it loses what is distinctive about it. (Parton and O'Byrne, 2000: 33)

The daughter

Mr Green's daughter Grace came to see Des following the planning meeting. She spoke about her efforts to give her father a good and consistent level of support and her difficulty in balancing this with other aspects of her life. Grace talked about the demands of her young family and her part-time job. She confided that her mother's illness, five years earlier, had placed a considerable strain on her marriage, as she was constantly having to make the 40-mile journey to and from her parent's home:

> Grace wanted to support her father and to respect his right to make his own choices, but she was also worried about having to become more involved in his physical care if he continued to live in the sheltered flat. She was finding it hard to see how this would be possible, as she already

had considerable family obligations and very little support in her own life. I could see that for Grace this situation was finely balanced. If she had to give more time to her father's care, there was a possibility of other tensions opening up in her life. Grace was also worried about her father's safety. On one hand she knew how happy he had been in the flat, on the other, she was afraid that he might wander off and put himself in real danger. If he were to move permanently to a residential home, at least she would know that there was someone to keep an eye on him all the time.

As a result of this conversation, Des was able to appreciate that Grace's perspective was influenced by a complex mixture of factors, involving her own needs as well as those of Mr Green. His ability to move beyond formal boundaries in facilitating open communication enabled Des to reach a fuller, more complete understanding of Grace's previous contribution to discussions about Mr Green's future.

The 'Safe Haven' unit

Mr Green's stay in the Safe Haven Unit had now exceeded the agreed 10 day period. Des was under increasing pressure to facilitate a solution for Mr Green so that the bed could be made available for someone else:

My role was to bring together and to try to resolve a number of different perspectives, but in Mr Green's case, as in many others, time was needed for this to happen. For me, the issue was getting the service user's voice heard and taken seriously – it was essentially an advocacy role within the assessment process. I knew that Mr Green might not be able to live independently for much longer and that the early signs of confusion would probably increase. At the time of the assessment the evidence for him needing a higher level of care was finely balanced, but for Mr Green the opportunity to return home and to try to regain his independence was an overwhelming priority. Part of my responsibility was to amplify his voice and ensure that it was heard as well as helping him to confront the reality of the risks he was facing. I met with my colleagues in the Safe Haven Unit to explore the dilemmas we were struggling with. It did seem that Mr Green's confusion was lessening as the GP had predicted, but this was very gradual and unlikely to result in a complete recovery. After much debate we agreed that Mr Green would find a temporary move to a residential home extremely disorientating and that he should remain at the Safe Haven Unit for a little while longer.

247

In negotiating a longer stay for Mr Green, Des and his colleagues were working together in an effective partnership, which involved crossing some agreed boundaries of service provision. Their discussions acknowledged the fact that the service would cease to be effective if it was not 'short term' in the majority of cases. They also recognised, however, that flexible boundaries are essential to genuinely person-centred practice. As Robert Adams suggests, good collaborative working involves staff being empowered to 'use their initiative to go beyond the boundaries of their job descriptions ... This may involve disengaging with embedded perceptions and practices and being willing to embrace new practice. This is an intrinsically anti-oppressive, equality-driven, non-stigmatising, person valuing process' (Adams, 2005: 113).

Mr Green

During the course of his assessment, Des had made several short visits to Mr Green in the Safe Haven Unit:

> He didn't always know who I was and sometimes he blamed me for the fact that he was there at all, but we did establish a pretty straightforward way of communicating. In spite of that, it took me a long time to realise that no-one was really talking to Mr Green about the issue of night time 'wandering', which was exercising the rest of us so much. He told me that he had been having difficulty sleeping for some time and often got up during the night to go to the toilet or just to stretch his legs. He found the unit a confusing place in the dark and sometimes had difficulty finding his way back to bed, but as Mr Green said: "I wouldn't call that 'wandering' would you?"

My conversation with Mr Green really brought home to me, the fact that 'wandering' is a socially constructed term, used by health and social care professionals to describe behaviour, which they see as inappropriate or inconvenient. This is not to deny that Mr Green's night-time behaviour had been risky and problematic for himself and for others. There were times during his stay on the unit when he had become seriously distressed and disorientated, trying to find his way back to bed. Similarly, before his admission to the Safe Haven unit, the warden had been called out on more than one occasion because Mr Green had mistakenly attempted to get into someone else's flat. What was achieved, by opening up the term 'wandering', however, was a way for Mr Green and I to have a frank discussion about his night time walks as an obstacle to his return home.

For the next four nights, staff on the unit did not report any incidences of 'wandering' on Mr Green's part. I am still not sure how far this was a result of my conversation with Mr Green and how far it was part of a natural process of recovery. It was, however, seen as a sufficiently positive sign for me to be able to go back to the warden, to the community psychiatric nursing team and to Mr Green's daughter Grace and begin to negotiate a firm plan for his return home.

One year later ...

It is now more than a year since Mr Green's admission to the Safe Haven Unit and he is still living in his sheltered flat. His confusion has increased and he receives considerable support from community nurses and support workers, but so far he has retained his cherished independence.

The discussions between Des and his colleagues, which began during Mr Green's stay, continued and have since resulted in the evolution of a more flexible approach to the use of the Safe Haven beds. This shared commitment to developing the service and learning from their collective experience is something which Des continues to see as central to the success of the Intermediate Care service:

> For me, partnership working in the Intermediate Care service involves being open to different ideologies and viewpoints, while maintaining the role of champion for social work values. Team members sometimes have different priorities and perspectives according to their different roles and training, but the challenge is to use those boundaries creatively and to know when to go beyond them. We have some pretty robust discussions and at times we have to agree to differ, but there's a real buzz about sharing ideas and making things happen. In the end it's about finding ways of working together for the benefit of service users.

REFERENCES

Adams, R. (2005) 'Working within and across boundaries: tensions and dilemmas' in Adams, R., Dominelli, L. and Payne, M. (eds) *Social Work Futures* (Basingstoke: Palgrave Macmillan)

Audit Commission (1998) *A Fruitful Partnership* (London: HMSO).

Barnes, D., Carpenter, J. and Bailey, D. (2000) 'Partnerships with service users in interprofessional education for community mental health: a case study' *Journal of Interprofessional Care*, 14, 2, 189–200.

Barret, G., Sellman, D. and Thomas, J. (2006) *Interprofessional Working in Health and Social Care: professional perspectives* (Basingstoke: Palgrave Macmillan).

Department of Health (1996) *Consultation Counts: Guidelines for Service purchasers and Users and Carers Based on the Experiences of the National User and Carer Group* (London: Department of Health).

Department of Health (2000a) *The NHS plan: A Plan for Investment, A plan for Reform* (London: Stationary Office).

Department of Health (2000b) *Guidance on the Health Act Section 31 Partnership Arrangement* (London: Stationary Office).

Department of Health (2001a) *Involving Patients and the Public in Healthcare: A Discussion Document* (London: Department of Health).

Department of Health (2001b) *The National Service Framework for Older people* (London: Stationary Office).

Department of Health (2002) *HSC 2002/001: Guidance on the Single Assessment Process for Older people* (London: Stationary Office).

Department of Health (2005) *Creating a Patient-led NHS: Delivering the NHS Improvement plan* (London: Department of Health).

Department of Health (2006) *Our Health, Our Care, Our Say: A New Direction for Community Services* (London: Stationary Office).

Harries, J. (1999) *Elephant problems and Fixes that Fail: The Story of a Search for New Approaches to Inter-Agency Working* (London: Kings Fund).

Harrison, R., Mann, G., Murphy, M., Taylor, A. and Thompson, N. (2003) *Partnership Made Painless: A Joined-up Guide to Working Together* (Lyme Regis: Russell House).

Leathard, A. (1994) *Going Interprofessional: Working Together for Health and Welfare* (London: Routledge).

Ovretveit, J. (1997) *Interprofessional Working for Health and Social Care* (Basingstoke: Macmillan).

Parton, N. and O'Byrne, P. (2000) *Constructive Social Work* (London: Macmillan).

Sullivan, H and Skelcher, C. (2002) *Working across Boundaries: Collaboration in public Services* (Basingstoke: Palgrave).

Tennyson (1998) *Managing partnerships: Tools for Mobilising the Public Sector, Business and Civil Society as Partners in Development* (London: The Prince of Wales Business Leaders Forum).

Taylor, C. and White, S. (2000) *Practicing Reflexivity in Health and Welfare: Making Knowledge* (Maidenhead: Open University Press).

14 Promoting best practice through supervision, support and communities of practice

JUDITH THOMAS AND KATE SPREADBURY

INTRODUCTION

Critical Best Practice (CBP) involves working with uncertainty and risk while maintaining open approaches to practice (Ferguson, 2003). For this difficult and demanding activity to be achieved effectively, a continuous, critically reflective examination of one's own and others' values, feelings and perspectives is needed. This chapter will explore a range of approaches to supervision as well as a number of other sites of support. Our aim is to illuminate some of the supervisory and/ or supportive practices which facilitate best practice through the development of engaged, self-aware and critically reflective social workers.

We (the authors) are both white women, who over the past 30 or so years, have been social workers, managers, practice teachers, trainers and lecturers. Judith currently works in higher education as a programme leader for a social work course and Kate is an adult protection co-ordinator and training officer in a local authority social services department.

Our starting point in this chapter, is a belief that practice which is 'critical' and 'best' is necessarily underpinned by protected opportunities for reflection, development, guidance and support. What we are *not* seeking to do however, is to provide a 'how to' guide or blueprint for good supervision. There are already many texts which attempt to do this, several of which helpfully review a range of different models and approaches to supervision (see for example, Brown and Bourne, 1996; Knapman and Morrison, 1998; Hawkins and Shohet, 2000; Parker, 2004). Our focus in this chapter is rather on a range of individual and group experiences (including some of our own), which we hope will provide the basis for reflection and learning about effective supervision, professional development and support.

THE CONTEXT OF SUPERVISION AND SUPPORT

Changes in social work practice and in the organisation of services, in the United Kingdom and elsewhere, are mirrored in arrangements for supervision and support. The traditional model of one to one supervision with a manager or more senior worker from the same profession, is increasingly complimented by a range of developmental opportunities, ranging from structured training programmes to spontaneous discussions about daily challenges and dilemmas. The fact that many social workers now practice in multi-professional teams, where they may be supervised by a manager from a different professional background, is another dimension of the changing context of professional practice.

In spite of organisational changes and new opportunities for development and support, some of which will be outlined in this chapter, there is a good deal of consensus in the literature about the nature of traditional social work supervision. Brockbank and McGill (1998) suggest that three roots in the worlds of industry, therapy and academia can be clearly discerned. While Brockbank and McGill translate these into the core supervision activities of 'overseeing', 'counselling' and 'learning', others use the terms 'managing', 'supporting' and 'teaching'. Some writers have accepted these core functions, but added 'mediation' between worker and agency (e.g., Morrison, 1993; Knapman and Morrison, 1998) or 'assessment' to the list (e.g., Sawdon and Sawdon, 1995). As these commonly defined characteristics indicate, supervision in social work has tended to integrate managerial and professional functions. In this respect it has differed from some other professions including nursing and psychology, where management and clinical or professional supervision have tended to be separate activities. The case studies discussed below cannot claim to be a statistically relevant sample, but they do indicate the potential for 'best practice' to include models other than the traditional all encompassing approach to manager–worker supervision and the importance of a critical approach to what supervision can and ought to be.

FORMAL SUPERVISION

Cliff

We decided to talk to Cliff about his experiences of supervision because we knew him to be an enthusiastic and forceful advocate for both social work practice and professional development. Since he returned to education as a mature student, first on an Access to Social Work programme and then on the qualifying Diploma in Social Work, Cliff has become an Approved Social Worker under the 1983 Mental Health Act, completed the Post Qualifying Award in Social Work and embarked on a Master's programme. He has built a reputation as a practice teacher and trainer in both uni- and multi-professional settings and in many respects fits the model of the sort of entrepreneurial, boundary spanning practitioner described by Pat Taylor and Karen Jones in Chapter 13.

Cliff is the only social worker in a multi-professional team; his manager is a nurse, who in turn is managed by a social worker. When we asked Cliff about sources of supervision and support, he identified the following:

- One to one manager supervision.

- Clinical or professional supervision.

- Informal support from the multi-disciplinary team and from other Approved Social Workers.

- Case discussions within monthly team meetings.

We will return to Cliff's list later, but our focus in this section is on the first two bullet points:

One to one manager supervision

The increasing dominance of managerialism in social work, through audit, notions of 'best value' and other bureaucratic tools (Leonard, 1997; Parton and O'Byrne, 2000; Webb, 2006) has arguably had the effect of boosting the managerial function of supervision at the expense of its educative and supportive roles. Cliff's supervision with his manager is typically dominated by the issues of workload management and the functionality of his role within the organisation. Cliff is perhaps unusual in not seeing this in negative terms. He told us:

> Health and social services departments are big organisations; they need an effective management structure so that social workers and others can do their job well. My line manager has an important job to do and sometimes that involves challenging me about my priorities and my use of time and sometimes it involves me challenging him about the priorities of the organisation and the team. It's taken time and effort on both sides, for us to build a good working relationship, but there's a mutual respect between us so even when we disagree, supervision's still basically a creative process.

Cliff is a confident, white middle-aged man. He is an Approved Social Worker, which his manager is not and he has a high level of expertise in relation to social work practice, policy and legislation. All of this, he says, helps to 'flatten the hierarchy' between himself and his manager. Clearly this is not the case for everyone. In other situations, the power differential between the manager and the supervisee can be acute and needs to be openly acknowledged and worked with. What is so valuable about Cliff's approach in terms of CBP however, is his preparedness to think critically about the management role in the organisation and to resist easy oppositions between practitioners and managers. As Harry Ferguson argues in Chapter 1, the conscious use of supervision and other development opportunities can enable social workers and managers to move away from the polarities of 'oppressive management systems/powerless victimised social worker'.

As we have seen from Cliff's list above, his experience of supervision, professional development and support, does not end with formal, line manager supervision. As a member of a multi-disciplinary team, comprised mainly of health professionals, Cliff, like the other qualified practitioners in his team, has access to regular professional or 'clinical' supervision.

Clinical or professional supervision

Cliff is something of an evangelist for professional supervision in social work. While this is common practice in the United States, the uniprofessional nature of social work teams and an adherence to the models of supervision outlined above, means that professional supervision has not traditionally been a feature of social work in the United Kingdom. Furthermore, social work was not until recently a 'registered' profession. Social workers have not therefore been formally account-able to a professional body and the responsibility for standards of social work practice has rested solely with employing organisations. It remains to be seen whether registration and the increasing professional-isation of social work in the United Kingdom through the establishment of a code of practice, leads to a shift in perceptions of accountability. Cliff certainly sees himself as being accountable to his profession *as well* as to his agency. As an ASW Cliff has a certain amount of individual accountability in law, but he also has a strongly developed professional social work identity and believes that the opportunity to explore prac-tice issues, is essential to his professional development.

It may be that supervision with one person, which balances managerial and professional issues effectively is the ideal, but Cliff sees real advan-tages in having a space for professional reflection, which is set apart from bureaucratic, managerial or administrative issues:

> Professional supervision goes to the heart of what I do and who I am. It gives me a chance to order my priorities. It also helps me to prepare for supervision with my line manager, which sometimes involves arguing for resources for a service user or for my own professional development or putting a case for doing things differently within the team.

Cliff sees his professional supervisor, who is a mental health social worker, every six weeks and discusses general and specific practice sit-uations including ethical dilemmas and his feelings about the work that he does. This experience is central to his development as a critically reflective and self-aware practitioner:

> It's a protected space which is about case work rather than case man-agement. It's a chance to look not just at whether I'm doing what I'm required to do, but at what kind of practitioner I am and what kind of practitioner I aspire to become.

SOME REFLECTIONS ON FORMAL SUPERVISION

Cliff's experiences of supervision with both his line manager and his professional supervisor are very largely positive. Cliff has the experi-ence and the confidence to take a lot of responsibility within his own supervision sessions and a well developed critical awareness of the interpersonal dynamics between himself and his supervisors.

Many practitioners are, however, less experienced or less fortunate than Cliff in their supervisory relationships. In order to provide a critical framework within which to address the potentially challenging dynamics of supervision, we therefore want to look briefly at some of the concepts that we have found useful in our own reflections on the dynamics of formal supervision. Our contention here is that the sensitive and well tuned awareness of self which is a characteristic of the critical practitioner (Brechin et al., 2000), emerges from an ability to reflect not only on relationships with service users, but also on relationships with colleagues and supervisors.

POWER

Julia Phillipson (2002: 246) observes that power dynamics, particularly in relation to issues of identity are increasingly acknowledged as important concerns in supervision. Differentials in terms of age, experience, gender, ethnicity, class, sexuality and disability as well as the power inherent in the supervisory role, all play apart in defining the supervisor – supervisee relationship and need to be openly acknowledged. It is beyond the scope of this chapter to explore these complex dynamics in detail (See Brown and Bourne, 1996 for a more detailed analysis). However, we would assert the importance of resisting a simple binary oppositional approach to supervision, which defines the social worker as powerless in the face of a powerful supervisor.

While it is important to bring issues of power imbalance to the surface and to work to counter them, it may also be necessary to find constructive ways of re-framing the supervision experience. The notion of professional responsibility is helpful here. Cliff does not believe that supervision with his line manager is simply about agency accountability. It is rather a site for negotiation with his manager about the interface between Cliff's responsibility to his profession and his responsibility to his agency. This is understood by both Cliff and his manager and within their interactions, Cliff sees his professional identity is a source of empowerment. At the same time, he acknowledges his line manager' experience, role and responsibilities and recognises that sometimes his manager's use of authority is necessary, appropriate and welcome. Julia Phillipson (2002) draws on Karen Healy's (2000) work on critical practice, when she suggests that supervision needs to consider the positive dimensions of power imbalances rather than simply seeing power as oppressive and therefore negative. While issues of power have the potential to manifest themselves in damaging ways within supervision, CBP involves resisting the simplification of power relations and embracing the considered and appropriate use of authority.

GAME PLAYING AND 'MIRRORING'

The word 'game' was used by the Transactional Analysis theorist Eric Berne (1964) to describe the defensive manoeuvres people make to avoid painful feelings. It is our contention that the 'best' supervision is that which does not deal in superficiality or simple managerialism, but which acknowledges the risky, complex and uncertain nature of social work practice. Within this context, there will inevitably be times when even the most highly skilled supervisors and committed practitioners find themselves playing 'games' as a way of coping with the difficult and often intense emotions which can be generated in supervision. The challenge for the critical practitioner, is to engage with what is really going on and to find ways of achieving a shared understanding of the games which are being played and how to move beyond them. We hope that the example below, which is taken from Kate's experience as supervisor, will help to illustrate this in practice, but first we will explain a little more about the theory of 'games'.

The idea of the game within Transactional Analysis is underpinned by the 'Drama Triangle' (Karpman, 1968; Hughes and Pengelly, 1997) within which complex emotions are attributed to roles in a dramatic scenario. The roles of 'rescuer', 'persecutor' and 'victim' reflect the way in which each player of the game interprets his or her experience and can be powerful enough to affect their perception of reality. Karpman's (1968) illustration of the drama triangle is shown below:

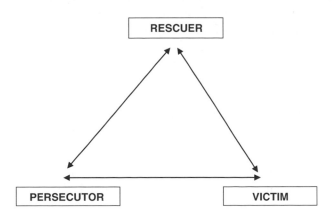

Karpman suggests that although individuals are likely to prefer one of the three roles, these can sometimes be switched quite quickly. While the roles of the victim, persecutor and rescuer are sometimes directly enacted in the relationship between the supervisor and supervisee, they can also 'mirror' experiences which are taking place outside of supervision.

An example that we have both come across on several occasions, is the social worker whose preferred role is that of a rescuer in relation to the service user who is perceived as vulnerable and a victim. The social worker then becomes alarmed to find that the 'victim', angry at being rescued is moving into the role of persecutor and making the social worker feel like a victim. Another possible twist in the game is for the worker to respond with feelings of anger resulting in persecution towards the service user who is now experienced as resistant, unreachable or ungrateful. These feelings can then be 'mirrored' in supervision, with the relationship between the social worker and the service user being reflected in the relationship between the social worker and the supervisor (Hughes and Pengelly, 1997).

Jane

Jane, a social work student, was frustrated by her attempts to work with Mrs Smith, who she felt was avoiding her. When they did meet, Jane felt that her suggestions were discounted or ignored, making it difficult for her to establish a relationship with Mrs Smith. The case was a recurring topic in supervision, but it took me (Kate) some time to realise that as Jane's supervisor, I was beginning to feel angry and persecutory towards her. Jane seemed reluctant to make eye contact with me and whatever useful suggestions I made, she ignored them or found reasons why they would not work. Eventually I explained my observations and feelings to Jane and asked her to respond. Jane told me that she felt I was not listening to her and that I did not understand her position as a student. It was clear that we both needed to develop a fuller and more critical understanding of the roles we were enacting, and to move beyond them to a relationship of greater openness and awareness.

I encouraged Jane to draw on her experience of me in order to reflect on how she might in turn be experienced by Mrs Smith. As we unpicked the two situations, we began to see that Jane's desire to 'rescue' Mrs Smith by finding solutions to her problems, was 'mirrored' in supervision through my suggestions about Jane's approach to practice. Mrs Smith was feeling angry at being treated as a victim by Jane and Jane was reflecting this in supervision through her anger towards me. Jane and I went on to look at the drama triangle together. Our discussion about its relevance to Jane's experience with Mrs Smith and to our shared experience of supervision, enabled us to explore both Jane' practice and our relationship in a more open and fruitful way.

What we hope that this example has shown is the importance within a CBP approach to supervision, of avoiding the polarising roles of rescuer, persecutor and victim, by openly reflecting on how and why we find ourselves thinking in these ways. Furthermore, understanding games and mirroring in supervision opens the way to exploring and working constructively with the emotional content of social work as a central component of best practice.

INFORMAL SUPPORT AND TEAM MEETINGS

Imogen

We also spoke to Imogen, a senior social worker in a mental health team, whose critically reflective approach to practice, was known to us through her work as a student of the post Qualifying Award and which led to her collaboration with Karen Jones on Chapter 3. We were interested to find out from Imogen about the support available to her in dealing with the sorts of practice issues and dilemmas she describes in Chapter 3. Like Cliff, Imogen is an Approved Social Worker and she too works in a multi-professional team. When we asked Imogen about the sources of supervision and support she identified the following:

- One to one manager supervision.
- Informal support from the multi-disciplinary team.
- Case discussions within monthly team meetings.

Imogen has about two hours supervision every six weeks, with her line manager who is also a social worker. These sessions focus primarily on accountability and the management of risk in relation to her caseload. While Imogen finds these sessions helpful and supportive up to a point, the *dominant* model here is managerial rather than supportive or educational. Much could be said about the shortcomings of Imogen's experience of formal supervision and the ways in which both she and her supervisor might work to make this a more satisfying and creative experience. Our focus here however, is on the two final bullet points on Imogen's list which reflect the enthusiasm with which she talks about the learning and support she receives from the multi-professional team:

Informal support from the multi-disciplinary team

Despite their heavy case loads, Imogen and her colleagues have developed a culture within which they consciously give each other time to reflect on the dilemmas, anxieties and uncertainties of day-to-day practice. Imogen told us:

> We do look out for each other. There is a kind of acknowledgement in the team that the work we do is emotionally demanding and we all need support. When someone's having a difficult day, one or two of the others will find space to listen and help work through the issues. We all know what it's like to be struggling and we know that tomorrow it could be us needing the extra support.

Imogen works mainly with older people with dementia and feels that it is essential to acknowledge the impact that this work has on her feelings about her own potential vulnerability in later life:

> You do identify quite strongly and see the loss of dignity and identity that older people can experience. Talking it over with people in the office helps me to hold it together. I'm doing a photo album of my life in case it happens to me, so people know who I am and what I've done.

Talking openly about these very personal feelings to colleagues who are dealing with the effects of similar experiences is something Imogen has found very beneficial. Finally, Imogen highlights the importance of the informal team support in identifying and celebrating that which is 'best' in her own and other's practice, 'We are quite careful to celebrate achievements within the team, even if they are quite small – it's part of validating our own and each other's practice and savouring the aspects of the work that we enjoy most.'

Imogen and Cliff both identified their immediate colleagues as an essential part of their support networks. The sort of day-to-day 'looking out for each other' which Imogen describes above is deceptively simple at one level, but it is also an important manifestation of the awareness of self and others and the commitment to emotional engagement, which is at the heart of CBP. Both of them feel fortunate to belong to a multi-professional team with a genuine commitment to partnership working, however, both of them also spoke of the struggle which has taken place within their teams to get to this point of openness and support.

Cliff in particular told us of the feelings of isolation he experienced when he joined the team as its only social worker:

> I needed to assert my role and identity to avoid being seen as generic worker and being 'dumped on' by other members of the team, but I also had to do my bit to help build good relationships in the team and try to learn about other people's role and values.

The ability to hold an awareness of one's professional role, responsibilities and values, within a context of supportive and effective multi-professional working, demands an ability to work openly with difference and uncertainty, which goes to the heart of CBP. As Pat Taylor and Karen Jones, writing about partnership working in Chapter 13 suggest, 'In order to be truly effective, (this form of) partnership across professional boundaries, requires social workers and others to be generous with their knowledge, imaginative in their engagement and open to new learning in their dealings with other workers' (p. 239).

In addition to the informal support from colleagues which arises within a shared office space, Imogen and Cliff both talked about the importance of discussing cases and sharing practice wisdom in the more formal setting of monthly team meetings:

Case discussions within monthly team meetings

Most of the chapters in this book have focussed on day-to-day examples of individual social workers, working effectively with individuals and families. While this reflects the casework oriented nature of social work practice in the United Kingdom and most other western countries, it was clear from talking to Imogen and Cliff, that for them, the team is also an important site of learning, development and support. It has been argued that teams rather than individuals are the fundamental learning unit within modern organisations and that unless the team can learn, neither can the organisation (Senge, 1990).

Cliff and his colleagues have consciously created an educative space within their team meetings to learn about each other's professional values and approaches by sharing their reflections on specific cases. This has not always been an easy or a comfortable process and has involved a willingness to be open to different practice perspectives and

261

priorities. As Cliff says:

> There have been moments of conflict and there will be again. We each bring our individual personal and professional perspective, so there are differences, but diversity and that range of skills is also our strength as a team. The fact that we see difference as a creative thing and something to be valued is also part of what enables us to be supportive of each other.

Imogen's monthly team meetings include similar discussions. Team members also regularly circulate articles that they have found in their own professional journals and discuss topics or ways of working raised by them. As Imogen explained:

> You need to be open to new ideas for it to work. I could just produce social work articles as 'evidence' that the social work perspective is best and argue my case. The occupational therapist or the psychologist could do the same, but we try to hold on to the importance of difference and learning from each other. I will always promote a social model in relation to dementia, but I've learnt some really useful things from my colleagues about the biological processes involved and about practical ideas for improving people's quality of life.

Cliff and Imogen have both succeeded in embracing professional difference as well as maintaining their own strong professional identities. The security they each feel in their role as social workers enables them to see the multi-professional team as a source of support and professional development rather than a source of threat or competition.

GROUPS, PEER LEARNING AND COMMUNITIES OF PRACTICE

It is our contention that peer groups of different kinds are particularly useful as sites of critical thinking, learning and development which can usefully supplement formal line manager supervision. Learning from peers through the sharing of experiences and dilemmas is widely recognised as a fruitful dimension of adult learning. Whether this takes the form of enquiry based learning groups (Burgess, 1992; Fook et al., 2000) or action learning sets (McGill and Beaty, 1998; Thomas et al., 1998), peer group learning has the potential to facilitate the exploration of practice issues in a mutually supportive environment and is a helpful model for support within social work practice.

Imogen and Cliff describe the role of the multi-professional team in ful-filling some of their educative and support needs in more or less formal ways. In both cases and to differing degrees, these compliment their experiences of formal supervision. As most social workers are based in either uni- or multi-professional teams, most are likely to recognise aspects of these experiences. However, there are other less familiar examples of peer group learning support and development, which may exist beyond the immediate team context.

Members of minority groups, such as black, lesbian and gay or dis-abled workers and staff recently recruited from other countries, have been at the forefront of developing systems of peer support within health and social care organisations. As well as offering mentoring and support, these groups can enhance agency practice by challenging inequality and ensuring greater representation of minority group mem-bers at management level.

The existence of support groups for black workers and members of other minority groups, represents an acknowledgement of social and institutional disempowerment. However, the fact that such groups have often been a catalyst for organisational change also highlights the importance of collectivity as a critical force in promoting best practice within agencies. Some writers have identified 'mediation' between the agency and the worker or the worker and the agency, as one of the core functions of supervision (Morrison, 1993; Knapman and Morrison, 1998). While this is an important aspiration within individual supervision, collective issues which challenge an employing organisation, may often be better raised from within the more power-ful and supportive context of a group.

A final example of the sites where practitioners may seek out effective supervision and support is the 'community of practice'. This may be a formal arrangement as in the example described below or something which emerges spontaneously from the needs of a particular group. Cliff for example, identifies 'informal peer group meetings with other Approved Social Workers' as one of his key sources of support. He finds the opportunity to meet with others who regularly encounter sim-ilar practice issues and dilemmas, essential in facilitating his own reflective processes and in providing the support which comes from shared experience.

Kate (the co-author of this chapter) has been instrumental in her role as an adult protection co-ordinator, in developing a more formal commu-nity of practice for professionals from a range of disciplines, with a particular interest and role in adult protection work. The impetus

263

behind the setting up of the group came from national policy requirements which demand a multi-agency response to the protection of vulnerable adults from abuse (DH, 2000, 2005). As the group evolved,
however, it has developed a two-fold purpose. First, it has helped to
promote mutual respect and common ground amongst its members. As
Smith (2003) suggests, the organisation of a community around an
area of mutual interest gives participants a sense of joint enterprise and
group identity. This has been an essential prerequisite for the development of effective systems of joint working in the area of adult protection. Second, the group has provided practitioners with the
opportunity to engage in learning and reflection on practice away from
the constraints of managerial supervision. Several group members have
talked about the significance of this as a source of individual support
and a focus for practice development.

The group meets once a month and is attended by 15–20 practitioners
from diverse statutory and voluntary agencies including the police,
health, social care and housing organisations. The presence of representatives from multiple professions means that multiple perspectives
and multiple practices (Taylor, 2004) are frequently reflected within
the room. At times this has been challenging. Issues of power associated with the professional role and perceived status of different participants have emerged, as have conflicts rooted in different professional
values and approaches. Brechin urges critical practitioners to create
connections with other professionals, 'through which real communications can occur, bringing opportunities to learn about others views and
perspectives and discovering ways of talking constructively about differences of opinion' (2000: 37).

'Real communication' has not always been easy to achieve, but over
time the group has developed a set of aims and ground rules, including
a commitment to what Eraut (2001) calls 'a blame free culture'. This
has helped enable group members to explore general practice issues
and dilemmas as well as their own feelings of ambivalence and conflict.
It also works against the tendency to assert a definitive professional
'line' which was observable in the early meetings.

The establishment of a shared and openly acknowledged group culture,
has been essential in developing a climate of learning and support
within which individuals feel comfortable with their own uncertainty
and ongoing learning. In this respect the group is committed to a collectively critical way of working, which not only informs the practice
of individual members but also supports the development of a negotiated, partnership approach to best practice in adult protection.

CONCLUSION

The context of social work is changing rapidly and this may, as Julia Phillipson (2002) suggests, indicate the need to consider new models of supervision and support. Phillipson discusses Jan Fook's (2002) idea of a new discourse of professional expertise, which values practice wisdom above externally imposed measures of performance. She suggests that this approach along with Nigel Parton and Patrick O'Byrne's (2000) notion of embracing ambiguity and uncertainty rather than attempting to eliminate it through managerial, decision-making processes, may offer a starting point for a new perspective on supervision.

These are certainly ideas which resonate with the best practice high-lighted in this chapter. The practitioners whose experiences we have described, share a commitment to the active promotion of their own learning and development through a process of critically reflective engagement with practice. In this respect our examples also have much in common with Sawdon and Sawdon's (1995) call for a creative approach to problem solving in supervision, which challenges taken for granted assumptions and refuses to deal only in easily accessible solutions. Practitioners like Cliff and Imogen, are not looking for a blueprint for social work practice, they are rather embracing existing opportunities and creating new ways in which to develop as critical thinkers in order to enhance their own and others' practice.

REFERENCES

Berne, E. (1964) *Games People Play: Psychology of Human Relationships* (New York: Grove Press).

Brechin, A. (2000), 'Introducing critical practice', in A. Brechin., H. Brown and M. Eby, (eds), *Critical Practice in Health and Social Care* (London: Sage).

Brockbank, A. and McGill, I. (1998) *Facilitating Reflective Learning in Higher Education* (Bristol: Taylor & Francis).

Brown, A. and Bourne, I. (1996) *The Social Work Supervisor: Supervision in Community, Day Care and Residential Settings* (Buckingham: Open University Press).

Burgess, H. (1992) *Problem Led Learning For Social Work: The Enquiry and Action Learning Approach* (Whiting and Birch: London).

Department of Health (2000) *No Secrets: Guidance on Developing and Implementing Multi Agency Policies and Procedures to Protect Vulnerable Adults from Abuse* (London: HMSO).

Department of Health (2005) *Action on Elder Abuse: Report on the Project to Establish a Monitoring and Reporting Process for Adult Protection Referrals Made in Accordance With 'No Secrets'* (www.dh.gov.uk accessed 30.12.05)

Eraut, M. (2001) 'Learning Challenges for Knowledge Based Organisations', in Stevens, J. (ed.) *Workbased Learning in Europe* (London: Chartered Institute of Personnel and Development (CIPD)).

Ferguson, H. (2003) 'Outline of Critical Best Practice Perspective on Social Work and Social Care', *British Journal of Social Work*, **33**, 1005–1024.

Fook, J (2002) *Social Work: Critical Theory and Practice* (London: Sage).

Fook, J., Ryan, M. and Hawkins, L. (2000) *Professional Expertise: Practice, Theory and Education for Working in Uncertainty* (London: Whiting and Birch).

Hawkins, P. Shohet, R. (2000) *Supervision in the Helping Professions: An Individual, Group and Organizational Approach* (Buckingham: Open University Press).

Healy, K. (2000) *Social Work Practices: Contemporary Perspectives on Change* (London: Sage).

Hughes, L. and Pengelly, P. (1997) *Staff Supervision in a Turbulent Environment* (London: Jessica Kingsley).

Karpman, S. (1968) 'Fairy Tales and Script Drama Analysis', *Transactional Analysis Bulletin* **7**(26), 39–44.

Knapman, J. and Morrison, T. (1998) *Making the Most of Supervision in Health and Social Care: A Self-development Manual for Supervisees* (Brighton: Pavillion)

Leonard, P. (1997) *Postmodern Welfare: Reconstructing an Emancipating Project* (London: Sage)

McGill, I. and Beaty, L. (1998) *Action Learning: A Guide for Professional, Management and Educational Development* (Kogan Page: London).

Morrison, T. (1993) *Staff Supervision in Social Care: An Action Learning Approach* (Pavilion: Brighton).

Parker, J. (2004) *Effective Practice Learning in Social Work* (Exeter: Learning Matters).

Parton, N. and O'Byrne, P. (2000) 'What do We Mean by Constructive Social Work?' *Critical Social Work*, **1**(2), Fall, 2000.

Phillipson, J. (2002) 'Supervision and Being Supervised' in R. Adams, L. Dominelli and Payne, M. *Critical Practice in Social Work* (Basingstoke: Palgrave).

Sawdon, C., and Sawdon, D. (1995) 'The Supervision Partnership: A Whole Greater than the Sum of its Parts' in Pritchard, J. *Good Practice in Supervision: Voluntary and Statutory Organisations* (London: Jessica Kingsley).

Senge, P. (1990) *Fifth Discipline: The Art and Practice of the Learning Orgnaisation* (Doubleday: New York).

Smith, J. (2003) 'Communities of Practice', *The encyclopedia of informal learning*. www.infed. org/biblio/communities_of_practice.htm. Accessed 22.5.06

Taylor, I. (2004) 'Multi-professional Teams and the Learning Organisation' in N. Gould and M. Baldwin (eds) *Social Work, Critical Reflection and the Learning Organisation* (Ashgate: Aldershot).

Thomas, J., Boutland, K. and Carlin, J. (1998) 'Learning Sets for Post Qualifying and Advanced Award Portfolio Development' in *Journal of practice Teaching in Social Work and Health*, 11, (1), 60–75.

Webb, S. (2006) *Social Work in a Risk Society: Social and Political Perspectives* (Basingstoke: Palgrave).

15 Best practice as skilled organisational work

BRUCE SENIOR WITH ELSPETH LOADES

INTRODUCTION

The organisational dimension of social work is often neglected in practice literature. While there are notable exceptions (for example, Lymbery & Butler, 2004), there is a gap between the realities of organisational life as a social worker and social work practice as presented in the literature. Discussions of organisations or management are not usually integrated with practice examples. Such integration would help social workers develop organisational skills and knowledge that would enable them to carry out their job more effectively. The stereotypical gap between social work theory and practice is in many ways a reflection of this lack of analysis and an insufficient understanding of the organisational realities in which social care staff operate. Furthermore, the common deficit model (Ferguson, 2003) is explicitly or implicitly applied to discussions about the organisational context of social work practice: the employing agencies are 'too bureaucratic', 'too managerialist' and so on. The organisational setting becomes an easy target to criticise, and this can add to the negative burden that social care agencies and employees have to carry with them.

In many ways there are good reasons for this absence of the organisational dimension. There are so many variables at play in considering examples of practice which are located in a specific organisational context. However, our thesis is that unless social work practitioners think about their own organisation, and how they both affect it, and are affected by it, then the possibilities of best serving the interests of service users are diminished.

One of our key points in this chapter is that aspects of the organisation provide both the opportunities for, and limitations of, best practice.

These opportunities are best seized by workers with an appreciation of how people operate within organisations and how those organisations themselves are structured and go about their business. This chapter encourages the reader to think about the agencies in which they themselves are familiar, either through employment or placement. We will develop our general theme, which emphasises the crucial importance of thinking about organisations, and then go on to look at more specific key aspects. We will examine the discourse around managerialism and bureaucracy; the pivotal position social workers hold between the organisation and the public; and consider the neglected emotional life of social care organisations.

In this discussion, we draw on our experiences as managers and educators, and as implementers of policy as well as policy producers. We have in recent times made a point of discussing many of the issues in this chapter with practitioners, and their contributions can be seen in quotes we use. In particular we draw on an interview with Alison Gardener, who also has her own contribution in this book.

THE NECESSITY OF AN ORGANISATIONAL PERSPECTIVE

The importance of understanding and being able to operate within a complex organisational web has never been more crucial than at a time when the organisational structures, policies and procedures of social work agencies (or rather agencies that employ social workers) have been subject to so much fundamental change. In the United Kingdom context (albeit with 'national' differences) there are many strands to this change. These include: the separation of children's and adult services, the integration of health and social care, the integration of social services for children and education, the emphasis on inter professional working, the increased emphasis on accountability, audit, performance and the service user voice, and the development of a range of private, voluntary and quasi government organisations. These all contribute to a rapidly changing organisational context in which social workers must operate.

Despite the differences in organisational cultures and structures, and increasingly complex legal frameworks, there is a common ground with regard to the crucial importance of considering organisational aspects. This commonality encompasses the differences between the statutory, voluntary and independent sectors and between the four countries that make up the United Kingdom and extends beyond the

United Kingdom to the organisational frameworks, wherever social workers and related professionals are employed.

Social workers need to understand how organisations function, and how common features of organisations, whatever their purpose, impact on their practice and services they provide. For example, how the agency is managed and led, how aspects of the organisation's culture restrict or encourage creative working practices. In the UK context this is of particular importance at this time because of the advent of professional registration for social workers, and the legal restriction of the term 'social worker'. Following the USA example, where the National Association of Social Workers obtained legal regulation of the title of social worker as part of strategy to attain higher professional status, and protect its domain from competitors (Resser, 1996), this same trend has taken place in the United Kingdom and more accountability is, therefore, placed on individual social workers. As the impact of registration unfolds we should see social workers being held to more account for their individual actions. This in turn will open up the possibility of social workers being able to adopt a more assertive stance in relation to their employers in the name of overarching law, policy and the Codes of Practice (GSCC, 2002), now all the more prescriptive in the United Kingdom than ten years ago.

If social workers are to make use of greater individual professional accountability rather than a localised accountability to their employer, it is even more crucial to understand how their employer's organisation operates, and how it impacts on their practice. The argument here is that the foundations to undertake social work, whether assembling community care packages or undertaking a child protection assessment, are based on a social worker's ability to work as skilled organisational persons, and not just as some free floating professional devoid of an organisational base.

The organisational context we refer to is widely defined and includes all aspects of organisations from structure to psychodynamic forces; from culture and gossip to leadership and management styles; from interpersonal relationships with colleagues and line managers to the power exercised in relation to service users see Sims et al., Fineman and Gabriel, 1993 for an unorthodox account of organisations and Mullender and Perrott, 2002 for a summary view of the social work context). In addition, a critical best practice (CBP) approach reminds practitioners to consider what they bring of themselves to organisational life. Consideration of who we are, our characters and personalities has been squeezed out of social work education and practice in recent times.

An awareness of our own impact on the people around us, and the organisation in which we operate, is crucial. How many social workers are subject to the unthinking whims and particular character traits of managers? Similarly managers have to deal with the various 'personalities' in their teams and departments. A little more insight on all sides concerning what individuals bring with them into organisations would be beneficial both for the organisation itself and the people who work within it, but also ultimately for the recipients of services.

MANAGERIALISM, PROFESSIONALISM AND BUREAUCRACY

In broad terms one can identify a shift from the 'bureau – professionalism' established through Seebohm to the current emphasis on managerialism and the voice of the consumer/service user (Harris, 1999). Our experiences suggest that both these generalised descriptions are relevant to understanding how organisations operate today. The language of both permeates throughout people's understanding of what they experience in the social care work place.

One of the hallmarks of a CBP approach is to examine terms such as 'bureaucratic' or 'managerialist' in more depth and detail. The apparent disaffection of social workers from organisational culture, and ways of working can feed into a crude polarisation between 'managerialism' and social work (Jones et al., 2006). This dichotomy seems to resonate with a reality that is reported by many social workers, yet a CBP approach may reveal that this is too simple a conclusion to draw.

Managerialism has many forms (Clarke & Newman, 1997), and not all are crude enactions of the oppressive macho manager only concerned with controlling the workforce and promoting their own career. Just as in any sector one can find aggressive managers who are only concerned with finances and the 'big picture', and who have lost all sight of day to day concerns of front-line workers and the public. However, one can also find many managers who are focused on balancing individual interests and best practice with a dependency on public funding and the concerns of key stakeholders such as local elected politicians or management boards. 'Managerialism 'has become a cliché and a term of abuse, and it may be useful for front-line workers to revisit Clarke and Newman's analysis as well as consider Trow's (1993) distinction between 'hard' and 'soft' managerialism. 'Soft' managerialism, according to Trow, is the recognition of inefficiency and ineffectiveness by all concerned and shared efforts to bring about change. This 'soft' managerialism is not necessarily incompatible with traditional notions of professionalism and meeting the needs of service users.

There is no doubt that 'managerialism' marks fundamental changes in the welfare state. One of the effects of which, as Hoggett (2000: 44) explains, is that 'A culture of audit, quality assurance, performance monitoring and evaluation has descended upon British public services in the 1990s.' However, the term has become overused and is now often a form of shorthand for an incomplete analysis, however much it appears to resonate with aspects of the working lives of social workers. It partly rests on a mistaken assumption that social care organisations somehow create a uniform and all controlling management front. As Evans and Harris (2004) argue, the idea that management somehow 'bends workers to its will' (p. 876) is far from the case. As one social worker ironically expressed to us a view of her own powerful position, 'What will they do, sack me?'

Furthermore, as any social worker knows there are huge differences between managers and how they operate. A united front of an all-powerful management is not the reality. If one digs a little deeper into the disaffection that many social workers indicate, one finds it is far from uniform or the only experience. Our discussions with social workers from a wide range of agencies revealed many differences. Social workers reported to us how much they value excellent team managers who are very supportive and key to the practice they carry out. One social worker stated, 'I couldn't do the job without their advice and support.'

Alison Gardener in an interview describes her team and the team management as being very supportive, 'The team I work for functions extremely well and we are very well managed ... managers are extremely supportive ... and there is sense in which our management is our foundation, that's how I feel it, that they are the bedrock.'

It is clear that not all social workers would report that same experience. So how do managers make a difference? Gardener emphasises the importance of the availability of team managers in order to provide the necessary climate for creative good practice in a testing and challenging environment. She goes on to comment that:

> You are left to get on with your work and use your own judgment, so you go to them when you need time rather than them coming to you and saying 'what are you doing?' So it's the right way round, you have a sort of freedom, but you have support as well.

In addition 'monthly in depth supervision is sacrosanct'. The interview revealed that as would be expected there is less engagement with and knowledge of senior managers. It is striking that senior managers in some agencies do not appear to take more steps to stay in touch with and engage with social care workers on 'the front line' or seem to be less aware, than they should be, about how middle managers actually manage. There are senior managers, however, who take the time to visit teams, and even read case files in order to stay in touch.

Discussions right across hierarchical levels reveal the strong commitment of staff at all levels to improve services and support each other and in many cases a widespread loyalty to the organisation even under stressful circumstances. In our experience social workers are generally looking to act creatively on behalf of service users albeit sometimes in the face of what they perceive as organisational obstacles. Many managers, despite the stereotype of managers not being really interested in specific service user needs, are looking for workers who act creatively within agreed organisational policies and procedures. At times there is a gap between these two realities and where this is not addressed social care agencies are more likely to be dysfunctional.

Bureaucracy has become a term that cannot be used positively. Anything that is 'bureaucratic' is by definition undesirable and unwelcome; paperwork for the sake of paperwork. Yet in our own everyday lives we welcome many aspects of bureaucracy. We like to be paid at regular intervals; we want organisations to have our customer records available. A CBP approach demands that at the very least we think through the easy condemnations of bureaucracy that pervade many discussions about contemporary health and welfare services.

On reflecting on the reality of working in a bureaucratic organisation, Gardener noted in our interview that things had changed even in the past two years:

> The new computer system has created quite a big change in the office – client balance of work, we all feel we are seeing fewer clients and I think that's real. There is less flexibility ... now a minor change to a care plan entails many more steps than in the past, but at same time I suppose the object of that is probably to make the audit trail more efficient ... if it [administration] has a point then I don't really have a problem with it.

In common with other social workers that we discussed these issues with, Gardener is not objecting in principle to administrative systems and recognises the advantages of some of the changes; namely, easier record sharing, transparency of process, clarity for service users about what services they will receive, clearer accountability for public expenditure. The problem with bureaucracy is often that the purpose is not explained or understood, or actually there is no point, or where it requires duplication of task and effort.

There are undoubtedly increasing administrative demands on social workers, but at the same time a generalised condemnation of bureaucracy is a convenient and easy target which ignores the importance of reliable and relevant administrative procedures.

Another angle on this discussion is the polarisation between bureaucratisation on one hand and professionalism on the other. Earlier we argued that professional registration might lead to strengthening the professional accountability of individual social workers rather than purely an accountability to a bureaucratic organisation. In a sense, however, any account that polarises bureaucratisation and professionalism is not helpful. Simpkin (1979) in his radical critique argued that professionalism and bureaucracy go hand in hand in contemporary society, and that any argument that they are logical or moral opposites is mistaken (p. 114). He argued that social democratic societies offer professionalism (discretion, greater flexibility) as an antidote to bureaucracy (organising activity of the state) (pp. 126–127). The GSCC registration may be the latest example of a trade-off between professionalism and a reinforced managerialism which in part promotes the agenda of consumer rights. Simpkin's analysis is worth revisiting, not only to understand a continuity of issues in social work but also to see where issues have moved on, for example, the expansion of post-qualifying social work education in the 1990s and the developing emphasis on evidence for practice.

It may surprise some readers to see that in the 1970s Simpkin (a social worker himself) discussed the advent of 'managerialism' in social work. For Simpkin, managerialism represented central planning, optimal use of resources, coordination and organisational unity (pp. 114–117). The radical agenda at the time was clearly in opposition to managerialism although Simpkin's wish that managers would actually concern themselves with managing and not trying to please everyone, and thereby satisfying no one, has perhaps more generally come to pass.

One of the reasons for the growth of managerialism and bureaucratisation, especially under New Labour, has been the attempt to more equitably focus resources by developing criteria of risk and need. This is seen by some as undermining the judgement of social work professionals; yet three related points need to be borne in mind. First, in our lives as citizens and customers we want to be dealt with fairly, and not at the whim of whomever we happen to come across or where we happen to live. Second, in the past social workers have engaged in long-standing dependent relations with 'clients' at the expense of meeting needs elsewhere in the community. Finally, clear policy and procedures for such work as child and adult protection are essential in order to provide effective safeguarding of individuals. These too can be described as 'bureaucratic' or 'managerialist'.

It may well be the case that in some areas of work the balance between organisational criteria and professional judgement is tilted too far in favour of the former at present (see, for example, Martin et al., Phelps and Kabana, 2004), but we should remember that a balance does need to be struck, and that too wide a sweeping condemnation of bureaucracy and managerialism can obscure this point. Furthermore, while 'bureaucratisation' and 'managerialism' can be seen as widespread and all pervading in the social work agencies known to us, the *experience* of these phenomena will be different depending critically on the management and leadership of immediate and more senior line managers. It also depends ofcourse on the characteristics of individuals, and the team in which they operate. A discussion with a group of social workers about the reality of their working lives, demonstrated how vital the team context is. One social worker commented that: 'A stable team provides fantastic training, nurturing and empowering'.

The context of local procedures and organisational culture has been hugely significant in understanding the work of social workers and how (for example) scandals erupt in some organisations at particular times. One key message of the various reports on the scandals that have besieged social work is that individual workers can get caught up in dysfunctional organisations. For example, whatever the weaknesses and poor judgement of individual workers, the results of enquiries from Pindown (Levy & Kahan, 1991) to Climbie (Laming, 2003) illustrate deficiencies of organisational culture and management. Inquiry reports inevitably consider individual responsibilities within an organisational framework, and therefore the question of individual discretion arises.

The notion of discretion and whether it still exists in social work practice is crucial to our previous discussion about accountability of front-line staff, and whether or not managerial bureaucracy is all powerful. It is crucial for new (and experienced) practitioners to consider the argument made by Evans and Harris (2004) that 'the proliferation of rules and regulations should not automatically be equated with greater control over professional discretion; paradoxically, more rules may create more discretion' (p. 871). In addition, they argue that discretion itself is not necessarily a 'good' or a 'bad' thing. It can be a welcome professional attribute 'or a cloak for political decision makers to hide behind or it may be an opportunity for professional abuse of power' (p. 871). Evans and Harris in their work on the exaggerated death of discretion constructively identify a gradient of discretion, rather than an all or nothing phenomenon and refer to Dworkin's (2000) three senses of discretion. One of these pertains to interpretation and use of judgement within the rules. Whilst this is not the only meaningful sense in which discretion continues to be the lifeblood of social work practice, this form of discretion needs to be borne in mind when social workers are confronted by literature that suggests that the age of professional discretion in social work has ended.

Discussions with social workers make it abundantly clear that discretion lives on. For example, Alison Gardener in our interview refers to her discretion, and use of her own judgement as a key component of everyday work. There are many times when 'you know what your decision is based on a sound assessment and then you have to find ways of backing up your own argument using the language of the local authority and the eligibility criteria'. CBP means using discretion (in a variety of forms) within the legal and policy framework to make sound value and knowledge-based decisions.

OPERATING AT THE EDGE

The notion of discretion(s) is of paramount importance because, as front-line workers, social workers patrol the boundaries of their employing organisations. The interactions of social workers with the public occupy the fluid spaces between the organisation itself, typically characterised as bureaucratic and monolithic, and the human encounters of everyday life. Inexperienced (and experienced) workers can be pulled too far in one direction or another. They can either become the 'bureaucratic' voice of the organisation that is too rule bound, or, as is often the case, they act out their own conception of their employing agency which may be far removed from reality. Professionals and others characterised by Lipsky (1980) as 'street level bureaucrats' often fall back on the organisation as an excuse for not responding in more sensitive and humane ways. 'I would like to provide this service, but it's not our policy.' This line can be heard when no one is clear whether it is policy or not.

Conversely any health or social care worker can get sucked into losing touch with their professional authority and the legal, policy and employment framework in which they operate. Thus, at times, they set up false encounters with service users where the power of the worker is effectively hidden from the service user. CBP here is about an appreciation and understanding of this space at the boundaries of organisations so as to maximise the possibilities of effective and skilled interventions within the legal and policy framework.

This is a point made by Charles and Butler (2004) in their discussion of a comparison between the 'accommodating' and 'reflective' practitioner. The former is said to achieve a sense of control by adopting the language, and standardised practices of the agency, 'they respond to the workplace's emotional intensity by bureaucratising difficulties' (p. 73). The reflective practitioner draws on a social work knowledge base to make considered decisions, carefully selects methods to apply and will 'relish the uncertainties inherent in working 'in the swamp', using these to increase their organisational power' (p. 72).

The comparison between these two approaches that social workers may adopt is a useful one to help us to think about how we operate in our employing organisation. However, a key point that Charles and Butler make is that an individual practitioner will constantly shift between patterns of 'accommodation' and 'reflection in action' in their daily working lives. In other words, most people are not either the supine organisational mouthpiece or the reflective hero or heroine. Most of us act in a rich variety of ways in the complex organisational worlds in which we live and work. This point needs stressing because the comparison between accommodation and reflection runs the risk of being just another good/bad dichotomy that leaves practitioners feeling inadequate about their working lives.

Social workers operate at the edges of organisations, and at times may refer to 'social services' or their employing agency as though to imply that they themselves were not really part of the organisation. This reflects the ambiguity that has always been inherent in social work between on the one hand focusing on the needs of service users and on the other acting as an agent of the welfare state and gatekeeper to scare resources. Understandably, social workers shift their ground between at times acting as (for example) a messenger from the agency, and on other occasions standing alongside service users. To take an example, at the beginning of an assessment a social worker needs to form an initial relationship, and to do that they may well need to try to occupy that space or middle ground between the organisation and service user rather than merely be a cipher of the agency. However, at another point in the process (perhaps with aggressive or vulnerable people):

> 'it can be important to be able to bring someone higher up the hierarchy into a situation and to have a clear, legally sanctioned procedure to follow and by which you are bound. In this sort of situation, you may then be more clearly acting as a mouthpiece for a statutory authority and using it to try to protect a service user (and yourself)'. (Gardener, this volume, Chapter 2)

We can see how social workers need to adopt different positions with regard to the service user and organisation if we look more closely at examples elsewhere in this book. Alison Gardener explicitly states that she sees herself as acting first and foremost on behalf of service users (Chapter 2). Indeed the social services perspective is clearly one that is external to the worker herself. However, in another example, Gardener rightly considers that she has to inform the authorities and ultimately the police about Simon's driving. We might conclude, therefore, that here she is clearly operating from within the organisation. However, both examples can be rooted in an understanding of being 'professional'.

There are potential difficulties in seeing ourselves as somehow outside the organisation when we take actions that are alongside the service user, and then retreating back inside the organisation when we need to use authority or take actions we may feel less personally comfortable with. We adopt this way of thinking partly because many of us want to distance ourselves from the organisation we perceive as bureaucratic and insensitive, and partly because some managers do not appreciate the need for sensitive and compassionate social work to take place in these swampy areas on the edges of organisations. We found one example where a social worker was not recording or reporting to managers that they were making follow-up visits to families where work had been formally completed. This was done in the name of good practice where it was felt that the organisation could not spare the workers' time to check that a family dispute had remained settled after an earlier intervention. This reveals the extent to which an experienced social worker may go to pursue their understanding of good practice even to the extent of placing themselves in a risky situation with regard to their employer. Martin et al. (2004: 484) report similar examples of care managers putting careers at risk to promote service user needs.

A thoughtful and considered recognition of the role of the social worker as operating on behalf of the employer at the edges of welfare organisational boundaries is necessary in order to provide effective services. As Gardener in our interview expresses it, there is no point in being simply a mouthpiece of the organisation 'if we don't in any sense stand back and critique the organisation there is not a lot of point in training for 3 years and calling ourselves social workers'.

We should be open to the possibility that organisations (and some managers within organisations) actually want good social workers to operate in that space, rather than see it as running counter to organisational priorities and concerns. This is the space where social workers have meaningful conversations with members of the public and where they can establish a purposeful relationship albeit in many cases a short-term one. In discussing this way of thinking about the work, Gardener explains in our interview that 'I don't actually feel that is in opposition to the organisation, I think that is what the organisation is asking us to do ... although maybe other agencies are more restrictive.'

Social workers pursuing best practice need to analyse how they operate at the boundaries of organisations. Here they are often in the position of negotiators. That is negotiation with other agencies and professionals, with members of the public as users of services and carers and with their own managers. Sometimes that negotiation takes place while clearly acting as the voice of the employer and the law; at other times while not acting counter to the law and employer, it clearly takes place from alongside the user of the service, at times advocating for that citizen against the employers' usual way of operating. This reflects the flexibility and true creativity required of social workers and a position that many social care organisations and managers would consider quite legitimate as well as consistent with the professionalism enshrined in professional registration.

THE EMOTIONAL LIFE OF ORGANISATIONS

Operating at the edges of the organisation, and engaging in personal interactions with the public gives rise to a wide variety of emotions. Coupled with this is the fact that emotions are rife even in the most sheltered recesses of formal bureaucracies, indeed in any organisation. As Gabriel (1999: 211) expresses the point: 'one only has to scratch the surface of organisational life to discover a thick layer of emotions and feelings, at times checked, at times feigned, at times timidly expressed and at other times bursting out uncontrollably'. The image of the organisation as a machine (Morgan, 1986), the impersonal bureaucratic stereotype, obscures the reality of our agencies as a hot bed of emotional life.

Many of the tensions and unproductive elements of organisations arise from a failure to recognise and deal with the flood of emotions that ebbs and flows though our working lives. There are two key points here in any pursuit of CBP. First, the relevance of the feelings and emotional life of all staff needs to be recognised in any successful social care organisation. After all feelings and emotions are part and parcel of the everyday work, and they need to be managed through supervision and organisational processes as well as more informal methods. For example, the 'bureaucratic' processes that shape child and adult protection work can also be an appropriate part of the organisations need to protect workers from overwhelming anxiety. Second, we must acknowledge that, nonetheless, the prime task of social work agencies is not to deal with the emotions of employees (or councillors or management committees come to that) and that people also have to take responsibility for the management of their own feelings and emotions.

Both these aspects of managing emotions need to be constructively handled so that the primary functions of the organisation are met. Where this is not done, psychoanalytic insight tells us that anxiety can rise to debilitating levels (Gabriel, 1999). This is of particular relevance to social workers who as we have seen operate at the edges of organisations which is usually the most challenging and anxiety provoking place to be (Froggett, 2002). Understanding anxiety, and the defences that individuals, teams and organisations construct in order to deal with it has over the years largely disappeared from social work education and supervision. We have lost sight of this dimension with an emphasis on outcome based criteria and performance management. The work of Menzies (1970) on nurses is as relevant to health and social care workers today as it has ever been. Her work on the defences that nurses can construct to protect themselves from the emotional realities of their work can resonate through any analysis of contemporary social care activity. One can still find in residential homes and social work offices those dreadful notices that say 'you don't have to be mad to work here but it helps'. Despite the rhetoric and changing realities around the voice of service users, we can construct all sorts of unhelpful defences to guard us against the feelings and emotions of our work.

Contemporary organisational thinking has recognised the reality and importance of emotions (Fineman, 1993). Instead of being denied and always kept in check they have become a resource to be managed. Fast food outlets may insist that the smile that greets a potential customer is 'sincere' (Ritzer, 2000). Emotions are no longer seen as dysfunctional. In a world of continuous change and uncertainty, management theory has embraced attributes such as commitment, trust, care, enthusiasm, pride and even fun as necessary for organisational success. At a different level social workers are expected to utilise emotions in pursuit of social work goals; indeed appropriate use and management of feelings is central to their professionalisation.

Charles and Butler (2004), in their very useful contribution to thinking about the organisational context, argue that hierarchical organisations are 'incapable of working constructively with emotions' (p. 81). We would argue that this may well be the case in many organisations as a generalisation, but the day to reality has to be different if any effective social work is to be carried out. The emotional life of any organisation is crucial in shaping the experience of front-line staff and users of services. A study by Leigh and Miller (2004) on first encounters between duty desk child care social workers and the public reveals the importance of that first engagement in shaping the subsequent satisfaction 'felt' by the service user.

An organisation is not one all-encompassing entity, and social workers (and managers) carve out their own emotional enclaves in order to meet the needs of the public, to survive, to be creative and, dare we say, even flourish. Social workers have to manage a range of emotions in the course of their working days, from fear to the pleasure of a situation handled well or satisfaction from the thanks of a grateful service user. As one social worker on a post-qualifying programme reported, 'A sense of achievement makes you want to carry on.' This sense of a job well done despite all the constraints and contradictions goes largely unreported. In discussing issues in groups of post-qualifying workers, it can be the negative voice that attempts to prevail and shape the emotional climate.

The interview with Gardener indicates a team environment that helps maintain a sense of calmness in the face of many competing pressures, not only of a stimulating job well done, but also of a more negative emotions such as anger. For example, while discussing what contemporary social work is like:

> This government's fixation on performance indicators can be a source of conflict, because one can feel that the concern of senior management is about the information that is churned out the other side; and getting those right boxes ticked sometimes does have a detrimental effect on the people on the receiving end, and that does get me very angry indeed.

These more negative emotions churned up by the organisation need to be recognised and dealt with by all concerned if they are not to diminish organisational effectiveness. Supervision is of central importance and a lack of emphasis on regular in-depth supervision can mark out a more dysfunctional social work agency. In addition, a functional team at formal and informal levels is crucial.

The centrality of emotions to the social work job has to be recognised, and we need to find ways to ensure they are worked with constructively in public sector organisations. The key is to consider and understand the part emotions play in our working lives, and crucially the emotions we ourselves bring to the work place, and the emotional impact our jobs have on us.

Psychoanalytic thinking is no longer part of mainstream social work as it has been in the past, but it can offer important insights into our understanding of organisations as well as ourselves. Gabriel has applied psychoanalytic concepts to the study of organisations. In terms of what we bring to our agencies he points out that: 'The way we perceive organisations, the way we try to find our place in them, the way we submit to or question their requirements, are influenced by our psychological development' (p. 60). In other words our own character is a vital component of how we operate within, and how we understand organisations.

So just as we need to have insight into ourselves in order to work on a face-to-face basis with vulnerable people, we require that insight in order to operate successfully within a complex organisational context, and to understand what we ourselves contribute to the puzzles, tensions and complications of that organisation.

It needs to be recognised that a decision that is eminently reasonable and fair to one person may be an erosion of basic principles and a personal affront to another. As Gabriel (1999) expresses the point: 'Different individuals, working side by side in the same organisation, may be working in organisations that are in effect different – one person may experience the organisation as a hostile and malevolent force, bent on destruction, while a second may experience the same organisation as a model of everything that is good and right, and a third is 'only doing a job' and does not care one way or another for the organisation' (p. 60). In our work with social workers and students we see these varying points of view on a regular basis.

A CBP approach demands that we recognise these differing perceptions of organisational reality and work with them to further social work goals as opposed to using them as a defence in order to justify inaction, or wrapping ourselves in the comforting blanket of a weary cynicism.

Engaging with the contradictions of policy, the difficulties of implementation, and resource constraints are not straightforward, but to do so is crucial to delivering and improving social work practice.

ORGANISATIONAL SKILLS AND UNDERSTANDING

An understanding of the wider policy, political and financial environment in which the organisation operates is an essential part of a CBP approach to social work. As the interview with Gardener demonstrates, 'What I find helpful is actually making myself look at things from a wider social policy and political perspective so I'm not just thinking it's so and so over there in senior management who can't see sense and is making this ridiculous decision.' We would argue that a political knowledge and understanding and an appreciation of the policy and implementation process are crucial to being an effective social worker, and indeed to organisational survival.

Some key factors that social workers should consider about their organisation include: how is it resourced, structured, managed and led; who are the key stakeholders, where does power lie; how would someone describe the culture of the organisation or the subcultures of particular teams? What are the levels of trust; how are emotions handled; how reliable is the gossip?

For newly qualified practitioners, the key consideration is about the team they join, and how that team is managed. Will you have to 'hit the ground running' (and what does this over-used phrase mean in *this* team at *this* time?) or will you be appropriately introduced to a workload, local policies and procedures.

The importance of language and the power of discourse are central to an understanding of CBP. Many experienced social workers may have missed out on the postmodern emphasis on discourse (Pease & Fook, 1999). To take, for example, the phrase in the previous section 'hit the ground running'. This will have different meanings: to some (newly appointed social workers) it means you will get a large complex case load and insufficient support, to others (managers) it means you need to be capable and qualified to do the basic tasks. In the same team, the reality of it may change in a matter of weeks as new staff are appointed or staff leave or the manager changes.

The effective social worker develops a sophisticated and detailed understanding of the complex nuances of organisational life; although as we stressed earlier, this sophistication is not present at all times. Like everyone else, the skilled reflective worker will take the easy way out and act unthinkingly. We have not intended to outline organisational practice in an idealised way so that practitioners feel inadequate.

The actions that practitioners can take to gain influence, and improve outcomes for service users are by themselves not dramatic or heroic. They stem from an understanding of how their organisation operates, and a degree of confidence in their sense of purpose, values and knowledge. These often small steps require the will to make a difference and a level of trust that these actions will not be seen negatively by people further up the hierarchy or indeed by peers. Some examples of creativity and acts of influence we have uncovered include contacting senior managers with suggestions for improvements; offering to help with new initiatives; contributing to policy documents (many front-line staff in their post-qualifying portfolios report contributing to policy formulation). Effective social workers often take a bit more time and trouble to track down who in the organisation can resolve an issue rather than despair too readily at the environment in which they operate.

In this chapter, we have discussed some of the main aspects of a CBP approach to any analysis of the organisational context in which social workers operate. This includes examining one's own assumptions and understanding of organisations, including one's own character and how one deals with such factors as anxiety and leadership figures.

It involves critically reflecting on how one acts and operates within the organisation and in relation to others, for example, analysing and recognising the power and authority one holds in relation to service users, carers and colleagues, and examining what stereotypes one operates with in relation to other professionals, managers and service users.

We have stressed the importance of developing a detailed understanding of *your* own organisation. Organisational thinking and knowledge can be generalised across agencies, but specific actions often require an analysis of a specific context. A detailed understanding of how a particular line manager operates, how they understand the organisation, the impact of senior managers, the culture of the organisation, levels of trust, power and commitment and your own character all come into play.

Finally, we hope we have furthered the recognition that not to understand the organisational context in which social work is carried out is a self-imposed burden on any social worker who seeks job satisfaction and who has service user interests at heart. CBP requires a continually developing understanding of the organisational context, and this is a key foundation for what can still be a fascinating and challenging job.

REFERENCES

Charles, M. and Butler, S. (2004) 'Social Workers' Management of Organisational Change' in Lymbery, M. and Butler, S. (eds) 2004, *Social Work Ideals and Practice Realities* (Basingstoke: Palgrave Macmillan).

Clarke, J. and Newman, J. (1997) *The Managerial State* (London: Sage).

Dworkin, R. (2000) *Taking Rights Seriously* (London: Duckworth).

Evans, T. and Harris, J. (2004) 'Street Level Bureaucracy, Social Work and the (Exaggerated) Death of Discretion', *British Journal of Social Work*, **34**, 871–895.

Ferguson, H. (2003) 'Outline of a Critical Best Practice Perspective on Social Work and Social Care', *British Journal of Social Work*, **33**, 1005–1024.

Fineman, S. (1993) *Emotions in Organisations* (Sage: London).

Froggett, L. (2002) *Love, Hate & Welfare: Psychosocial Approaches to Policy and Practice* (Bristol: Policy Press).

Gabriel, Y. (1999) *Organisations in Depth* (London: Sage).

General Social Care Council (2002) *Codes of Practice* (London: GSCC).

Harris, J. (1999) 'State Social Work and Social Citizenship in Britain: From Clientalism to Consumerism', *British Journal of Social Work*, **29**, 915–937.

Hoggett, P. (2000) *Emotional Life and the Politics of Welfare* (Basingstoke: Macmillan).

Jones, C., Ferguson, E., Lavalette, M. and Penketh, L. (2006) 'Forward Thinking', *The Guardian* 22.3.06

Laming, H. (2003) *The Victoria Climbié Inquiry: Report of an Inquiry* (London: Stationary Office).

Leigh, S. and Miller, C. (2004) 'Is the Third Way the Best Way? Social Work Intervention with Children and Families', *Journal of Social Work*, **4**(3) 245–267.

Levy, A. and Kahan, B. (1991) *The Pindown Experience and the Protection of Children: The Report of the Staffordshire Child Care Inquiry* (Stafford: Staffordshire County Council).

Lipsky, M. (1980) *Street Level Bureaucracy: Dilemmas of the Individual in Public Services* (New York: Russell Sage Foundation).

Lymbery, M. and Butler, S. (2004) *Social Work Ideals and Practice Realities* (Basingstoke: Palgrave Macmillan).

Martin, G. P., Phelps, K. and Katbamna, S. (2004) Human Motivation and Professional Practice: of Knights, Knaves & Social Workers, *Social Policy & Administration*, **38**(5) 470–487.

Menzies, I. (1970) *The Functioning of Social Systems as a Defence Against Anxiety* (London: Tavistock Institute of Human Relations).

Morgan, G. (1986) *Images of Organisation* (London: Sage).

Mullender, A. and Perrott, S. (2002) 'Social Work and Organisations', in Adams, R., Dominelli, L. and Payne M. *Social Work: Themes, Issues & Critical Debates* (London: Macmillan).

Pease, B. and Fook, J. (1999) *Transforming Social Work Practice* (London: Routledge).

Resser, L. (1996) 'The Future of Professionalism and Activism' in Raffoul, P. R. and McNeece, C. A. (eds) *Future Issues for Social Work Practice* (Allyn & Bacon, Massachusetts).

Ritzer, G. (2000) *The McDonaldization of Society* (Pine Forge Press: London).

Simpkin, M. (1979) *Trapped within Welfare: Surviving Social Work* (London: Macmillan).

Sims, D., Fineman, S. and Gabriel, Y. (1993) *Organising and Organisations: An Introduction* (Sage: London).

Trow, M. (1993) *Managerialism and the Academic Profession: The Case of England* (Stockholm: Council for Studies of Higher Education).

Concluding reflections on the nature and future of critical best practice

KAREN JONES, BARRY COOPER AND HARRY FERGUSON

The aim of this book has been to provide examples of best practice in social work seen from critical perspectives. The book has drawn upon and sought to develop existing literature on how social work is created through interactions between practitioners, service users, managers, values, the law and organisational rules and procedures. In some key respects, however, what has been presented in the book constitutes a new way of thinking and writing about social work, given the paucity of literature which has focused in a systematic way on accounts of best practice and the almost complete absence of such narratives in the critical practice literature. In this conclusion we want to draw together the various strands of the book and reflect on the present and possible futures of critical best practice (CBP) perspectives.

THE ORIENTATION OF CRITICAL BEST PRACTICE PERSPECTIVES

The central approach of this book has been to produce accounts of theory and practice which focus in a sociologically critical way on what actually gets done well in social work, why and how it gets done, and with what consequences – a CBP perspective. We hope that the chapters can help to promote discussion and open up processes of critical reflection on best practice amongst groups of practitioners, managers, academics and students. The book has shown that CBP perspectives are concerned with the short and long-term processes of intervention, as well as with what makes up the components of practice at each stage of the intervention process, from referral, assessment, through to long-term work and the organisational structure, culture and processes which enable (best) practice to go on. In a variety of ways the book has demonstrated the practicalities of how the organisational context, inter-agency structures and rules and resources within which social work goes on are drawn upon by practitioners in their work. The chapters have been situated at the inter-face between organisations and service user's lives and have sought to sensitise readers to the legal and procedural realities of social work while focusing on how they are turned into practice – on the detail of what can and needs to be said and done in particular situations; on how social work is *performed*.

Ideally discussions of best practice need to be communal (or at least include that dimension), where story-telling about best practice experiences informs and inspires the entire group/team, making an impact on the organisational culture as well as individual knowledge and practice. We were able to engage in such a process in the planning and writing of the book. As all the contributors came from the same region, we held regular meetings which involved detailed discussions of the meanings of critical thought and best practice, both in a general way and as applied to each chapter, drafts of which were discussed and critiqued at the meetings. Whatever coherence of theme and content the book has managed to achieve is heavily due to the collective work that went in. What has also, with hindsight, proved crucial is our unity of purpose as an editorial team and commitment to advancing the topic, which has grown significantly and enjoyably through the process. It has been a deeply satisfying project to work on as the significance of this 'strengths perspective' (Saleebey, 2006) for social work practice has developed. On reflection, a good reason for this is that engaging in producing knowledge of best practice is a refreshing and rewarding thing to do. It can be just the same for any group of people who choose to do it.

This is not the same as saying that engaging in CBP analysis is necessarily an easy thing to do. What the chapters individually and collectively show is that engaging in CBP analysis is not simply about assembling a random celebration of 'good works' in social work, but demands a rigorous sociological approach which discovers, analyses and profiles practice which is skilfully supportive, therapeutic and challenging of power structures, yet where good authority is exercised. It can be shown to deserve to be called 'best' because of how it contains aspects of all these. Nor, as the contributors consistently have shown, is the emphasis on best about being unaware of or avoiding constraints on good practice. It is about best practice within those constraints while being critical of the constraints and working to transcend them. CBP refers to the ways in which professionals work creatively with and within structures to carve out actions which make a positive difference to service user's lives, while seeking to extend the boundaries of what can be done and reformulate structures in enabling ways.

We are against notions of 'best practice' that are equated with some notion of 'ideal practice'. Such a 'counsel of perfection' approach is not helpful, either for users or providers of social work services, as it only adds to a view that the profession is constantly failing and the service delivered is never (quite) good enough. The critical accounts produced here are illustrations of good practice skills and strengths that have been revealed in working from the assumption that workers 'do their best' in most, if not all, circumstances. In other words, the positive and creative encouragement arising from a strengths perspective should apply to service providers and social work practice as well as service users. So, 'best' in this definition does not mean 'this could have been best if only this, that or the other had been the case'. It is recognising the actualities of practice, within which 'best' is simply the best that could be achieved at that time. It is 'best' taking a reality check. 'Best' in terms of what was achieved despite and because of all of the complexities and difficulties. This has resonances with what Webb (2006), drawing on notions of 'virtue ethics' and 'good judgement', calls 'the practice of value'. For this *is* social work doing its best and doing pretty well because there probably is not any other profession or person that could or would have done this any better.

However, this realist definition of 'best' should not be construed as an excuse for poor practice. This has certainly not been the intention of this book. It is perfectly possible to take a best practice approach and still recognise that 'not good enough' practice exists. Our aim rather has been to hold up examples of best practice to promote learning, debate and place social work under a positive sign. Nor are we saying that the best practice featured here is possible and should be going on in all contexts at all times and if it is not then there is something wrong with those practitioners, managers, agencies, service users and so on. The contributors have been careful not to extrapolate from their own examples to practice contexts in general. What we learned while in the process of producing this book is that to have maximum impact in providing plausible accounts and promoting learning, it was best for the theorising and drawing out of implications not to go beyond the detail of the practice contained in the examples given. CBP analysis must provide 'situated' accounts that are grounded in the social and organisational realities and the diversity of individual styles, temperaments, skills, knowledge, passions that professionals and service users embody. They must be grounded in what Healy (2000: 52) calls 'the politics of detail' and the possible, while at the same time seeking to extend the boundaries of what is thinkable and is demonstrably possible. It is not only sufficient but also commendable to draw out the practical and theoretical implications of the practice under analysis without trying to explain and generalise beyond the contours of that experience. To do so is to wander into the realms of the kind of prescriptive writing where practitioners are told what they *should* be doing, but never how, or considering even if it is possible that has dogged the radical/critical tradition in social work and led to 30 years of exasperated practitioners responding to 'radical' academics with, 'it's all right for you to talk!' (Cohen, 1975).

This is not to say that there are no general implications that can be drawn. There is a paradox that the more detailed the analysis of particular situations, the more some key general issues that arise across the chapters in this book can be seen. This includes the centrality of meaningful relationships between professionals and service users, and between professionals; the high level of skill, professionalism and deep humanity that are at the heart of social work encounters; a reflective understanding of the emotional dynamics of these relationships; the informed use of extensive knowledge about service user's social contexts, problems and application of methods of helping them; a deep understanding of the organisational context and procedures and rules which regulate practice and management and other organisational supports as a constructive resource which can enable best practice; a conception of the exercise of power in social work which is based on an understanding of the deep ethical complexity which is at the heart of all practice.

The existence of such key components means that an approach to generating particular kinds of knowledge, a critically informed 'best practice' perspective that is generalisable to all aspects and contexts of social work is possible. In adopting it the book has aimed to provide a detailed description and analysis of social work – or at least some aspects of it – by 'unpicking' what is done well within a realistic representation of the contexts of practice. It is beyond the scope of a single book to focus on all aspects of social work, and there remains much to be done to open up social work to CBP perspectives. Social work reveals itself 'best' when the veil of normative assumptions is lifted so that the unacknowledged realities of underlying networks of power and skilful action can be exposed. In this way, the best social work can often be *tacitly* skilled and sensitive, critically aware and knowledgeable of intricate social complexities, with a strong sense of human values and competing ethical imperatives. It is this level of detailed engagement with the day-to-day connection between theory and practice which has been drawn out in this book. Because of its detailed focus on actual people's lives and interventions, we hope that the book provides a more intimate sociology of social work practice than is typical, where deeply personal stories rub shoulders with theoretical perspectives in ways which allow actions, feelings, vulnerability, risk, pain and power relations to gain expression and produce a lived sense of how (best) practice goes on. Exposing these riches, which are too often buried within and by the literature, and within the culture of practice itself, is the central aim of all CBP analysis.

TOWARDS A NEW ETHICS OF CRITICAL SOCIAL WORK PRACTICE

This is the domain of practice-based knowledge or 'practice based evidence'. It constitutes a form of 'evidence' which needs much greater formal recognition in understandings and debates about 'evidence based practice' in social work. It does not deny the validity of scientifically produced evidence produced by experimental research designs such as randomised controlled trials. Far from it, as some of the practice documented in the book took such knowledge into account. But at the centre of best-practice-based evidence is the practitioner voice, together with that of the service user and any other stakeholders who contribute to and co-construct the practice. A key focus here is on those actions and processes which may not be amenable to or even seen as relevant to measurement but which are the essence of what social work is. Best practice analysis is about more than just outcome, dealing with social action, process and the nuances of how practice is done. It is the execution of countless tasks made up of acts of skill, intellectual and political vision, generosity and courage which individually and collectively create best practice.

The chapters suggest the need for a diversity of forms of theory and sources of social work knowledge. What they broadly have in common is their location within 'critical' and 'constructive' theoretical frameworks. Both individually and taken together the accounts assembled in this book add up to some serious challenges to social work. A key one lies in current orthodoxies surrounding an anti-oppressive practice (AOP) framework, the validity of which must be seriously questioned. While the principle of working anti-oppressively must be maintained, the intimate accounts of practice in this book suggest that what is needed is a much stronger focus on ethical dilemmas (Banks, 2006; Beckett and Maynard, 2006). The book has given countless examples of practitioners having to grapple with how to use their powers and judgement in situations to which there were no straightforward right or wrong answers or winners and losers. All practitioners appear to shift between patterns of passivity and acceptance of things as they are and a critical stance which embodies reflection in action in the way they handle their organisations and everyday interventions (Charles and Butler, 2004). The crucial thing here is the need to embrace complexity: this involves an understanding of professionals and service users as capable of being not only cooperative and constructive but also resistant, hostile and destructive, of love and hate in welfare relationships (Froggett, 2002), and of organisations, agency rules and office cultures as enabling as well as constraining. The evidence accumulated in this book suggests that 'pure' critical or best practice is not possible, or at least not without a process of uncertainty, struggle, false starts and unintended consequences. Achieving CBP depends on enacting a constant cycle of reflection, on what must be done (well), as well as thought, and what must be done now in the light of that new understanding.

One of the strengths of critical theory has always been the way in which it demonstrates the workings of power, the inequalities it produces and the need for social change. This book has shown that in applying such analytical frameworks and insights, social work theory needs to (re)capture the essence of what it is about in terms of helping living, breathing people; it needs to rediscover its soul. The key shift within critical practice this book has attempted to push forward has been to contribute to a knowledge base around ways in which critical practice in social work can best be actually done and the fact that helping individuals, groups, and/or communities to change and/or improve their lives is a radical thing to do. This is a 'critical' shift for social work to make in the sense that it is urgently necessary for those in need. Contrary to the impressions often given, effective critical practice which makes a real difference to the lived experiences of people's lives is not a soft option but is invariably a difficult thing to achieve. It is precisely the huge achievements of social work in promoting vulnerable people's well-being and the common good that make it worthy of pride and celebration.

REFERENCES

Banks, S. (2006) *Ethics and Values in Social Work* (Basingstoke: Palgrave, 3rd Edition).

Beckett, C. and Maynard, A. (2005), *Values & Ethics in Social Work: An Introduction* (London: Sage).

Charles, M. & Butler, S. (2004) 'Social Workers' Management of Organisational Change' in M. Lymbery & S. Butler (eds) (2004) *Social Work Ideals and Practice Realities* (Basingstoke: Palgrave Macmillan).

291

Cohen, S. (1975), 'It's all right for you to talk' in Bailey, R. and Brake, M. (1975) *Radical Social Work* (London: Edward Arnold).

Froggett, L. (2002) *Love, Hate and Welfare* (Bristol: Policy Press).

Healy, K. (2000) *Social Work Practices: Contemporary Perspectives on Change* (London: Sage).

Saleebey, D. (ed.) (2006) *The Strengths Perspective in Social Work Practice,* 4th edition (New York: Longman).

Webb, S. A. (2006) *Social Work in a Risk Society* (Basingstoke: Palgrave).

Index